THE TWO DANTES

and other studies

KENELM FOSTER, O. P.

THE
TWO DANTES

and other studies

UNIVERSITY OF CALIFORNIA PRESS
Berkeley and Los Angeles, California

UNIVERSITY OF CALIFORNIA PRESS
Berkeley and Los Angeles, California

ISBN: 0-520-03326-4
Library of Congress Catalog Card Number: 76-24581

© Kenelm Foster, 1977

Cum permissu superiorum Ordinis

Printed in Great Britain

CONTENTS

For
UBERTO LIMENTANI and **PATRICK BOYDE**
with gratitude and affection.
And to the memory of
BENET WEATHERHEAD

PREFACE

The title I give this book is that of the last and longest of the essays that compose it, but what holds the book together, it seems to me, is simply an interest, maintained over many years, in the workings of Dante's highly unusual mind; an interest which I can hardly separate from the endless delight I find in the study of his poetry.

While writing the 'Two Dantes' essay and the study of *Paradiso* XIX (here ch. 9) I had the present book in mind: the rest were written, on various occasions, for publication on their own. And some were written a fairly long while ago, so that I cannot read them now without a certain embarrassment, a sense of their immaturity. This is the case, certainly, with the first two essays. And perhaps the second in particular calls for a word of apology to any scholars in the field of 'courtly love' who may happen to read it; and who will no doubt find it, to say the least, inadequately documented. But I would ask them to consider that this piece was not written for specialists: it is merely an outline analysis, reduced to the simplest terms, of a single text, familiar to them indeed but generally little known (the *De Amore* of Andreas Capellanus). The presence, on the other hand, of this modest piece in a bundle of Dante studies hardly needs defending, I suppose, in view of the European literary tradition within which and out of which Dante's poetry took shape.

The 'Two Dantes' essay and that on *Paradiso* XIX were finished without my having taken account in them of relevant work of high quality done by two of the younger Italian Dantists: I mean Giorgio Padoan's well documented study 'Il Limbo dantesco', now available in *Il pio Enea, l'empio Ulisse: tradizione classica e intendimento medievale in Dante*, Ravenna, 1977, pp. 102–104, and Angelo Jacomuzzi's very perceptive reading of *Paradiso* XIX, in

L'Ahlighieri, Rome, XIV, 1973, 2, pp. 3–24. While I differ on points of detail from these two excellent scholars, I am happy to find myself in broad agreement with their respective conclusions.

For permission to reprint already published material, my thanks are due to the following: to The Oxford University Press, for 'An Introduction to the *Inferno*'; to the editor of *New Blackfriars*, for 'St Thomas and Dante' and 'Courtly Love and Christianity'; to the editor of *The Downside Review*, for 'Dante and Eros', to The Dante Society of America, the proprietors of *Dante Studies* (State University of New York Press), for the four pieces reproduced from that journal: 'The Canto of the Damned Popes, *Inferno XIX*'; 'The Human Spirit in Action, *Purgatorio XVII*'; 'The Celebration of Order, *Paradiso X*'; 'The Son's Eagle, *Paradiso XIX*'. Finally, a word of sincere thanks to my publishers, and in particular to John Todd and Robin Baird-Smith, without whose encouragement this book would never have seen the light.

K. F.

Blackfriars
Cambridge
18 March, 1977

AN INTRODUCTION TO THE *INFERNO*

Written over the gate of Hell Dante read, 'The primal
LOVE made me'; and long before Dante the fearful
paradox expressed in these words had been written in-
delibly into Christian minds as a mystery which no theologian dared
to think he could fully explain. Nor did the great poet, of course, explain it or even try to; but for our part, as readers of the *Inferno*, we
do well to bear in mind that initial extraordinary declaration. Certainly we shall not read aright this third of the *Comedy* unless we
bear in mind both Purgatory and Paradise; or at least have some notion of what Dante conceived goodness to be, before we read his
description of evil. Evil can only be the negation of good; it is only
conceivable in terms of goodness; and the whole *Inferno*, from this
point of view, is nothing but a picture of the thwarting or destruc-
tion of types of goodness which are to be reaffirmed triumphantly in
the *Purgatorio* and the *Paradiso*. I say the *Purgatorio* also, because
the goodness that gives indirectly its meaning to the *Inferno* is
human as well as divine; it is represented by the Earthly Paradise at
the end of the *Purgatorio* as well as by the heavenly Paradise
beyond. Indeed, to a large extent it is already represented by the
Good Pagans of Limbo (canto IV). As I have said elsewhere, most
of the people whom Dante represents as damned 'would be sinners
in any world that was human at all'[1] ; their guilt, I mean, need not
presuppose a specifically Christian standard of judgement. Most of
the evil we meet with in the *Inferno* is ordinary human wickedness
which any man, whatever his faith, could in theory recognize as
such. Removed from the moral and poetic intensity of its setting in
the work, much of it would even seem rather trivial – gluttony, for
example, or ill-temper, of flattery, or thieving, or squandering, or

1. *God's Tree*, London, 1957, p. 54.

various kinds of faking, or fortune-telling. There is nothing 'mystical' or sublime about all this. Indeed, everywhere in the *Inferno* the reader will do well to keep a critical eye on his sense of the admirable; otherwise he may miss the sense intended by the poet, and much of his deep irony. The high heroic colouring of parts of the *Inferno* belongs to the attitudes assumed by the sinners, not to the sins in themselves. Was Francesca's adultery admirable in Dante's eyes? Was Farinata's materialism heroic? Or Jason's random seductions, or Pier delle Vigne's suicide, or Brunetto Latini's sodomy, or the cunning of Ulysses, or the intrigues and betrayals of Ugolino? If these figures strike us as superb poetic creations, if they touch us as tragic heroes do, we need not suppose, indeed we do better not to suppose, that the poet thought them heroic as sinners. Dante was no romantic but a medieval Catholic with an extremely sharp eye for the irrational in human behaviour. The nobility and dignity of some of the sinners, the pity or admiration they arouse in the Dante who encounters them, these things are part of the action of the *Inferno*, of its 'plot'. We should not forget that the Dante who goes through Hell is himself a character in the poem; moreover his character is that of a sinner in the poem (he starts in the dark wood), though in process of conversion and purification. And the point of view of this character is determined by his situation in that process; it cannot, therefore, be the point of view of the poet writing as if *post eventum* and describing the process. While the process is continuing the character called Dante is subject to feelings of pity and admiration for sinners whom the poet Dante, who selected them as symbols of evil, regarded quite differently. In the traveller Dante's surrender to the seduction of Francesca, in his eager response to the greatness of Farinata and Ulysses, we must recognise – the plot requires that we do – a good deal of illusion: for according to the plot the traveller is a man still deeply disturbed by evil, still only in the early stages of moral recovery, still undergoing a moral re-education; which will only be completed at the summit of the mountain of Purgatory. Here and now, in Hell, he is undergoing the only remedy left to him, 'so low had he fallen'; he is being taught to know evil, he is being shown 'the lost people' (*Purgatorio* XXX, 136-8). It was his last chance.

In short, Dante's Hell is not only a picture of sin as it is (as one man saw it) but of sin as it would like to appear.

And the sin he encounters on his way is, I repeat, largely sin against the light of reason alone, apart from any 'higher' considerations. It is wrongdoing very much on the human level and in the give and take of ordinary social intercourse. A strong social emphasis marks the *Inferno*; and, since the poet was deeply involved in politics and his world was that of the medieval Commune, the more or less self-governing city-state, a strong political emphasis too. It is true that all wrongdoing, however social or political its circumstances, had for Dante a deep religious significance. Since human nature is God's creation, to injure man is to offend God. And certainly the *Inferno* could only have been written by a believing Christian. Nevertheless the measure of right and wrong that governs, immediately, the greater part of it is a rational, not a specifically Christian, measure; it is drawn from moral philosophy (especially Aristotle's) rather than from the Gospels.

A corruption of reason, then, rather than a refusal of grace; not an adequate summary, this, of the content of so rich and subtle a work (but the subtlety is far more in the presentation than in the content, complex though this certainly is) yet it may give us our bearings. We must not expect much explicit Christianity here. It seems a strangely un-Christian world through which pagan Virgil guides his Christian pupil — Virgil, symbol of the soul of man poised in a perfect yet limited equilibrium between animality transcended and divine grace not yet received, though glimpsed from far away and longed for:

> tu modo nascenti puero, quo ferrea primum
> desinet ac toto surget gens aurea mundo,
> casta fave Lucina . . .

This 'Virgil' believes in God. He knows that an original Goodness glows through all creation; moreover he knows how creatures can deny and dishonour that Goodness and besmirch and violate its effects, particularly the noblest effect of which man has experience, his own rational nature. Virgil even knows something of the fall of the angels. 'Behold Dis', he says at the end, pointing to Satan; and we can suppose that he, like his pupil, knew that it was through pride that 'he who was so fair . . . raised his brow against his Maker'. He is aware too of the Church even if, in the great ecclesiastical canto XIX, he will tactfully step aside and leave that

unforgettable indictment of clerical materialism to flow from
Catholic lips. But Virgil only knows *of* the Christian revelation, he
has not personally received it; and though familiar with the
topography of Hell, there is something about damnation itself that
always escapes him. No wonder; never having known God incarnate, how could he understand a condition which is only definable
as the consequence of a rejection of that God?

But one might ask whether Dante himself assessed it in these
terms; for certainly, as I have said, all specifically Christian concepts
remain, through much of the *Inferno*, well in the background. But
two reasons can be given for this. First, as a medieval Christian
Dante was not in the least inclined, as the modern reader is, to
find the very idea of damnation unacceptable. He could take the
idea for granted, and this left him free to elaborate it in his own
way, a very personal and original way. And secondly, this distinctively Dantean way of representing evil was naturally coloured by
the poet's temperament and special interests and experiences. An obvious point, to be sure; but worth some attention in detail. Two
minor stresses and a major one are discernible in this Dantean 'way'.
The first apears in canto III, in the very characteristic contempt
for the neutrals, for the inert 'who never were alive'; and it led to
three lines (37-9) of rather queer theology.

Another relatively minor stress, though more frequent and important, can be felt in Dante's strictures on the clergy, which, after
some preliminary sniping in cantos VII and XI, rise to a crescendo
in canto XIX, and again in canto XXVII. It would be misleading
to call Dante an anticlerical, but he was very much disposed to find
fault with priests, or at any rate with prelates; and there were
political as well as religious reasons for this. As for the major stress,
which is Dante's dominating and pervasive concern in the *Inferno*
with *injustice*, this was affected through and through by his political
experience and especially by the circumstances which led to his
banishment from Florence early in 1302. It is true that behind
Dante's concern with political justice was a purely religious impulse,
such as breaks through, magnificently, in canto XIX; but on the
surface at least the chief moral theme of the *Inferno* is social justice in
the human order. The concept of justice can serve, in fact, as the key
to the poem's moral pattern, at least from canto XI onwards.

This pattern may strike us as strange, and it is certainly an original one so far as the bulk of Hell, comprising the whole of the City of Dis (i.e. from canto IX to the end) is concerned. Outside that city – if we exclude the neutrals and Limbo (cantos III and IV) – Dante seems to have been working with the traditional Christian scheme of the seven 'capital vices', the scheme he was later to use for the *Purgatorio*. But from canto IX on (omitting the heretics of canto X, who form a group apart – an important one as we shall see) Dante is using a scheme of his own based on an analysis of injustice, a vice not included in the traditional seven *vitia capitalia*. This new scheme represents in the main a free handling of Aristotle's *Ethics*, blended with a pregnant hint from Cicero's *De Officiis* and having the Bible as its presupposed background. As expounded, drily and lucidly, by Virgil in canto XI it all centres on one term, *malizia*, understood as a force aimed against one or other aspect of total reality – one's own self, or other men, or the order of nature, or God. *Malizia* indeed is virtually injustice in the widest sense of the term. Its special 'end' is *ingiuria*, 'wrong done to someone' ('injury' would be too weak a rendering); and the wrong is done, Virgil continues (and here comes in the hint from Cicero) either by violence (*forza*) or by craft (*frode*); which are then correlated as respectively less or more evil and analysed into subdivisions. Craft is worse than violence as involving a deeper corruption in the agent, a misuse of the gift of reason that both defines man and is his special likeness to God. When crafty *malizia* is aimed against one who 'trusts' the wrongdoer it becomes *tradimento*, 'betrayal', the sin of those damned to the icy lake at Hell's base. But the extreme of *tradimento* is to betray one's benefactor; hence ingratitude is the worst sin of all; its embodiment is Satan who had been the fairest work of God (cf. *Paradiso* XIX, 46–8). From another point of view Satan's sin was pride, and this aspect is stressed in the *Paradiso* (ibid.) but in the pattern of the *Inferno* it is rather an ultimate ingratitude, a total break off from and scorn of the primal Love, which is symbolised in that frozen and ferocious colossus of canto XXXIV. Three-faced, to suggest an anti-Trinity, Satan gnaws the three ultimate human traitors: Judas, who betrayed God made Man; Brutus and Cassius who betrayed God's regent, the founder of the Roman Empire. And here, I suppose, every modern reader will wonder what in heaven's name the assassins of Julius Caesar are doing at the bottom of the Christian Hell! The choice is certain-

ly surprising and may have an anti-climactic effect, as of a sudden
narrowing of vision. Well, we must take Dante as we find him; but
we should also try to understand that for him loyalty to the Empire
was no narrowly political issue, but essentially a loyalty to reason
and so a moral issue too. Indeed, it was a loyalty to God.

As mankind is one race in virtue of the common gift of reason, so
it should, Dante thought, form one political community obeying one
ruler who would represent both God who creates reason and man
who receives it. The ideal is not ignoble, whatever may be thought
of the historical Empire or of the appropriateness of so weighty an
allusion to it at this point in the poem. In any case its sudden
appearance here, at the end of the *Inferno*, is only the most striking
manifestation of a social and political concern – a concern essentially
with justice – which pervades all this third of the *Comedy*. In view
of its subject-matter the *Inferno* may well seem curiously 'secular';
but then for Dante the secular was also sacred. Both Church and
State were sacred, though in different ways. Everything was sacred
through its relation to God: reason, the human body, the family, the
State, the Church; each through its own relation to the primal Love.
For it is that Love that glows through all things, *in una parte più e
meno altrove*, 'here more, there less' (*Paradiso* I, 3); and sin is
nothing but the wilful thwarting, misuse, or denial of this or that
aspect of that manifold glow.

We have Dante's word for it that he had taken Virgil as his
literary model before he began the *Comedy*. 'From you alone', he
declares to Virgil at their first meeting, 'I learned *lo bello stile che
m'ha fatto onore*'; words which place the whole poem, in a sense, under Virgil's patronage. Yet there is nothing evidently Virgilian
about Dante's earlier poetry; and, given the metrical forms that it
took (canzone and sonnet) there hardly could have been. Yet in the
De vulgari eloquentia, written certainly before the *Inferno*, we find
Dante strongly recommending his fellow poets in the vernacular to
take the Latin classics (not Virgil only) as their model; for classical
verse was written with art, *arte regulari*, but vernacular verse, hitherto, only in a random sort of way, *casu magis quam arte*. Implicit in
this judgment – which raises questions we cannot stop to examine –
is certainly an aspiration to lift vernacular poetry to a dignity that
would rival the poetry of Rome; an aspiration that will later become
explicit in *Inferno* IV, 97-102 and XXV, 94-102. The classics,

then, had set the standard for writing as an art; and for all Dante's passionate cult of the Italian vernacular, (which was later to lose him credit with Petrarch and the Humanists) he remained faithful to this classicism. And as time went by and the *Comedy* took shape in his mind he doubtless turned more and more to the example and the study of Virgil. Ovid, Statius, and Lucan he continued to revere with what Saintsbury called 'the touching humility of the Middle Ages'; drawing much on them for images and allusions in his poem. But Virgil, 'our greatest poet', became the master pre-eminent. Dante's motive in so revering Virgil was not, of course, a merely literary one. There was, to be sure, a decisive literary influence; it was largely by attention to Virgil's style that Dante brought his own to maturity; the terseness, the sonorous pregnant brevity, the prevailing *temperateness* of the style of the *Comedy* owe much to the Latin master. From the *Aeneid*, again, especially from Book VI, came much of the material for the *Inferno* – Charon, Cerberus, the Harpies, Phlegyas, the rivers Acheron and Phlegethon, and Cocytus, now become a lake, and Styx, now a swamp. Of more stylistic interest is the way Dante will echo – and this happens at some of his intensest moments – a Virgilian phrase, or appropriate a Virgilian episode and charge it with fresh significance – compare, for example, *Aeneid* III, 310-16 with *Inferno* X, 67-9, or *Aeneid* VI, 679-94 with *Paradiso* XV, 25ss. There is no better example in literature of one man's art being fertilised by another's than Dante's use of Virgil.

But, as I say, the relationship is not merely literary in the narrow sense; there is also Virgil's representative value for Dante. He borrowed from Ovid and Statius, but they did not represent anything to him as Virgil did. We think of Dante himself as representing his own age, and we may think of Virgil as representing his; but if we do, is it not because we still see Virgil partly through Dante's eyes? He has 'placed' Virgil so decisively that it is not easy to see him in a quite different way. Of course that placing was normally the medieval Christian one; but it came to life in Dante's art.

It came to life in the conversation we overhear through two thirds of the *Comedy*. And this conversation is a crystallization in art, and to some extent a conscious one, of an immense historical relationship, the relationship between the old pagan world and the

Christian West. In literary history the *Comedy* depends on the *Aeneid*, and in Dante's mind it was intended, I think, as a sort of continuation of the *Aeneid*. In the poem Virgil guides Dante to a point beyond which the pagan cannot go but the Christian can; there is dependence and then a release from dependence, an experience shared and then – farewell. Thus the external historical process is mirrored *within* the poem; the historical relationship between the poets is turned into an imaginary dialogue: in which more is involved than the minds of two individuals. For the play within a play, which is the poets' conversation through Hell and Purgatory, was Dante's way of representing the vast historical change from B.C. to A.D. His Virgilianism was one thing with his sense of the Roman past as a providential movement towards Christ; and it was in becoming conscious of this movement that Dante remembered Virgil. Or rather, perhaps, *vice versa*; in any case this movement is what Virgil, more than any other historical figure, came to represent for Dante. Hence the Roman poet's function in the *Comedy* from the moment when Beatrice, now in eternity, sends him to Dante's rescue with a movement which seems to cancel the centuries and yet leaves intact the spiritual difference between pagan master and Christian pupil. Something in the ambivalence of this relationship – in which the pupil reveres a master who knows less than he does – recalls the position of Aquinas with respect to Aristotle. But Aquinas did not make poetry out of the situation.

At this point I am reminded of an interesting essay by Ulrich Leo, published some years ago, on 'The unfinished *Convivio* and Dante's re-reading of the *Aeneid*'[2] In this essay Leo suggested that Dante broke off his Italian prose work the *Convivio* and began the *Comedy* when two things dawned on him: first that his own sense experience, especially visual experience, must be made the matter of his art; and secondly that the Latin poets, and Virgil in particular, could be imitated on a far greater scale than was possible within the narrow limits of the *canzoni* which Dante had been writing so far. The first of these realizations caused him to turn from the prose of abstract theory (the philosophizing of the *Convivio*) to the poetry of vision; that is, so far as the unseen world was concerned, from talking about it to imagining a direct sight of it. And the second realiza-

2. *Medieval Studies*, Toronto, XII (1951) pp. 41-64.

tion impelled him to compete with the old poets on their own ground of poetry, and on a grand scale, instead of continuing merely to take arguments and examples from them for his prose treatise. And the two together – the new stress on vision and a new sense of the imitability on a large scale of the classical poets – would have a particular relevance to Virgil; for the climax of Virgil's art, *Aeneid* VI, describes an experience of the unseen world.

Leo argues plausibly for the view that Dante reread the *Aeneid* in the course of writing the fourth and last book of the *Convivio*, and he suggests that Dante now read *Aeneid* V to XII for the first time. However that may be, the *Aeneid*, especially books IV, V, and VI, certainly moves into the foreground in the later chapters of the *Convivio*; and it does so as an allegory of human life considered as a sequence of change from youth to old age. This sequence Dante distinguishes into four 'ages', but these matter less than the statement that the *Aeneid* is an allegory of the process as a whole and that the central books, IV to VI, represent the age of ripe manhood (*gioventute*) when the soul is in 'the middle of the way' through mortal life; and Dante attempts to show how the conduct of Aeneas, in these central books, displays the qualities appropriate to middle age.

There are difficulties against Leo's view (though other good scholars strongly hold it) that the *Comedy* was begun soon after the *Convivio* was interrupted and left unfinished; but I personally find it plausible to take that allegorical reading of Virgil, which we first meet with explicitly in Dante towards the end of the *Convivio*, as a pointer to the impulse which set Dante to work on the *Comedy*. It seems to me likely, that is, that he deliberately set out to complete Virgil's allegory. He had already, no doubt, the motive hinted at the end of the *Vita Nuova*, the glorification of Beatrice; but surely the Virgilian allegory was relevant too. Virgil meant so much to him. He read the *Aeneid* as an allegory of man's life in time, of the process from birth to death; he would now write his own poem about the relation between temporal life and eternity, embodied in a description of a man's journey into eternity. Again, Virgil's allegory had to do, not with an individual's life only, but – and much more – with social life.

The *Aeneid* is the story of a search for a city and a homeland, a promised land. The city is Rome, seat of the Empire, the common homeland of all mankind 'bounded on every side by the Ocean's

shores'; and this Rome, the capital city of mortal man, becomes in
Dante's imagination a figure of the city of God, the true home of
man as immortal: *quella Roma onde Cristo è romano.*[3] So now
Virgil's Christian pupil would describe the substance that his
master's ideal had foreshadowed. As Virgil's successor and 'son' (as
he so often calls himself in the *Comedy*) Dante would complete the
earthly allegory with a heavenly one; he would draw a vertical line
from man to God, to complete the design begun with Virgil's
horizontal line from youth to age. And because Virgil, in drawing
this line, had sketched the providential preparation of the world for
Christ; because he was the prophetic voice of the Gentiles in the
fourth Eclogue; because he had travelled in imagination into the
world beyond the grave (*Aeneid* VI); because he was *nostra maggior
musa*, − for all these reasons he was the man best fitted to guide a
child of God into the other world, though he could not take him to
the end of the journey.

And this way of regarding Virgil in Dante's thought can help us
to see what he symbolises as a character in the *Comedy*. This is commonly said to be 'human reason', and the phrase will do well
enough, provided we extend the term 'reason' to cover things that
are not commonly included in it. If the term be stretched to mean
the human spirit touched by intimations of immortality and yearning for a lost Eden which it dimly remembers as a dream is
remembered in daytime, then Virgil does symbolise reason. But in
no less extended sense of the term. If Dante has a symbol for reason
in a more restricted sense, that symbol is Aristotle, whose
characteristic task it was precisely to define the limits of human
endeavour *as human*, or better, *as proper to man within the limits of
temporal existence*. Aristotle is 'the master and leader of the human
reason' because he succeeded in defining 'the good for man', which
consists in being humanly virtuous, with *hē anthrōpikē aretē* (*Nicom.
Ethics*, I, 13), and which issues in 'the happiness of this life . . .
symbolised by the Earthly Paradise'.[4] · And just because that is what
Aristotle represented, he could not be the guide into the world
beyond death. As a teacher, an author, he had nothing to do with
the world beyond death. Not so Virgil: he had sent Aeneas into the

3. 'that Rome where Christ is a Roman', *Purg.* XXXII, 102.
4. *Convivio* IV, vi, 6-16; *Monarchia* III, xv, 7-9.

world of the dead; and he had dreamed, on Parnassus, of a bliss before the Fall.

'The world of the dead' brings back to mind those heretics whose position in the *Inferno* (in canto X and immediately inside the wall of the City of Dis) has been, it will be remembered, left unexplained: and it does so because Dante's heretics are precisely defined as Epicureans 'who make the soul die with the body'. This is an extremely interesting fact. Why did Dante, who had all the aberrant Christian sects to choose from, select the pagan Epicurus 'and his followers' to represent heresy in the *Inferno*? It was no doubt fitting that a Catholic poet, in describing Hell, should allot a place therein to heretics of some sort, but there was nothing either in ecclesiastical or literary tradition to compel or even incline him to choose heretics of this particular sort – who were not even, theologically speaking, heretics at all but unbelievers; for in strict theology a heretic is still a sort of Christian. Why then Epicurus? Why the special stress, implied in the poet's deliberately choosing to cross the circle of heresy at precisely *that* point, on the evil of denying the soul's survival of bodily death?

The answer, I think, lies deep in Dante's individual outlook and experience. His choice at this point in the invention of the plan of the *Inferno* was dictated by an intimately personal concern – a concern that had already been apparent, in an ecstatic visionary way, in the second half of the *Vita Nuova*, and that had blazed out, with sudden and significant violence, in one chapter of the *Convivio*. Now in both of these places it was Beatrice whom Dante had in mind. The meaning of Beatrice is too large a matter to discuss *in extenso* here. Enough to say – what I suppose hardly anyone would deny – that the Beatrice of the *Vita Nuova*, whether originally a real girl or an allegory, functions in that work as a 'showing' to the young Dante of the divine light of heaven. And when she dies her soul naturally goes to heaven; and Dante's love follows, drawing his thoughts 'upwards' as a 'new' (or 'strange') understanding, *intelligenza nuova*, that enters paradise and glimpses her there. So the *Vita Nuova* ends with Beatrice in glory and with the poet resolving to prepare himself, by study, to write one day of her 'what was never yet written of any woman'. This phrase has naturally been understood to refer to the *Divine Comedy*, and clearly it must refer to some germinal idea, at least, of the *Paradiso*; to which, years later,

Dante may well have returned when he began to work out the
whole poem in his mind – writing it, in this sense, backwards. But
the point to note here is the close association of life after death, the
eternal life, with Beatrice; the two ideas seem to have gone together
in Dante's mind from the time of the *Vita Nuova* onwards.
Associated, they triumph in the *Comedy*. Now one has only to read
carefully the last five cantos of the *Purgatorio* to realise that Dante
saw religion, the Christian religion of course, both in its moral and
its intellectual aspects, as in some sense symbolised in Beatrice. The
poet takes every care to leave the reader in no doubt on this point.
Beatrice, borne on the chariot of the Church, is the centre of the
allegorical procession, the total meaning of which is certainly the
Christian revelation. Her own special meaning here, to judge by
XXXI, 121-45, is sacred teaching or theology. In her eyes Dante
sees Christ reflected, now under the human nature, now under the
divine; from her lips he hears the bitter reproaches which identify
his moral backslidings with unfaithfulness to her – and to her as
'risen from flesh to spirit', that is, as having passed from mortal life
to eternal life. In short, Beatrice is being presented as the chief symbol of Christianity inasmuch as Christianity impinged on Dante
Alighieri, and at the same time she is vividly and fully retaining her
close association with the life after death. Beatrice, dead to this
world, had been the reminder to him of the eternal life of glory and
was now deliberately made the symbol in the poem of Christianity
advancing to meet him, rebuking, reconciling, and enlightening him.
Surely the inference, on the evidence of this central scene of the
Comedy – central both literally and metaphorically – is plain: that
Dante saw the Christian religion as the way into eternal life after
death and that he laid particular emphasis on this aspect of it.
Characteristic of his religion was a stress on the life of glory and the
vision of God – on *vision* above all. This emphasis had its ebbs and
flows; among his works the fourth book of the *Convivio* and the
whole of *Monarchia* represent periods of relative this-worldliness,
when the tension towards the ultimate vision was temporarily relaxed. But Dante was always a man who had seen Beatrice (whoever
or whatever she may have originally been) and who now knew she
was dead, and whose hope of recovering that experience and ex-
hausting all its implications was absolutely conditional on there being a future life to look forward to. It is wholly characteristic that

his supreme statement on religion should have been all explicitly and directly about what happens after death.

Thus the suggestion that the soul might not, after all, survive the body was emotionally, as well as rationally and religiously, intolerable to him; it struck him at the heart. In the great germinal experience of his adolescence, recorded in the *Vita Nuova* and recalled — and with such emphasis — at the very centre of the *Comedy*, Dante saw love in time as an incitement towards the eternal joy, as a transitory glimpse of 'the love that moves the sun and the other stars'. The idea that there might not after all be an eternity for his soul was perhaps of all ideas the one he was least able to discuss calmly. When he turns to it in the *Convivio* how quickly the sparks fly! 'Since the immortality of the soul has been mentioned I will digress to say something on this matter; because to do so will be a suitable conclusion to what I have to say about that living and blessed Beatrice, since I intend not to speak of her again in this book. I say then that of all basely stupid opinions (*bestialitadi*) the belief that after this life there is no other life is the stupidest, the vilest and the most pernicious . . .' (II, viii, -8). It is not, then, surprising that just this 'heresy' should be the one we encounter in *Inferno* X; that Farinata and his companions, who denied the life beyond the grave, should be in *tombs*. And my opinion, for what it is worth, is that this denial is the hidden meaning of the Gorgon's head which the Furies threaten to show Dante in canto IX. Had he once looked on the Gorgon there would have been for him, as Virgil said, no going back, *nulla sarebbe del tornar mai suso*; and no going forward either; for he would have been turned to stone; stone dead.

We do not know exactly when Dante began the *Inferno*. Boccaccio claimed to know that the first seven cantos were already written before the poet's banishment from Florence at the beginning of 1302; and that after some years Dante resumed the work with the appropriate phrase that opens canto VIII: *Io dico seguitando*. The story, though *prima facie* not implausible, is generally rejected nowadays and we can safely discount it — though this need not mean discounting altogether the hypothesis (to which I have already alluded implicitly) that an important alteration in the design of the poem may have been introduced at canto IX. In any case the *Inferno* as we have it was almost certainly all composed in exile, and of course before the *Purgatorio* and the *Paradiso*. It seems to have been

published separately and to have been circulating in Italy by
1313-14. It is hard to date it more precisely than this. Today the
more usual view is that it was composed between, roughly, 1307
and 1311. This dating, besides other advantages, would of course
allow time for the great labour of composing the rest of the *Comedy*
and would also account for the interruption of the prose works, the
Convivio and *De vulgari eloquentia*, which can both with certainty be
dated to between 1304-1307, and were both left unfinished.

2

COURTLY LOVE AND CHRISTIANITY

No doubt the French historian who called love 'une invention du douzième siècle' did not stake his academic reputation on this epigram; yet it has its grain of truth. For certainly, with the close of the eleventh century and on through the twelfth a heightened awareness of love comes into western literature – and not perhaps only on its more secular side – and this awareness brought into circulation ways of thinking about love which in some respects were undoubtedly new. This novelty, as expressed in the poetry of the troubadours, has recently been called 'merely a new literary fashion'; yet even regarded as a fashion the troubadour love-theme was an immensely influential one, as most of the literature of Europe goes to show, down to the Renaissance and beyond; but in fact to dismiss courtly love – as this theme has come to be called a little misleadingly – as a mere fashion is to risk failing to do justice to the enduring interest, and importance, of the idea and ideal that it contained.[1]

It is this idea and ideal that I propose to examine briefly in this paper; but since I am concerned with courtly love as an idea, and not directly with its literary expressions, I shall take as my text, not any samples of troubadour poetry, but the prose treatise *De Amore* in which Andreas Capellanus, chaplain to Marie de Champagne, drew this idea out into a system and code of conduct, probably in the 1180s. My purpose is to outline the main ideas contained in this work and touch briefly on their relation to the Christian ethic.[2] This

1. M. Valency, *In Praise of Love. An Introduction to the Love-Poetry of the Renaissance*, New York, 1961, p. 1. For a very different and more interesting view, see P. Dronke, *Medieval Latin and the Rise of the European Love-Lyric*, 2 vols., Oxford, 1965.
2. Critical edition by E. Trojel (1892). There is an English translation by J. J. Parry, *The Art of Courtly Love*, New York, 1941. For the circumstances and background of Andreas I draw largely on F. Schlösser, *Andreas Capellanus. Seine Minnelehre und das christliche Weltbild um 1200*, Bonn, 1960.

aspect of courtly love, its relation to Christianity, is the one I find
most interesting, and, as we shall see, it has particular relevance to
the work of Andreas. The question is, of course, in the first place
historical: how did a work of this kind, apparently so pagan in content and spirit, come to be written, and written evidently in response
to a demand, in the overwhelmingly Catholic world of twelfth century France? But behind this historical question lurk more practical
and urgent issues. If I venture to say that I regard courtly love as in
some sense a contemporary issue, the reader may be inclined to discount this as a medievalist's attempt to persuade himself that his
professional studies are not merely 'academic'. But let the reader be
patient; let him wait until he has heard Andreas. To indicate,
however, at the outset the sort of issue I want to raise, let me say
that it seems that there are not many fundamentally different ways
in which men and women can try to organise and direct sexual
desire, and that one of such ways is represented, essentially, in the
code of human love expounded in the *De Amore*. It is in this broad
sense that my subject has, I think, an interest for students of human
behaviour and for Christians in particular.

The author of the *De Amore* was a French cleric, almost certainly
a priest. His mind had been formed by a Christian education and
naturally he knew some theology; and of course the Christian ethic
was the traditionally accredited norm both for himself and his
readers. Yet it was a norm from which the love-ethic outlined in his
book sharply deviates in important respects; and of this disagreement Andreas was fully aware. This he shows with disconcerting
clarity in a sort of epilogue added to his book, in which he utterly
repudiates, in the name of religion, everything he has said therein.
The *De reprobatione amoris*, as this retraction is called, is relatively
short[3], amounting to hardly a sixth of the work it is intended to re-
cant, and it is as stereotyped and conventional as the *De Amore*
itself is individual and original. But, such as it is, the *Reprobatio* adds
both interest and difficulty to the study of Andreas: interest, because
it brings the conflict between courtly love and Christianity — at least
as Andreas understood these things — into the open, and because it is
clear evidence that the conflict was felt as a real one in the world for
which he wrote; and difficulty because it raises the question of our

3. It is usually printed as Book III of the *De Amore* (so in Trojel's edition). I have,
however, taken the liberty of restricting this title to Books I and II.

author's sincerity. Andreas upholds, successively, two absolutely opposed views on life; he says 'Yes' and then 'No' about the same thing. Was then his 'Yes' sincere and his 'No' insincere? Or *vice versa*? Or did he perhaps sincerely hold both positions, in the sense that he saw that certain consequences followed logically from two distinct premisses and, being genuinely unable to reconcile these premisses, he contented himself with arguing logically from both — in the one case as the spokesman of his lay patrons, Marie de Champagne and her circle, and in the other case as spokesman of the Church whose minister he was? Interpreted in this last sense his position would be an early instance of the kind of thing we meet a century later among the radical Aristotelians, or Averroists, at Paris and Bologna, the so-called principle of 'double truth'.

But I raise the question of Andreas's sincerity only to set it aside, for I am concerned with his ideas themselves rather than with the way he held to them. It should be noted however, that so long as Andreas is expounding courtly love (which he called simply love, *amor*) he writes with a zest, a fluency and a resourceful dialectic which are sadly lacking when he speaks from the other side. Yet this is fortunate for the historian, for while the *Reprobatio Amoris* is a mere jumble of early medieval common-places against love and against women in particular, the *De Amore* is not in the least commonplace: it presents a very clear and detailed picture of an attitude and state of mind that was still relatively new and 'modern' when Andreas was writing and which no other document of that time reflects with anything like the same completeness. It is to Andreas's interest in the love-theme that we are largely indebted, in fact, for what we know of the climate of opinion that nourished the beginnings of vernacular literature in Europe, to the extent that this was secular in outlook and tendency — secular I mean not only in the sense of being written for men and women of the world, but also more precisely in the sense of disregarding the teachings of Christianity.[4] This is not of course to proclaim the *De Amore* as a sort of *résumé* of twelfth century lay mentality, even in its more sophisticated manifestations. Andreas was evidently something of an

4. This 'disregard' is not of course, in the *De Amore*, inadvertence. A feature of Andreas's manner is a curious playing with Christian themes and texts, amounting occasionally to downright parody (e.g., p.32); and there are moments of discreet polemic against the Christian code (e.g., p. 162).

extremist. He liked to push ideas as far as they would go. As I shall have occasion to note again, his love-ethic is more secular, more 'pagan', that that, for example, of his great contemporary Chrétien de Troyes. But Andreas is certainly a most important witness to what a section of lay society in France, and a socially very eminent and influential section, thought about love and the conduct appropriate to lovers. The tone and allusions of his work make it clear that he wrote within and for a definite aristocratic 'set', the countess of Champagne's in fact; and she was one of the greatest ladies of her time, a daughter of Louis VII of France and Eleanor of Aquitaine. Moreover, the ideas of Andreas are broadly in harmony with those of the twelfth century troubadours, so far as ideas of any kind are discernible in their lyrics. In this sense, at least, the *De Amore* is certainly a representative document.

What then does it teach? But before turning to our text it may be convenient to have before us the outline description of courtly love proposed by the learned Canadian priest Fr A. J. Denomy.[5] His description will suit my purpose because, besides being an exceptionally qualified witness, Denomy was particularly interested (as one would expect) in the aspect of the matter that concerns us at present, the relation of courtly love to Christianity. This relation he saw as a decided antinomy, an opposition, and he very clearly and candidly said so. Perhaps indeed he over-stated the opposition, but from my point of view his downrightness is valuable; it provides me with a sharply defined starting point for reference and comparison.

Denomy, then, distinguishes three 'basic elements' in the heresy, as he calls it, of courtly love.[6] (1) human love is regarded as 'an ennobling force'; (2) the beloved, the woman, is regarded as superior to her lover; (3) the love itself is regarded as an 'ever unsatisfied, ever increasing desire'. These three elements he says, 'make courtly love to be courtly love and set it apart from all other conceptions of love' — whether classical, medieval or modern. He then distinguishes four features of courtly love, to bring out more clearly the implications of these basic elements. First, love is the source of all the goodness in man: no man is worth anything without it. 'Nuls om ses

---

5. Fr Denomy's work on courtly love was published as articles in *Medieval Studies*, Toronto, in vols. 6, 1944; 7, 1945; 8, 1946; 11, 1949; 13, 1951; 15, 1953. cf. also *Speculum*, 28, 1953, and *The Heresy of Courtly Love*, New York, 1947.
6. *The Heresy of Courtly Love*, New York, 1947, p. 20 ff.

amor re no vau' (Bernart de Ventadour), so that in some sense it is a matter of moral obligation; a most important point as we shall see. Secondly love has nothing to do with marriage; again a fundamental point to which we shall return. Thirdly love is not an end in itself but a means to 'progress and growth in virtue, merit and worth'. And fourthly the effective intrinsic agent in this growth in virtue is *desire*: 'it is not the beloved that ennobles the lover, but the love of her'; from which, as we shall see, the troubadours implicitly and Andreas quite explicitly drew the conclusion that love was the more excellent, the more 'fin', the more true to its essence in the degree that it was 'pure', i.e., that it withheld from carnal union. And so Denomy sums up: 'That is courtly love. It is neither Christian *caritas* nor platonic love ... neither mystical love nor lust, but a special type of love ... divorced from physical possession ... (yet) based on the desire for it, practised by people of worth (an élite) and regarded as productive of every virtue and every good'. This conception of love, he goes on to say, cannot be traced to classical sources (which would mean Ovid especially) nor to the Catharist heresy as some writers have maintained.[7] Its true source, he thinks, is to be found in Arab literature and particularly in a treatise on love by Avicenna.[8]

Myself, I think that this last part of Denomy's thesis begs more questions than it solves; but the problem of sources need not detain us here. Denomy's description of courtly love itself we can provisionally accept. As for the wider problem of the relation in general of courtly love to Christianity, this, I am sure, calls for a more extensive and detailed treatment than Denomy ever provided. Here of course I can hardly do more than define the terms of the problem: and the little I have to say will amount in fact to hardly more than a sort of footnote to a remarkable work by a German scholar which appeared since Denomy's death a few years ago: I refer to Felix Schlösser's *Andreas Capellanus. Seine Minnelehre und das christliche Weltbild um* 1200.[9] This book comprises, first, a thorough analysis of the doctrine contained in the *De Amore*, and then an extremely interesting and, it seems to me, largely convincing

7. Notably D. de Rougemont in *L'Amour et l'Occident*, 2nd ed. Paris, 1956.
8. Trans. E. L. Fackenheim: 'A Treatise on Love by Ibn Sina', *Medieval Studies*, 7, Toronto, 1945, pp. 208-28.
9. v. note 2. p. 15 above.

attempt to place Andreas in relation to his background, social, literary and above all religious. Schlösser has the merit (not so common among learned men) of taking both human love and Christianity seriously; moreover he is well read in the Catholic theology of sex and marriage, both medieval and contemporary. I owe much to his learning and judgment.

But now to Andreas. An early, perhaps thirteenth century, manuscript of the *De Amore* begins thus: *liber amoris et curtesie ab andrea capelano regis francie compositus* [10], a well chosen title since Andreas's principal theme is love as the way to acquire the qualities which should distinguish a gentleman and are indicated here by *curtesia*, a term derived from the late Latin *curialitas*. *Curialitas* is frequently employed by Andreas and it may be rendered as 'courtesy'. Only we should beware of taking this term in too narrowly 'courtly' a sense, as though the love-ethic proposed by Andreas were merely the conduct appropriate to courts, whether feudal or royal; or, more generally, were conduct only befitting the upper classes. If such were the case the *De Amore* would be a less interesting work than it is. In fact, however, the feudal and aristocratic colouring of the book is only incidental to its basic argument. Though Andreas belonged to a feudal court and wrote for the upper class in the first place, his mind is notably free from class prejudice. He believes in the natural equality of all men (*uno . . . ab initio stipite derivati*),[11] though he balances this view with the seemingly naive (but where does naivety end and irony begin in Andreas?) remark that class distinctions came in as a result of some men's exceptional virtue.[12] In any case he envisages members of the middle class (*plebei*) as just as capable as the nobility (*nobiles*) of giving and receiving the sort of love he is concerned with. It is true that he excludes peasants (*rustici*) but that is simply due to the material conditions of peasant life. Andreas's basic argument has nothing to do with class at all. For him the true love-ethic, loving intelligently, *sapienter amare*, consists in directing sex in harmony with human nature precisely as human; it is conduct befitting the nature of the rational animal, man, *quae rationis differentia nos a cunctis facit animalibus separari*: [13] and to denote the worth of goodness to be

10. See Trojel ed., p. xxiv.
11. ibid., p. 17.
12. ibid., p. 23.
13. Trojel ed., p. 13-4; 'which distinguishes us from all other animals by the gift of

acquired by such conduct his favourite term is *probitas*, a word
which even for him had probably less upper-class association than
curialitas, and in any case refers to a more interior moral quality.
One might say that either term denotes, for Andreas, both morals
and manners; but *curialitas* (or *urbanitas*) especially manners, and
probitas especially morals.

There is nothing, then, essentially feudal about the theory of
courtly love. Of course it had feudal origins in the sense that it arose
among the southern French nobility at the end of the eleventh century, and of course this circumstance affected its outward forms and
expressions; but it did not make it an intrinsically feudal thing.
There is much to be said indeed for calling it anti-feudal, or at least
'a phenomenon of the decline of feudalism': [14] for it emerged within
the feudal structure as an order of feelings and attitudes that in some
respects went clean contrary to the external order imposed by
custom and law. In this external order the ruler was normally and
emphatically the male; medieval society was by and large
patriarchal. But in the order of courtly love we find the ruler, the
belted knight, habitually on his knees before a woman. 'Whereas in
the material world' says Mr Valency, 'a vassal paid homage to his
lord — the source presumably of all his good — in the world of love
his homage was paid to his lady, the source of all his joy.' [15] Further,
this homage, since it was normally paid to another man's wife, involved the steady threat of a sanctioned adultery — sanctioned, that
is by the code of love. And adultery of course was a sin as well as a
social disturbance; and so we return to the non-Christian aspect of
the love-cult. Its intrinsically non-feudal character is a minor matter
sub specia aeternitatis: and yet it has its importance; for unless we
grasp the fact that courtly love had roots that went down deeper
than any class differences or particular social structure, we shall fail
to do it full justice. The cult of the feminine that it entailed had
nothing, I repeat, to do with social status. It is true that some of the
troubadours were the social inferiors of the women they
worshipped; but some were not. It is likely that most of the women
were well born, but this is only to say that twelfth century courtly
love was mainly an upper class occupation, patronised by great

reason'.
14. M. Valency, *op. cit.*, p. 84.
15. ibid., p. 83.

ladies like Eleanor of Aquitaine and her daughter, Andreas's patron. But there was no intrinsic reason why the love-cult should not spread into the middle class, as later it did to some extent, particularly in Italy — though always retaining clear traces of its aristocratic origins. And there is no reason why the theory that underlay it should not reappear, in other forms, in any age.

The entire doctrine of Andreas rests on two principles which are really two ways of regarding the same basic thing. This thing is love, and love is both observed as a fact given in nature and evaluated as a principle of moral development. As a fact in nature it is sexual attraction; personified sometimes as Venus but more characteristically as *deus amoris*, 'the god of love'. As a fact in human nature love is sexual attraction operating as conscious desire for one of the opposite sex. Love cannot, for Andreas, be homosexual, because homosexuality is a deviation from nature and love is essentially in line with nature: *res enim est amor, quae ipsam imitatur naturam*.[16] Let us note this stress on nature; one implicit consequence of it is that Andreas's system has no place for a love directed towards God. And the emphasis on sex should be noted too, for it defines the field which Andreas is observing: when he says *amor* he excludes everything except the sexual relation between men and women. And this marks him off, not only — as is obvious — from Christian mystics like his near-contemporary St Bernard, but also from ancient writers like Plato and Cicero with their relatively small interest in heterosexual love. Andreas's chief classical source, by the way, is naturally Ovid (*mirificus Ovidius*). Plato was perhaps only a name to him. But Cicero's *De Amicitia* he knew well and at one point he draws an interesting parallel between his own 'love' and Cicero's 'friendship': as the latter had distinguished friendship from blood-relationship, so Andreas will distinguish between love and *maritalis affectio*, the feeling that should unite man and wife. In either case the sentiment that is thus marked out and set in relief — *amicitia, amor* — is represented as more personal, more subject to free choice and so in a sense more noble than the feeling it is contrasted with, the tie of blood or the domestic tie.[17]

Against this entirely naturalistic background, then, Andreas develops his dominant theme: love as the principle of ethical perfec-

16. Trojel ed., p. 37-8: 'love is a thing that follows nature'.
17. Trojel ed., p. 142-3; cf. Cicero, *De Amicitia*, v. 19.

tion, of a growth into the full round of the natural virtues – minus, St Thomas would have said, the natural virtue of religion.[18] This may seem odd: how can sex of itself flower into the four cardinal virtues? But of course it doesn't, just of itself; Andreas insists again and again on a second factor: intelligence. His 'love' is desire carefully controlled and directed by reason; his ideal lover, man or woman, is a *sapiens amator*, one who uses his or her brains all the time. There is nothing 'romantic' in Andreas's attitude, nothing magical or fatal in the love he defines and defends. The *emotional* atmosphere of the *De Amore* (as distinct from the concepts it brings into play) is quite different from that of Beroul's *Tristan*, for example, or from that which Dante evokes in the Francesca episode. Much of the *De Amore* consists of dialogues between *homo* and *mulier* in which the concept of love is elucidated and applied to various possible situations; and the speakers reason over and about their desires with the coolest civility, the most pedantic precision; one understands the French critic's remark that theirs was 'un amour de tête'.[19] The basis certainly, and the motive, of all this reasoning is frankly sexual; but elaborated in a highly conscious conceptual way and with a persistent demand for clearly defined rules for different situations: in short, with a markedly casuistical tendency which is one of the several aspects of courtly love that reflect the Catholic milieu in which it was born and bred; for of course casuistry, the consideration of how general rules apply to particular cases, is freely used in moral theology. And if this parallel between courtly love and theology seems far-fetched (though indeed it is not) let me point, at any rate, to the general intellectualism that marks Andreas as a writer on love. A striking sign of this, besides the bent to subtle casuistry already mentioned, is what he says to justify love-making by the clergy (*clerici*). The clergy, Andreas observes, are made of flesh and blood like other men, and this already is some excuse; but, further, they are better educated than other men, and this is likely to give them an advantage as lovers. The *clericus* is normally 'more cautious and prudent' in his behaviour than the layman, more 'accustomed to regulate himself in all things with due measure and moderation'.[20] Clearly this stress on 'measure' is a stress on in-

18. *Summa theol.* II, IIae, 81.
19. P. Zumthor, *Zeitschrift f. rom. Philologie*, 63, 1943, p. 183.
20. Trojel ed., pp. 185-9.

telligence. It is extremely characteristic.

But to return to the basic principle of all this, the conception of love, in the sense indicated, as the source of all good in the world, as 'fons de bontat'. Andreas takes this for granted and assumes that his readers do so too: it is a point on which all agree, it need only be stated, not proved: *universis constat hominibus, quod nullum in mundo bonum vel curialitas exercetur, nisi ex amoris fonte derivetur. Omnis ergo boni erit amor origo et causa.*[21] Let us note that *bonum in mundo*; it is the goodness of this world, the world of nature, that love causes; and implicitly the goodness of human nature, growth in virtue. It is seldom that Andreas shows excitement about anything but here this cool-headed writer permits himself to exclaim 'O what a wonderful thing is love that causes a man to shine with such virtues and teaches him to abound in all goodness!' It even, he continues, 'adorns a man with an almost chaste-like quality' (*castitatis quasi virtute decoratum*)[22] – surely a revealing touch, and not only because of that rather engaging 'almost'. Andreas is recommending love to readers who could hardly, after all, not remember that they were Christians. His 'chastity', in any case, simply means fidelity to one woman, or one man, at a time. And in this there is surely nothing to mock at. The effort to keep licence out of love was perfectly genuine – so evidently so that Schlösser, for example, sees a discrepancy between the brief opening chapters, which present love quite frankly as carnal appetite, and the long chapters that follow, and compose the body of the work, in which love is continually associated with moral ennoblement and growth in virtue. There is not, I think, any logical inconsistency here; but it is obvious that the simple concept of *amor passio* given in chapter one (which agrees more or less with the theologians' *amor concupiscentiae*[23]) did not *need* to be drawn out into the refined and elevated considerations that follow. A theologian would have developed it in a quite different way. Taking it as his starting point Andreas drew it out into a natural morality, following the path already vaguely yet

21. *ibid.*, p. 29; (cf. pp. 10, 63, 86-7); 'All men agree that there is no goodness, no courtesy in the world that does not stem from love. Love then is the source and cause of all goodness.'

22. *ibid.*, p. 10.

23. The agreement consists, not precisely in the sexuality of the love in question, but in its inherently selfward egoistic character. cf. St. Thomas's definition of '*amor concupiscentiae*' *Summa theol.* Ia, IIae, 28, 1; II, IIae, 23, 1. cf. E. Gilson, *L'ésprit de la philosophie médiévale*, Paris, 1944, p. 266-7.

powerfully indicated by the troubadours. Sexual attraction, elevated
and refined by reason, becomes the principle of morality. This idea
of sublimated sexuality was not exactly Platonic and it certainly was
not mystical, either in the sense of presenting human love as
somehow *dispositive* towards divine love or as an *image*, an analogy,
of that love. Both of these ways of regarding human love are possible in Catholicism (granted that grace does not destroy but rather
perfects nature): the *Divine Comedy* is a Catholic poem and it takes
human love as a starting point – grace and repentance from sin
presupposed – on the soul's way to God; and St John of the Cross
used it as an image of the union with God. But neither way of
regarding love is to be found in Andreas; and neither is
characteristic of the main currents of medieval courtly love
literature. Until Dante any association of human love with charity
remained only marginal in that literature. And it is totally absent
from Andreas; for on the one hand his *amor* is firmly placed within,
and limited by, nature, and on the other hand (and this is the
decisive point) he has only the paltriest conception of grace – even
and indeed most evidently, when he speaks as a theologian in the
Reprobatio Amoris. Yet he has, within his limits, a high and humane
conception of human nature, so that in the event his love-ethic is
developed with sufficient force to compel both the historian and the
theologian to treat it seriously.

The historian will be fascinated by Andreas's silences. He leaves
so much unexplained; partly no doubt because he was himself only
half conscious of what he was doing – of the transposition, I mean,
that he was effecting, or continuing, of values recognised and sanctioned by Christianity into a system that was in principle non-Christian. But to say this is, of course, to raise the question how far some
of these 'values' were in practice recognised by Christianity; a question that presents itself most evidently and acutely, as we shall see,
with regard to the compatibility of love and marriage. And even
with regard to Andreas's basic principle – 'die Grundthese des
ganzen Traktates' as Schlösser says – that love is the source of all
good in the world, even with regard to this it is not a simple matter
to draw a clear line between pagan and Christian influences. Taking
'love' to mean sexual attraction, the principle itself sounds pagan
enough; it certainly lacked any theological authority. Yet in this
way of regarding love there may well be some reflection of the

Christian exaltation of *caritas*. And what about the virtues which, according to Andreas, spring out of love; generosity, courage, gentleness, truthfulness, courtesy, humility even? In part this list is just what we might have expected; sexual desire, tempered by a severe social etiquette, clearly could to some extent be sublimated to such results. But it is also clear that Andreas is thinking and writing in a mental climate deeply affected by centuries of Christian living, so that some such transposition of values, as I have suggested, there must surely have been — of values not, indeed, specifically Christian, but given, in fact, a Christian significance through their assimilation into Christian life and thought. Yet by Andreas they are transposed into a system largely *alien* to Christianity in principle though it emerged within and, largely, out of a Christian environment: at once a product and a negation of the Christian world. Hence, inevitably, certain distortions and ambiguities. One example of such has been noted already: the 'chastity' of Andreas's lovers. Another appears in his listing among the qualities of a true lover that he should be a good Catholic, go frequently to Church, speak respectfully of priests and religious. High among the reasons that would justify a woman in breaking off an attachment is that her lover 'be found to err from the Catholic faith' — a very awkward text for those who would connect courtly love with the Catharist heresy.[24] Again there is the bland way in which *amor* and *caritas* are correlated and compared at a certain point in the discussion: as good works without *caritas* are of no avail before God (a clear echo of 1 Corinthians 13) so the works of *amor*, unless they come 'from the heart', are of no avail before the god of love.[25] But such ambiguities or inconsistencies, though significant, are relatively superficial. We get into deeper water as we approach the central themes of the Andrean love-ethic.

Three such themes can be distinguished (all presupposing the principle that love is the source of all good): (a) a condemnation of mere carnal enjoyment and a consequent duty of self-control; (b) love as continual never-ending desire; (c) love as a free spontaneous gift. A little reflection on each of these themes should bring out more clearly the nature of love *secundum Andream* and at the same time its points of contact with, or difference from, the Christian ethic.

24. Trojel ed., pp. 248 and 68.
25. *ibid.*, p. 123.

(a) *the duty of self control.* This theme has already been touched on. Andreas distinguishes, sharply enough for his purposes, between love and lust, *amor* and *libido*.[26] Promiscuity is ruled out. Love requires strict fidelity: one man to one woman, one woman to one man. The man who becomes a lover engages himself thereby to keep a strict control over his male instincts, while the woman on her side must say goodbye to wantonness. As we should expect the man's duties in this respect are rubbed in harder than the woman's. And really, when one considers the inclinations of the average male, it says something for the courtly lovers that they cheerfully underwent (if any did, of course) the discipline required by their code — at any rate in its strictest form, that 'pure love', *amor purus*, to which I shall turn presently. For the moment however let us stress the woman's role in this business of chastening and bridling *impetuosa voluptas*. For if the man's duty was to learn self-control, the woman's was largely to teach it. Her task was, first, to assess the fitness of a wooer (had he enough *probitas*?) [27], and then, if she accepted him, to lead him through nicely calculated stages towards intimacy; always with an eye to his moral qualifications, at each stage, for a further advance.[28] And if the reader is surprised by this moralisation of adultery or fornication, I can only say that it is there in the texts, and further that it was, speaking generally, just this mixture of the erotic and the ethical that gave courtly love its enduring influence in the literatures of Europe. At the beginning and the end of love-making, in this system, is both a moral element and a sensual element: at the start is the sexual attraction, but a man may only respond to this, or the woman allow him to respond, if he is *probus*: and at the end is sexual intimacy (more or less, as we shall see) and this in turn connotes a final *probitas* which is the crown of love (*amoris digna corona*).[29]

Two further observations seem called for on the woman's place in this system. First, courtly love in general obviously reflects an enhancement of the position and influence of women in medieval society, in the sphere of sexual relations. The main stress falls on courting, not on coition, on desire, not on possession (whether mere-

26. Trojel ed., p. 66, cf. p. 13
27. In this matter Andreas may be echoing Cicero on the care required in the choice or friends, *De Amicitia*, cc. xvii and xxi.
28. Trojel ed., p. 32-3.
29. Trojel ed., p. 61.

ly carnal or also juridical and sacramental). Thus the sphere of *senti-ment* is enormously enhanced. The predatory aggressive male is systematically tamed. He is required to adopt an attitude to sex that is perhaps less naturally congenial to men than to women, so that the general result might be called a certain 'feminisation' of the sex-ual relation. On the other hand – and this is the second point – it can be misleading to stress, as Father Denomy and many other writers have done, the *superiority* of the woman in this system. It is true that the troubadours commonly look up to their ladies in a worshipping sort of way; and that in Andreas the woman always enjoys a certain initiative and authority in the process and discipline of loving. Indeed, one may go further and say that she holds this position because it is assumed that somehow she is privileged to have a sort of initial affinity with love itself, enabling her not only to take the lead as guide and umpire in the problems raised by love (in Andreas, the final appeal, in casuistical problems, is always to Queen this or Countess that) but also somehow to embody in her own person the complex of values which is love's total meaning in the system, a blend of nobility and joy.[30] Yet it is precisely this idealisation of woman which proves that it is not this or that woman in the concrete who is being worshipped, but the love-idea that she embodies. The prose of Andreas brings this out more clearly than it appears in the troubadours, because, being prose, it is analytic: it shows the woman, the beloved, clearly distinct from and subor-dinated to love itself. Like the man she also is servant to the god of love; and is answerable to him for her conduct in loving. Love then, not the woman, is the source of all good.[31] (b) So the individual woman of flesh and blood is the servant and instrument of something greater, of the love-power (which is a power for good) that she represents for the man. She is always, in Andreas, an *occa-sion* for his being touched and transformed by that improving power; she is never seen merely as something for him to enjoy, nor as a future mother of his children (children are never mentioned), nor as his partner in the Christian sacrament; but *only* as the re-quired condition of his growth in natural virtue. And so we pass on naturally to the theme of love as 'ceaseless desire, a yearning that is

30. A century after the *De Amore* this latent idea took shape in Dante's *Vita Nuova* and in a form that might have astonished Andreas.
31. This comes out most clearly on pp. 80-110.

unappeased', to quote Denomy again. True, one may be surprised, after reading the troubadours, to find Andreas apparently making so little of this theme. Yet it is certainly in his book, but by implication rather than by explicit statement. It comes nearest to the surface where he speaks of 'pure' and 'mixed' love (*amor purus, amor mixtus*). The derivation of these epithets is disputed but Andreas makes their meaning perfectly plain. Mixed love is love that is permitted to reach its term in coition; pure love is love that is deliberately withheld from coition; though it can go a fair way towards this end, so that its 'purity' from the Christian point of view, remains ambiguous. To the extent stated however it is non-carnal, and as such it could be held up as love *par excellence* (*fin amors*), the love that can realise most perfectly the ennobling effect of love. And this it can do precisely because the renunciation that it entails renders love more stable and enduring; because desire is maintained by *not* being satisfied: 'This love', says Andreas, 'increases endlessly, and we know that no one has cause to repent of its actions, and the more one obtains from it the more one longs to have'.[32] Here again it is plausible to suspect a transposition of a religious and mystical theme, itself derived from the Canticle of Solomon and from the text of Ecclesiasticus which Dante was to use when he saw Beatrice as the symbol of revealed Wisdom: *qui edunt me adhuc esurient, et qui bibunt me adhuc sitient.*[33] Too much must not be made of such echoes, but we should bear them in mind.

(c) *Love as a free spontaneous gift.* An important consequence of Andreas's so closely associating love with virtue, and in particular with generosity (*largitas*) is his stress on its spontaneity, on love's not being necessitated by any law extrinsic to itself. True, this stress is balanced by the characteristic emphasis on clear-sighted caution, on prudence. A woman should only accept a lover after coolly assessing his qualities. 'Whoever loved that loved not at first sight' is not a thing we can imagine Andreas saying. He has a Gallic taste for rationality in all things. But in fact these two balancing stresses, on *largitas* and on *sapientia*, are not inconsistent; rather, the one implies the other. To love with *largitas* is not to love on blind impulse: it is to love because one has consciously and freely chosen to and not

32. Trojel ed., p. 183.
33. Eccles. 24, 29; 'they who eat of me shall yet hunger and they who drink of me shall yet thirst'; *Purgatorio* xxxi, 128-9; cf. *Paradiso* ii, 11-12

because there is a law which says that one must, or even because the candidate for one's love shows every sign of deserving it. So *largitas* is linked with the phrase *ex gratia* in a passage in which it is impossible not to hear an acho of St Paul's doctrine opposing the works of the law to grace. 'You ought to love me', says *homo* here, and he states the reasons why; but he then goes on: 'Nevertheless it would be more praiseworthy in you if you gave me your love purely out of good-will (*ex tua gratia tantum*) rather than as a return for anything I have done in the past'.[34] This is to identify the freedom of loving with a certain indifference even to moral merit: and it clearly seems, I say, to connote a transposition of a Christian idea, an imitation of the order of *caritas*. But it is more to our immediate purpose to note the opposition of love, in Andreas, not to preceding merit but to external law; for this brings us directly to his sharp division of love from marriage.

This important issue is very frankly stated and firmly resolved in the *De Amore*: one feels that the question was a live one in the circles for which Andreas wrote and that he particularly wished to settle it. His own view, that love was essentially an extramarital relation, was by no means unquestioned in those circles, as we know from the works of Chrétien de Troyes, in only one of whose many tales – the 'Lancelot' (the 'Chevalier de la Charette') – is the hero definitely an adulterer.[35] By and large Chrétien 'did not like adultery'[36] and tried to reconcile love with wedlock. In his *Cligès*, for example, the hero marries his mistress and goes on loving her all the same:

> De s'amie a feite sa feme,
> mes il l'apele amie et dame. (6753 – 4)

Now precisely the same effort to reconcile courtly love and marriage appears in one of the dialogues in the *De Amore*, where the woman declares that she will only give herself to one who is both lover and

34. Trojel ed., p. 29.
35. This strange story – which Dante was to use in his critique of courtly love (*Inferno* V) – has been called 'the high-water mark of courtly love' (H. J. Weigand), or again 'La victoire de l'amour sur la chevalerie, de la féminité sur la virilité jusqu'a l'abaissement et l'humiliation totale' (G. Cohen). It is significant that in a preface to this poem Chrétien says that he owed the idea of it to 'la contesse', that is, to Marie de Champagne, the patron of Andreas.
36. T. P. Cross and W. A. Nitze, *Lancelot and Guenevere. A Study in the Origins of Courtly Love,* Chicago, 1930, p. 69.

husband (*maritus et amans*). The man argues against this view and
the discussion continues pro and con until they agree to refer the
matter to the judgment of a competent authority. The judge chosen
is the Countess of Champagne. Andreas gives their letter to her and
her reply. This reply, dated 1 May, 1174, and drafted with all the
formality of a legal sentence, is a decision against the woman's
opinion: love is *totally incompatible with marriage*. The Countess
bases her judgment on three reasons, but these can all be reduced to
one: that whereas married people are bound to one another by external law, lovers are united by free choice. 'We declare and firmly
decide', she writes, 'that love can have no place between husband
and wife: for lovers concede everything to one another *gratis* and as
constrained by no necessity; but a husband and wife are obliged to
obey each other's will, they are not permitted to deny each other
anything.'[37] And from this contrast, between spontaneity on the
one hand and strict obligation on the other, she goes on to draw a
consequence that would seem to imply that extra-marital love was
morally superior to marriage. Since, she says, the mutual self-giving
of a married couple is imposed on them by law, it can effect no increase in their personal *probitas* – as of course it would, on the
countess's view, were they merely lovers.[38]

It is worth noting that Andreas never explicitly states that love is
morally superior to marriage; he is content simply, but very decidedly, to separate them, to declare that love has nothing to do with
marriage. Courtly love, as he presents it, is, says Schlösser, '*aus-
sereheliche*' rather than '*antieheliche*'. All the same it is obvious that
his doctrine implies at least, or easily could imply, a contempt for
marriage; for it places, implicitly, all the moral value of sex in extra-
marital relations, reducing marriage to a purely institutional and
juridical state which only engages the personality in a relatively
superficial way. Underlying this is the very specious sophistry that
in the degree that one is obliged to do anything one must do it the
less freely; which is to confuse physical and moral compulsion. And
this sophistry, it is clear, could be applied all over the sphere of
morals. No need to limit it to sexual relations; it could, for example

37. Trojel ed., pp. 143-55.
38. *ibid.*, p. 154: *Praeterea quid jugalis crescit honori, si sui conjugalis amantium more fruatur
amplexu, quum neutrius inde possit probitas augmentari, et nihil amplius augmento videantur
habere nisi quod primitus jure suo tenebant.*

(as St Thomas saw) take the merit out of *any* obedience to law.[39]

But, as regards love, the emergence of this distinction between obligation and freedom and the use made of it to divide love from marriage indicates, it seems reasonable to suppose, a certain unrest, a *malaise*, in the society that was adopting courtly love — even if only as a superior sort of game. Even games have their unconscious motives, and this one, of regarding sex as a matter of high and serious human interest (making possible an ideal relationship between two autonomous personalities), could hardly have arisen in the way it did if people had not felt that something was lacking in the *status quo*. In other words, courtly love, I think, was in part an assertion of personal values against a social and juridical order which in some respects had come to appear excessively impersonal. Behind the ideas we have been examining there must have been strong currents of feeling. A section of lay society — an exceptionally cultivated section — was reacting against established opinions on sex because it felt that these were somehow inhuman, did not adequately reflect human realities.[40] But in effect this reaction involved a depreciation of marriage. The high French society of the twelfth century was Catholic and intended to remain Catholic, and could hardly imagine itself as anything else; yet, in the sphere of feeling, a part of it had apparently become alienated from the ideal of Christian marriage. How far this may have been the fault of the theologians is a question that inevitably arises, but one too complex for detailed treatment here.[41] We should, however, not fail to note

---

39. *Summa theol.* II, IIae, 104,1. The essential distinction comes in the reply to objection 3: it goes to the heart of the matter and is worth citing both in the Latin and in translation. *Aliquid potest judicari gratuitum dupliciter: uno modo, ex parte ipsius operis, quia scilicet homo ad id non obligatur: alio modo, ex parte operantis, quia scilicet libera voluntate hoc facit. Opus autem redditur virtuosum et laudabile et meritorium praecipue secundum quod ex voluntate procedit. Et ideo, quamvis obedire sit debitum, si prompta voluntate aliquis obediat, non propter hoc minuitur ejus meritum, maxime apud Deum, qui non solum exteriora opera verum etiam interiorem voluntatem videt.* 'Anything (i.e., any action) can be accounted gratuitous (or spontaneous) in two ways: either as regards the action in itself, inasmuch as one is not obliged to do it; or as regards the doer of the action, inasmuch as he does it of his own free will. Now what makes an action virtuous, praiseworthy and meritorious is chiefly its proceeding from the will. Therefore, although one is obliged to obey, it does not follow that there is any loss of merit, provided one obeys with a ready will; particularly in the sight of God who sees not only the outward deed but also the inward will.'
40. This may seem an overstatement, but it seems to me arguable from the emphasis laid by Andreas on the *human-ness* of the kind of love he advocates.
41. It is fairly thoroughly discussed by Schlösser, *op. cit.,* pp. 261-90. The reader who

another passage in the *De Amore*, where the half-concealed conflict
between courtly love and current theology comes more clearly into
the open. One of Andreas's arguments against bringing love into
marriage is a *reductio ad absurdum*: if, he says, you attempt to do this
you will necessarily make married people sin. For the only reason
for their having sexual intercourse at all is to pay their mutual debt
and beget children. It cannot in any sense be simply the pleasure
they take in one another. So he concludes: 'whatever pleasure
married people give to and receive from one another, apart from the
desire for children, cannot be free from sin (*crimine carere non
potest*)'.[42] Here again Andreas is using current theology as a foil for
his own thesis. And one can hardly accuse him, here at least, of
caricaturing his foil. He could have adduced plenty of texts for his
purpose. A haunting fear of letting concupiscence into marriage was
undoubtedly a powerful element in traditional marriage theology,
and one backed by the greatest names, St Augustine's, above all, and
St Jerome's. And with this fear went an implicit refusal to consider
sex in any other than one of two ways: either as pleasant *and*
procreative – and from this point of view the use of sex was justified, in marriage, by the intention to procreate; or as *merely* pleasant,
and from this point of view its use was never justified whether in
marriage or not. This was the traditional doctrine which St Thomas
was to resume and repeat in his Commentary on the Sentences (now
available in the Supplement to the *Summa Theologiae* QQ.xli to xlix).
In the twelfth century things were a little confused in some quarters
by an uncertainty as to whether the right to use sex were of the essence of Christian marriage or only something added on – a sort of
faute de mieux for those who were too weak to live according to the
pure essence and ideal of the sacrament. This was roughly the theory
of virginal marriage elaborated by Hugh of St Victor; an extreme
de-sexualisation of marriage which, despite Hugh's authority, found
little favour with subsequent theologians.[43] It remains only as an
interesting witness to the mystical or spiritualising trends which

---

desires to get his bearings on the subject may be recommended, however, to start with the
excellent articles on the history of marriage theology in the *Dictionnaire de théologie
catholique*, vol. ix, especially that by G. le Bras, col. 2077-2317.
42. Trojel ed., p. 137.
43. cf. Schlösser, *op. cit.*, p. 267-9. The relevant texts are in Migne PL, 176, col. 859-76
(*De B. Mariae virginitate*). cf. also Schahl, 'La doctrine des fins du mariage dans la
théologie scolastique'. *Etudes de science religieuse*, vol. 6, Paris, 1948.

were so characteristic of the early twelfth century and which were probably not without some influence on the rise of courtly love itself. But is is clear that in so far as courtly love was an attempt to vindicate for the sexual impulse an intrinsic value, a potential moral worth apart from its procreative purpose, it could look for no support from contemporary theology. Traditional theology took no account of any such value or worth. Theologians were then much less sympathetic than they are today to the 'personal' side of sex, to its connection with love. We today may be shocked to hear Andreas excluding love from marriage, but there is no reason to think that an average twelfth century theologian would have been in the least shocked by this — once he had understood what Andreas meant by love, namely sexual desire regarded as morally valuable apart from its term in procreation. Andreas belonged to one world and the theologian to another. More than a century was to pass before Dante drew the two worlds closer together in his poem.[44] In real life the separation continued.

To carry this discussion any further would overstep the limits of this paper. I have already perhaps started too many hares, at the risk of concluding with an anti-climax. It would be interesting to trace — but the evidence seems scarcer than one might have expected — the reactions of the Church to courtly love. Why, for example, did the De Amore escape condemnation until it suddenly turns up in 1277, a century after its composition, in the prologue to the famous condemnation by Tempier, bishop of Paris, of the 219 naturalistic and Averroistic theses current in the Arts faculty of the University? [45] And what is the precise significance of this condemnation? Again, there is the vexed question of the sources of courtly love; or again, that of the Christian transformation it underwent in the mighty and passionate mind of Dante. So many topics that would outrun my competence and perhaps the reader's patience. Let me reach my conclusion through a paragraph from Gilson which, for all its generality, and though I would question some of its phrases, comprises as good a brief definition of courtly love as one is likely to find. Courtly love says this great scholar, was neither a utilisation of themes

44. But Dante almost entirely ignores marriage: an interesting point of difference between him and the puritan Milton.
45. Text in *Chartularium Universitatis Parisiensis*, ed Denifle and Chatelain, vol. 1 p. 543 ss. cf. E. Gilson, *La Philosophie au Moyen-âge*, Paris, 1944, pp. 558-66.

from Christian mysticism nor a reaction against asceticism (but we have seen that in some sense it might be called a reaction of this sort): 'placé hors de l'une et de l'autre, il exprime bien plutôt l'effort d'une société polie et affinée par des siècles de christianisme pour élaborer un code de l'amour humain qui fût, non point mystique ni même spécifiquement chrétien, mais plus raffiné que la grivoiserie d'Ovide et ou le sentiment prît le pas sur la sensualité. C'est là, semble-t-il, qu'est sa signification historique propre. La sensualité au service de sentiment, et parfois des plus exquis comme chez Jaufré Rudel, ou même de la raison comme chez Chrétien de Troyes.' [46] An effort, within Christian society, to elaborate a code of human love; yes, but of purely human love apart from any consideration of the concrete claims and call of divine love; and therefore moving inevitably into positions at variance with the Christian ethic upheld by the Church — such at least is how courtly love appears in the fullest theoretical statement of it that we possess, the *De Amore* of Andreas. But to say this is not to deny that one may detach from the troubadour poetry, from Chrétien, even from Andreas himself, certain features, a certain attitude to sex and love which would not be incompatible with Christianity. In Andreas the two clearly non-Christian elements are his general this-wordliness and his implicit approval of adultery; but neither element is inseparable from a recognition that sexual attraction has, potentially, great moral and spiritual value; which when all is said, would seem to be the enduring essential 'message' of courtly love.

This 'message' came, naturally, from the laity. Yet its chief doctrináire spokesman was a cleric, our Andreas; and this fact has its own interest for the historian. For it means that we see the theory of courtly love through the mind of a man whose culture could not help being largely ecclesiastical. In reading the *De Amore* this is a fact we must allow for. And undoubtedly it is in one sense an advantage to view courtly love through the eyes of a worldly priest. As expounder and advocate of his thesis Andreas deliberately speaks as a man of the world; but since his clerical training keeps peeping through, we are never in danger in reading Andreas (as we might be in reading some of the troubadours) of forgetting the Catholic setting within and from which courtly love developed. It did so in

46. *La théologie mystique de saint Bernard*, Paris 1934, p. 193.

some degree as a non-Christian enclave within medieval christendom; yet the currents of thought that formed this enclave moved
from principles which, so far as they were truly rational and human,
no Catholic philosopher can allow himself to abjure; for we must
believe that all that is authentically human can be brought within the
sweep of grace. Certainly in their actual movement those currents of
thought and feeling could easily, as we have seen, issue in heresy and
immorality. Yet who would be so inhuman as to damn the whole
thing root and branch? Dante, it is true, damned Francesca, and in
doing so passed the most searching *literary* judgment on courtly love
that it ever received. But the heaven of Venus (*Paradiso* VIII and
IX) balances the zone of damned carnality (*Inferno V*); and Beatrice
far outbalances Francesca. When all is said, courtly love was an effort to bring sex into harmony with the spirit; it was an aspiration
to refinement and, as such, part of that general aspiration towards
intellectual, emotional and spiritual refinement which marked the
wonderful century in which it was born – the century of St Bernard
and the Victorines, of Abelard and the school of Chartres. In this
context courtly love becomes intelligible. Let us agree to call it a
heresy of a sort; but there were elements in it that cannot be dismiss-
ed as merely pagan.[47]

47. Dante, incidentally, never mentions the *De Amore*, but there is evidence that he
knew the work and made use of it, especially in his earlier writings: see M. Simonelli,
'Il tema della nobiltà in A. Cappellano e in Dante', *Dante Studies* (U.S.A.). LXXXIV,
1966, pp. 51-64; D. De Robertis, *Il libro della "Vita Nuova"*, Florence, 1961.

3

DANTE AND EROS

By 'eros' I mean here an inclination of the human psyche as a whole to satisfaction or fulfilment. So used, the term is roughly equivalent to St Thomas' *amor naturalis*, 'natural love',[1] when the nature referred to is human. This use of terms is open to question, of course. Is there in fact a common impulse — love, *amor, eros* — involved in all our desires? And if there is, what does it imply in terms of our place in the universe? Is there some basic 'goodness' in reality that draws us all the time and through all our faculties? And supposing there is, how should we define it? These are philosophical questions, and I am not writing philosophy. Still, my subject does indirectly raise them, since Dante's work is clearly a major expression, to say the least, of the erotic theme; and an essential element in its greatness was surely the intensity of his conviction (or better, the *quality* of that intensity) that all human desires *are* radically one, as stemming from a substance that is one. This conviction I will try to analyse and illustrate, in the hope of at least offering a challenge to reflexion. Great art is perhaps the best witness we have to the whole nature of man, and it is chiefly as such a witness that I wish to present Dante — as a 'case', let us say, and a rather extraordinary one. What is extraordinary about him, in this context, is that his poetry is so complete an expression of a trans-sexual idea of love. More particularly, I would say that he merits the attention of modern students of Christianity, and of religion generally, because a main theme of his poetry is *eros*, natural love, as related to the love of God; and because in pursuing this theme he was led to reflect profoundly on certain problems in ethics and psychology. I hold no special brief for Dante precisely as a theologian. I am aware that the theology of the *Comedy*, so far as it directly con-

1. E.g. *Summa Theol.*, 1a 2ae, 26, 1 and 2.

cerns the relation of nature to grace, is not only alien to the Protestant tradition but is also unlikely to commend itself today, without
considerable qualification, to educated Catholics. But it is above all
as a poet bearing witness that I present him – his burning witness,
from within the Catholic tradition, to the common nature of man.

Let us turn then to the *Comedy*; and since this is so evidently a
work that climbs to a climax, let us begin right at the end, at that
superb close *l'amor che move il sole e l'altre stelle*. Questions at once
arise. Why, for example, does the conclusion of so religious a poem
as this is generally held to be, lay that stress on the physical world,
on the sun and the stars? It is clear, of course, that *amor* is here a
synonym for God; clear too that love's presence in the created
world is in some sense only secondary and derived. But it is also
clear from the whole context that the 'rightness' of this world lies in
a certain conformity to divine love, and moreover that this conformity is given as *already* realized in the physical world, its actual present achievement being in the human spirit alone: the God-swayed
motion of the stars is an established fact to which a newly achieved
state of one human soul is now being likened. That is a first point to
note. But if we turn back from the last canto of *Paradiso* to the first,
we shall see that the relation of the physical and spiritual orders in
creation is not only one of likeness; it is also, and primarily, one of
co-existence as parts in a whole – the whole described by Beatrice in
canto I as an 'order' which forms the universe into a likeness (this
time) of God; a likeness consisting precisely in the ordered interrelation of the parts of the cosmos.[2] And the common measure and rule
of all the parts, both the physical and the spiritual, the principle that
holds them in unity, is God – both in the last tercet and the first
canto of *Paradiso*.

A difference worth noting, however, appears in the way the
different levels of reality are poetically represented. At the close of
the final canto the ultimate measuring of creatures by God is stated
with a stress on their passivity: the poet's will is impelled by the
love which also turns the stars in their courses. And the wheel image, introduced at this point, accentuates the note of passivity, with
the metrical stress falling on the passive participle: *sí come rota*

2. *Par* I, 103-08. (It would be interesting to follow up the Dantean stress on *order* being a
'likeness' to God; it has to do with his concept of goodness and, I fancy, with his reading
of Boethius in particular.

ch'igualmente è mossa; the poet's spirit moves as a wheel is moved, as the wheeling heavens are moved, by a force from outside. A spiritual state is reduced, as it were, in imagination, to a physical movement, the poetic effect being a sense of absorption into a totality entirely controlled *ab extra*. But such elimination of differences, so apt at the *Paradiso's* close, would be out of place at its beginning; and in fact Beatrice's discourse there on the dynamic cosmic order, while it places all this under an original and continuing impetus from God, goes on to show creatures taking their own directions within the system, each intrinsically impelled towards the eternal Good, and each therefore tending to its own distinctive approximation – near or far-off – to that Good, *più al principio loro e men vicine*. Far from assimilating these various movements to a single 'type', Beatrice is at pains to distinguish them in terms of degrees of affinity to the Creator:

> onde si muovono a diversi porti
>   per lo gran mar dell'essere, e ciascuna
>   con istinto a lei dato che la porti.[3]

'Thus things move over the great sea of being to different harbours, and each with the impulse given it that bears it along.' So the generalised *istinto* becomes in creatures with 'intellect and love' – angels and men – a conscious attraction towards the light that is perfect joy and is identified with the highest heaven, the 'happy target', whither Dante and his guide are now voyaging. A main effect, in short, of this opening passage is to prepare for the description, which in fact will fill the rest of the poem, of a particular kind of movement, a special sort of desire, the desire characteristic of intelligent beings. It is Dante's thought about this that we must now try to grasp.

This is not easy, for his whole philosophy of man is involved. For Dante, as for St Augustine and Freud, love was the absolutely central topic. At the heart of his thought, and so of his poetry, is a conception of the soul as appetitive, as *attracted*. It is no accident that the numerically central cantos of the *Comedy, Purgatorio* 17-18, contain Virgil's discourses on love; and nothing in the *Comedy* is more characteristic, in respect of content, than two tercets from them, the

3. *Par.* I, 112-14.

first declaring the absolute universality of love, the second showing its emergence in the human psyche. Here is the first:

> 'Né creator né creatura mai',
> cominciò el, 'figliuol, fu sanza amore,
> o naturale o d'animo; e tu 'l sai . . .' [4]

And now the second:

> 'L'animo, ch'è creato ad amar presto,
> ad ogni cosa è mobile che piace,
> tosto che dal piacere in atto è desto.' [5]

In the context these two statements are related dialectically, for the second introduces a discourse on free will and moral responsibility, the effect of which will be to distinguish the universal love-principle, as working through the human psyche, into contrasted acts or movements – the necessary and the contingent. At first sight free will is incompatible with that universal principle; for on the one hand every movement of the psyche springs from love of some kind, and on the other hand all the psyche's actual loving is a response to some *external* stimulus, to some object met in experience. How then can it ever love, or choose, as from itself, freely and responsibly? [6] This way of putting the problem was perhaps due to a tension in Dante's mind between an Aristotelian stress on the passive element in experience – if all knowledge starts in sensation, so too does every actual desire – and his Christian-Neoplatonist conviction that the world only existed as a process of necessary reversal to its divine source. But the point to note at the moment is the distinction drawn, within the psyche, between its inborn, necessary drive towards self-fulfilment, and its reactions to this or that thing met in experience. Free will is a dialectical, self-critical relation, in the living human soul, between itself as *simply* loving and itself as loving – or not – this or that particular thing. Thus the moral life is a continual measuring of particular attractions or repulsions against a single deeper attraction. Now this deeper attraction precedes con-

4. *Purg.* XVII, 91-93: 'Neither Creator nor creature, my son', he began, 'was ever without love, whether natural or rational; and this you know'.
5. *Purg.* XVIII, 19-21: 'The soul, as created ready for love, responds to all that gives pleasure, as soon as this stirs it to action'.
6. *Purg.* XVIII, 40-45.

sciousness; when conscious life begins we find ourselves *already* inclined in certain ways, prior to any act of choice: hence this inclination is not under our control. Dante calls it *la prima voglia*, the
'primary desire', and sees it as involved in all our particular aims and
activities.[7] But it is clear, I think (though he does not say this explicitly), that he understands the *prima voglia* as bearing radically on
one object, not many. What this object is will appear presently.

The 'primary desire' is not within our control because we cannot
deliberate about it. What we do deliberate about is our appetitive
reactions and responses to particular experiences precisely as such:
we find ourselves submitting these to an inward, innate power of
deliberation and decision: 'inborn in you is the deliberative power
(*la virtú che consiglia*) which should hold the threshold of assent'[8]
Now this power pertains of course to mind or reason; and
elsewhere, when speaking of free will, Dante will stress this intellectual element. But here in *Purgatorio* 18 his special concern, I think,
is to show choice as an activity integral to human desire itself, as a
factor which emerges in and from the spontaneous craving for happiness, and which in turn gives this craving its moral quality as, at a
given moment, ethically either right or wrong. The main stress here
is on the moral implications of free-will, and so on its
volitional-appetitive rather than its rational-cognitive aspect. And
what is most interesting, I feel, in Dante's thought at this point is his
conception of the *prima voglia* as the ultimate interior 'measure'
which not only — with rational deliberation playing dialectically
against it — makes free choice possible, but which also provides this
choice with its moral norm or rule. The norm of morality, as here
presented, is not then sufficiently described as right reason; nor,
much less, any abstract idea of duty; it is first and foremost the living soul itself as innately and spontaneously craving for happiness
through its confused apprehension of some final fulfilment —

> ciascun confusamente un bene apprende
> nel qual si queti l'animo, e desira . . .[9]

That this fulfilment is in fact to be found only in God will be the

7. *Purg.* XVIII, 49-72.
8. *Purg.* XVIII, 62-63.
9. *Purg.* XVII, 127-8: 'Everyone apprehends, confusedly, a good that would bring the
soul to peace; and this everyone desires'.

lesson of the *Paradiso*; but it is already implicitly such here, in
Virgil's affirmation of the inviolable moral authority, the sacredness,
let us say, of the primary desire: 'Now in order that every other
desire be gathered in (*si raccoglia*) to this one, innate in you is the
deliberative power that should hold the threshold of assent'.[10] For I
take this to mean that the moral acceptability of particular desires
consists in a certain relation to the primary desire, which in this
sense is normative and supreme. As a rule for conduct it takes effect,
of course, only through deliberation, but the whole purpose of
deliberation, *consiglio*, is to mediate between the basic *prima voglia*,
whose rightness is *not* in question, and all other, particular *voglie*
whose rightness is much in question.

Observe however that the rightness of the *prima voglia*, though it
underpins morality, is not in itself ethical, for it does not follow
choice but precedes it. Being in no way the product of free will, it
cannot incur praise or blame: *merto di lode o di biasmo non cape*.[11]
What is praiseworthy is any choice in conformity with it; what is
blameworthy is any other choice. Its rightness is ontological. It has
to do with what man is, prior to anything he does; with man as
God's product, not as his own. The 'rightness' Dante sees at the
roots of our nature is simply the effect of the divine Goodness which
created it.

Before pursuing this point further let me place what has been said
in some historical perspective. First, it is clear enough that Dante's
general theory of love is a variant on the Platonic tradition. Plato
taught that human love, *eros*, could become a love of ideal goodness
and beauty. The later Platonists, in particular Plotinus, developed
this teaching by combining their master's idea of the absolute Good
with his ideas about human *eros*.[12] Thus in Plotinus the Deity, the
One or Good, becomes not only the universal source of goodness,
but also — which is the crucial point — the source of *eros* itself, of an
aspiration in all things towards the absolute Good: 'the soul loves
him (God), moved by him to love from the beginning'.[13] Moreover
God, as the source of *eros*, may be called not only lovable but love,

10. *Purg.* XVIII, 61-63.
11. *Purg.* XVIII, 60.
12. See A. H. Armstrong, 'Platonic *Eros* and Christian *Agape*', *The Downside Review*,
LXXIX, 1961, pp. 105-21.
13. *Enneads*, VI, 7, 31.

eros itself: 'he is at once lovable, and love, and love of himself'.[14] In Aristotelian terms, the ultimate final cause of *eros* has become its efficient cause too; the upward path from the many to the One now implies a prior downward path. *Eros* moves in a circle; through *eros* things return to God because they came through *eros* from God. It only remained for Proclus to draw out more clearly the implied affinity between the One and the many.[15] Whatever proceeds from the One is in one sense the same as it, in another sense different: as the same it 'remains' in its Source; it differs only as proceeding from it. But the remaining (*monē*) takes effect dynamically as a natural trend in each thing to complete the movement of 'proceeding' (*próodos*) by one of 'turning back' (*epistrophē*). The whole cosmos follows this triadic pattern, the unifying principle of which is love, *eros*.

A fairly direct line leads from this later Platonism to Dante, though the way lies through Christianity. The religion of the Bible had its difficulties with Neoplatonism, but not in respect of the basic triadic pattern of procession and return through love. The differences concerned, not the reality of the cycle, but now it took effect. For Christians the *próodos* from God entailed creation in the strict sense, an idea foreign to the Greek mind.. And the *epistrophē* to God entailed the incarnate redeemer, a 'folly to the Greeks'. Nevertheless for Christianity too, indeed more emphatically, love was the principle of both *próodos* and *epistrophē*; and, so far, the tradition of *eros* was congenial to Christian theology. It could reappear therein in ways that were less than authentically Christian, but I do not think we need be concerned here with such deviations. Dante's love-doctrine was articulated under Neoplatonist influences; but in itself it did not – or at least need not – imply any weakening of Christian dogma; any more than similar influences did in the case of William of St Thierry or St Thomas Aquinas, both of whom, like Dante, took much from the Pseudo-Areopagite. What they – with other Christian thinkers of that time – took from Neoplatonism, as filtered through the respected Dionysian medium, concerned especially two vital points in Catholic theology, each connected with a key text of Scripture: the identification of God with love (I John iv, 16) and the identification of man with God's image (Genesis i,

14. Ibid. VI, 8, 15.
15. Proclus, *Elements of Theology*, Prop. 30-35.

27); and not only were both doctrines easily to be found in Denys's work but also the *eros*-link between them.[16] God is *eros* and its cause; which in St Thomas's scholastic diction becomes, 'God is *amor* both *essentialiter et causaliter*'. God *is* the love whereby he loves himself; therefore whatever he makes will be a created image of absolute love, and as such a lover of absolute goodness; so that from this point of view it will mean exactly the same to say, 'I am created', and 'I am a lover of God'; to say, 'I come from God', and 'I am returning to God'. To discover oneself as a creature is to discover oneself desiring one's Creator — and *vice versa*. With this we are already back in Dante's company, though certain special Dantean themes have yet to be touched on. But the general pattern has emerged. When in his prose *Convivio* Dante says, 'the chief desire in everything, and the first given it by nature, is to return to its source (*principio*), and since God is the source of our souls and made them in his likeness . . . the soul desires above all else to return to him',[17] when he says this, Dante refers to the Genesis text on the image, but he certainly had also in mind the Neoplatonist *Liber de Causis*, and he may well have been thinking too of the *Divine Names* and the Thomist commentary on it. The pattern in any case is the same circular one explicitly noted by St Thomas in this work: *quaedem enim circulatio apparet in amore, secundum quod est de bono in bonum*. Metaphysically speaking, the divine goodness is the reason why God first loves himself, and then of his consequent self-expression in creatures which of their nature must love him in return: *ex isto bono (Deus) emanavit in existentia, et iterum in existentibus participatus convertit se ad suum principium, quod est bonum*.[18]

By now the reader may be asking when I am going to mention a woman, other than Beatrice. But this is a study of Dante's ideas, not an essay in biography; and the feminine figures that appear in his lyrics — Violetta, the Pargoletta, the Pietra lady, Beatrice herself under this aspect — these can only concern me as a background to his theorizing about love. Yet it must of course be emphasised that before Dante set his hand to the 'sacred poem' he was already famous as a poet of 'profane' love in what is called the courtly tradi-

---

16. Cf. St Thomas, *Expositio super Dionysium, De Divinis Nominibus*, c. iv, lectio 11 *passim* (ed. Mandonnet, Paris, 1927, pp. 399-403).
17. *Conv.* IV, xii, 14.
18. St Thomas, op. cit., p. 403.

tion; and there would be much to say, had I space, on this aspect of
my theme. But I must stick to the bare essentials; which means,
from the point of view I have adopted, that I can attend only to
that element in courtly love which is most directly and dramatically
relevant to the mature Dante's effort in the *Comedy*, to correlate the
religion of *eros* with Christianity. I refer of course to the sexual element.

The question touched on here is a complex one and all I can
attempt is to indicate certain salient points that need, I think, to be
borne in mind in approaching it. And first one obvious consideration. When, in the *Comedy*, Dante came to record and take stock of
all his manifold experience, it was inevitable − given his milieu and
temperament − that what he said or implied about love should have
been largely critical and self-critical. The Dante who makes that
journey through the after-life is a sinner when he begins it, and the
whole point of the journey, as we learn in the poem itself, is to effect
a conversion in the will from sin to God; and this through a growth
in knowledge of good and evil. Hence the *Inferno,* giving a
knowledge of evil, and the other two *cantiche* giving knowledge of
good. And all this, in one way or another, was a study of love.
Metaphysically, for Dante, it had to be so, as we have seen; and in-
trospection showed that it was so, that as Virgil declares:

> . . . esser convene
> amor sementa in voi d'ogni virtute,
> e d'ogne operazion che merta pene.[19]

Amor here is *eros* in the wide trans-sexual sense already noted. But
as Virgil's discourse develops into the argument about free will a
specific sexual reference is discernible − naturally so, given that
Dante was a man of the world before he turned to theology, and a
poet of sexual love before he set out to sublimate *amor* into *caritas.*

Of course, the whole courtly love tradition was already a kind of
sublimation: see Andreas Capellanus on the manifold virtues required of the *sapiens amator*[20] But the ethical side of sublimation is
perhaps less noteworthy, in Dante's pre-*Comedy* writings, than the
connected, but logically distinct, idea of natural nobility. 'Nobility'

---

19. *Purg.* XVII, 103-05: 'love must be the seed in you of all virtue, and also of every deed
that deserves punishment'.
20. *De Amore*, virtually *passim*. See above, ch. 2, 'Courtly Love and Christianity'.

appears in things in the degree that their 'nature' is perfectly realized. Human nature is rational soul informing appropriate matter.
Whenever, then, these two principles fitly and harmoniously in-
terrelate, there is a noble man or woman, there is *gentilezza*. This is
not a moral quality precisely, since — like the *prima voglia* itself —
gentilezza pertains to the 'nature' one originally receives prior to any
act of the will. Still less does it depend on class or wealth. The long
and brilliant analysis of *gentilezza* in *Convivio* IV is a great document
of humanism just because it focuses so intensely throughout on what
is essential to common humanity. And in doing so it gave, for the
first time, to the literary and vaguely erotic notion of *cor gentile* a
central place in a philosophical treatise *de homine*. Here is perhaps its
chief historical importance — if what is novel and creative in the
work is not merely the fact that it is philosophy written for laymen
(and women) by a layman, but the fact that this layman was a poet
nourised on a literary tradition which had hitherto had only
marginal connexions with philosophy and virtually none with
theology. True, Dante's own interest in theology proper appears
only fitfully in the *Convivio*; for the book, while obviously the work
of a Christian, celebrates the discoveries of reason far more than the
mysteries of faith. Nevertheless, it is just where the argument
touches, or approaches, theology that Dante develops his ideas on
love in the most interesting ways.

I have in mind two developments in particular — one (I, xii-xiii,
III, ii) on love as a cosmic force deriving from the nature of God;
the other (II, v) a digression about astral influences. A glance at the
first may give more precision to what has been said about Dante's
love-metaphysic, while a brief consideration of the second bring out
more distinctly his teaching on free will.

We have seen from *Paradiso* I how Dante relates love to God
through the moving order of the cosmos: all movement in creation is
the effect of God's love and the resulting order is his 'likeness' in the
universe. This passage can send us back to the *Convivio* for more
light on the process involved, so far as the human spirit is concerned.
All love, we are told towards the end of *Convivio* I, is an attraction
to some 'goodness' in an object, and it grows in proportion to the
object's 'nearness'. And to a sentient or intelligent being things
become 'near' by being known; hence *ceteris paribus* the more
knowledge the more love.[21] Now love, Virgil will tell us on Mount

Purgatory, has three successive moments: first, apprehension; then desire, *ch'è moto spiritale*; thirdly, possession and enjoyment – the soul, once moving with desire, being unable to rest 'until the loved thing bring it joy'.[22] But it is with this last stage that Dante, in *Convivio* III, ii, identifies love as such, defining love as the *union* to which desire tends – *unimento spiritale de l'anima e de la cosa amata*; and to this *unimento*, he adds, the soul 'runs of its nature, and swiftly or slowly according as it is free or hindered'. Why 'of its nature' ? Because, quite simply, this nature comes from God, who is the primal unity. As deriving from God each creature has a natural affinity to unity, to *unimento*. Moreover, in God unity and being are one, and with a oneness that is precisely a loving. The soul then has a natural affinity to, and love of, being; and since God gave it being, its very nature must draw it towards God to maintain and strengthen itself in being. Note that this 'drawing' is the soul's basic and primary desire: it is only in *consequence* that it cleaves to its fellow-creatures, inasmuch as through them the divine goodness is 'shown' and more or less clearly known. Thus man as appetitive has a different natural relation to God from man as cognitive. As appetitive we are attached to God directly and from the start; as cognitive we must approach him indirectly through the piecemeal medium of experience in time – that is, as Dante puts it, through the 'showings' of God which are the forms of goodness we apprehend in external nature or in our minds.[23]

All this is clearly a variant on that triadic or cyclic pattern which Western philosophy and theology derived no doubt originally from Plato, but which has surely some claim to be simply an essential articulation of religious experience in any age. The same cannot of course be said of the part played by astral influences, for Dante and his contemporaries, in that cyclic pattern or movement. There is no doubt Dante believed in such influences. An individual had certain propensities because he was born under this or that star or constellation. Dante himself was born under the Twins and thought he owed much to them; and he also acknowledges emphatically the influence of Venus, the star of love, *lo bel pianeta che d'amar conforta*.[24] It is

---

21. *Conv.* I, xii-xiii; cf. III, ii, 8.
22. *Purg.* XVIII, 22-33.
23. *Conv.* III, ii, 2-9; cf. iv, 9; *Par.* IV, 40-42.
24. *Purg.* I, 19; cf. *Par.* XXII, 112-20.

easy to smile at this view of things, but it has most interesting implications. For the present it will be enough to note three points in Dante's thought on this topic in general and on Venus in particular.[25]

1. First then Dante insists that in all this process of 'influencing' the physical heavens are only instruments; the principal agents are the great Intelligences that move them, 'whom the common folk call angels' — the good, not the fallen, angels; Dante's universe is entirely controlled by good powers. Moreover these powers are all in direct contact with God; it is from him they draw the 'virtue' which they in turn pour down through the heavens. So it is with all the astral influences; so, explicitly, with that from Venus, 'by which souls (anime) here below are kindled to lve according to their dispositions'. But Dante goes even further; he makes the Venus-influence derive precisely from the third Person of the Trinity, inasmuch as the angelic Order which moves the third heaven — that of Venus — has for its special object of contemplation 'the supreme and most fervent love of the Holy Spirit'. Since the term 'souls', anime, in the phrase I have quoted certainly refers to the principles of all physical life, not in man only but in beasts and plants as well, it follows that by way of the Venus heaven and its angel-movers Dante is relating sexuality, plant, animal and human, to the Holy Spirit. It is with this in mind that we should understand those otherwise strangely 'erotic' declarations, in Paradiso 9, of Cunizza and Folco. Both of these blessed souls, now appearing to Dante in Venus, had been overcome on earth by the light of the love-star, and both now rejoice in the fact; not indeed in the faults that this occasioned, but in the amative influence itself which they were able, through repentance, to turn to good effect:

> non de la colpa, ch'a mente non torna,
> ma del valor ch'ordinò e provide.[26]

Sexual attraction, like everything else, is providential and should find its issue in charity, as the poet's attraction to Beatrice did.

2. Another important implication, for Dante, of the doctrine of

25. Conv. II, iv, 2. The sketch that follows, of the role of the angels in transmitting influences through the stars and planets is based chiefly on: Conv. II, iv-v; Par. II, 127-44; VII, 130-41; VIII. 97-148; XIII, 52-78; XXVIII, 64-78.
26. Par. IX, 104-05: 'Yet here we don't repent; rather, we smile, not at our fault (which is forgotten) but for the Power which directed and foresaw': cf. ibid. 32-36.

astral influences has to do with his interpretation of pagan religion as known to him through the Latin classics: an extremely interesting but still rather neglected matter.[27] Briefly, Dante saw the polytheism of the *gentili* as due to a mistake about natural forces arising from ignorance about the angels – from the lack of divine teaching that obtained in the world, outside the Chosen People, before the Incarnation. The pagans, or most of them, were vaguely aware of influences and powers in the heavens, but in their ignorance of the angels – the controlling, but themselves created and controlled Intelligences – they turned these heavenly forces into gods:

> questo principio (the fact of star influence), male inteso, torse
> già tutto il mondo quasi, sí che Giove,
> Mercurio e Marte a nominar trascorse.[28]

It was both religious and moral error; with idolatry went immorality, for Dante as for St Paul, and we are not surprised that he pauses to stress this fact as he enters the heaven of Venus, of *eros* –

> Solea creder lo mondo in suo periclo
> che la bella Ciprigna il folle amore
> raggiasse . . .[29]

To think that a love-influence came from the third heaven was not false, but it was a mistake to derive *'folle* amore', insane irrational love, from the heavens; and a still worse one to divinize the source of sin, putting a goddess, the fair Cyprian, a mere human fantasy, in a place really occupied by angels of the true God. And as the two Venus cantos continue we can see Dante quite evidently correcting this error with allusions to the angelic hierarchies, and so, implicitly, to the Providence that governs the star-influences generally. It is in effect a Christian de-mythologizing: the veil of fable is removed, the goddess dethroned, and her planet revealed now in its true relation to the angels, and through them to their Creator.

3. And this critique of paganism was in effect a putting of the physical world not only in correct relation to superhuman powers,

27. See especially P. Renucci, *Dante, juge et disciple du monde gréco-romain*, Paris, 1954.
28. *Par.* IV, 61-63: 'This principle, wrongly understood, once misled almost all the world, so that it ran off course, calling on Jupiter and Mercury and Mars'; cf. *Conv.* II. iv, 6-7.
29. *Par.* VIII, 1-3: 'The world once believed, to its peril, that the fair Cyprian rayed down mad love' . . .

but also in its due relation to the human spirit, especially to free will.

The question of free will is so prominent in the *Comedy* chiefly, I think, for two reasons — the prevalence of a certain astral determinism, derived largely from Arabic sources, and the fact that in the *Comedy* Dante is reacting against a strain of fatalism in the courtly love tradition, a fatalism he had himself encouraged in some of his lyrics. Astral determinism as such he confronts directly in *Purgatorio* 16, affirming, through Marco Lombardo, that the human mind depends immediately on God, and so is not subject, in principle, to the 'heavens'. The other — but connected — psychological fatalism which saw the will as powerless against passion, had of course a more literary, less scholastic background. Dante himself had given it powerful expression in some of his lyrics, notably in the 'Montanina' canzone and in a famous sonnet to Cino da Pistoia, *Io sono stato con Amore insieme*; and perhaps the best and briefest way to bring out his mature critique of this fatalism is to contrast the denial of free will contained in that sonnet with the assertion of it in the central discourse of *Purgatorio* already in part analysed. For in effect the latter text recants the former.

The gist of the sonnet, stripped of its grand imagery, is that the poet knows by long experience that reason is powerless against love, that where love is at work free will is extinguished and all deliberation useless:

> però nel cerchio de la sua palestra
> liber arbitrio già mai non fu franco,
> sí che consiglio invan vi si balestra.[30]

'. . . within his (Love's) arena free will was never free, so that in vain is deliberation shot forth there'. So Dante answered his friend who has asked whether he (Cino), having been the lover of one woman, should yield to the love he had begun to feel for another. The answer is 'Yes — for you cannot help it'. It is worth noting that in a prose letter accompanying his sonnet Dante does not mention free will, but rests his answer on the natural changeability of the *potentia sensitiva* which is 'the seat of love', *sedes amoris*.[31] This love is of course sexual, located in the animal body which, as material, is subject to the physical heavens. Thus the phrase in the sonnet, *nel*

30. *Rime* CX1.
31. *Epist.* III.

cerchio de la sua palestra refers to this world as subject to Venus influences. Our free will is located in this world, and whether or not it
is by nature subject to Venus — a point ignored in the sonnet — it
cannot in fact resist her; the force of concupiscence, aroused by her
influence, is too much for it. Now it is just this doctrine that the
Comedy corrects — first in *Purgatorio* 16, as regards the basic *natural*
independence of free will in relation to the 'heavens', and secondly
in *Purgatorio* 18 as regards its ability to resist passion. And the wor-
ding of the latter correction very strongly suggests that Dante had
precisely that sonnet of his in mind. In any case, without this assertion of the power of free choice against the pull of sense appetite the
'sacred poem' would have lacked an essential doctrinal component.
Hence, no doubt, the explicit association in this passage of free will
and Beatrice:

> la nobile virtú Beatrice intende
> per lo libero arbitrio . . .[32]

The allusion here is to Beatrice in her quasi-symbolic function as
the voice of Christian wisdom, of *sacra doctrina*. But in the *Comedy*
as a whole she is not only Dante's teacher about moral freedom (and
other things); she actually confers freedom upon him —

> tu m'hai di servo tratto a libertate —[33]

and we have already begun to see what she freed him from — subjection to the stars and to errors about them, and from his own carnal
appetite. Error, sensuality and servitude, these three themes are intimately connected, and they come to a focus in a female symbol
which, of all the figures in the *Comedy*, is the most clearly and directly opposed to Beatrice; I mean the Siren, who makes her
appearance, significantly, in the canto immediately following the
discourses on free will which had ended on the name of the heavenly
victorious liberator.[34] The Siren is born of sleep and dream, the
second dream on the Mountain — *mi venne in sogno*; and born, at
first, hideous; and her rebirth into beauty is a purely psychic process
proceeding from the dreamer himself. As Dante gazes at her she is
transformed, and by his gazing: thus he gives her beauty and falls

32. *Purg.* XVIII, 73-74: 'this noble faculty is what Beatrice means by free will'
33. *Par.* XXXI, 85: 'You have brought me to freedom from slavery'.
34. *Purg.* XIX, 1-33.

under a spell of his own making. Even the sweetness of her song comes from him, the song in which she exults over her prey:

> 'io son', cantava, 'io son dolce serena
> che i marinari in mezzo mar dismago;
> tanto son di piacere a sentir piena.' [35]

The whole stress then of this wonderful episode is on the *subjectivity* of carnal sin, and so on the delusion involved in that 'twisted love', *amor torto*, which in the canto on charity, *Paradiso* 26, will be directly contrasted with *amor diritto*, 'straight love'. [36] The metaphor implies that in loving creatures to excess the soul deflects from the way to God marked out by and in its nature — by that original and basic drive towards God which the *prima voglia*, as we have seen, involves. But note particularly the element of error involved. All sin implies an initial mistake. At its most venial — at a scarcely culpable stage at all — this appears in a child's turning to 'little goods' as though they were final, as though in fact they were the uncreated Good it already unconsciously desires. [37] At a more conscious and culpable level the mistake will be that of Francesca da Rimini, deluded by her literary romanticism, by the strain of illusion in courtly love of which the canto in which she appears, *Inferno* 5, is so discreet and telling a critique —

> Amor, ch'al cor gentil ratto s'apprende...
> Amor, ch'a nullo amato amar perdona... [38]

And behind this critique lies the psychology of moral error already worked out in the *Convivio*. Man has both sense and reason, but his rational 'eye' — which should see further and deeper than the senses, seeing in things an intrinsic order of means to ends, and so an objective goodness and badness — this 'eye of reason' remains dim in most men most of the time; and this because subjective emotion confuses and distorts judgement; and the more so as emotion increases — that is to say, as the outward object causing the emotion draws near to the subject apprehending it: 'the more', says Dante, 'the agent unites

35. 'I', she sang, 'I'm that sweet siren who leads sailors astray in mid-sea, so delightful is my song'.
36. *Par.* XXVI, 55-63.
37. *Purg.* XVI, 85-93.
38. *Inf.* V, 100-5: Love, kindled so quickly in the noble heart ... Love, that spares no loved one from loving'...

with the patient, the more passion is felt ... hence the closer the desired thing comes to the desirer the more desire grows, and the soul ... ever more identifies itself with the sense appetite and ever more abandons reason'. The result in fact is a lapse from the human to the animal level: 'so that now the soul no longer judges in a human way ... but in a more or less animal way, merely by outward appearances and with no discernment of truth'.[39] *Non discernendo la veritade* – the phrase is pregnant indeed on Dante's lips, for truth is 'the good of the intellect',[40] and this ultimately is God. To lose sight of truth is to begin to miss the way to God. It is also, we have seen, a lapse from humanity. And the general cause of such lapsing is now sufficiently clear. It is that desire always tends to outrun knowledge – the soul as appetitive being irresistibly pulled towards a final 'good' which, as cognitive, it only vaguely apprehends, and the real identity of which, and means to which, it is ever in danger of misapprehending; and this precisely because of that initial imbalance in it of cognition and appetition. Since knowledge begins in the senses, in the animal part of man, the misjudgments due to that imbalance tend as such to be subhuman – involving, as we have seen, both illusion and loss of freedom. And what particularly loses freedom in the process is the faculty of free will itself. It is the situation summed up in Book I of the *Monarchia*: 'If judgment moves the appetite it is free; but just in so far as appetite, taking the initiative ... moves judgment, the latter cannot be free, for then it does not act of itself but is drawn to act as captive of another'.[41]

For this 'other' – the force that, outrunning reason, drags it awry or down – the usual Dantean name is cupidity (*cupidigia, cupiditas*), and the principal symbols in the *Comedy* are the Siren and the She-Wolf; the one set over against Beatrice in particular, the other over against Justice. With respect indeed to the temporal political order, cupidity is directly destructive of justice between man and man;[42] but in respect of the eternal order and man's relation to God, what it corrupts is the natural desire for God impressed on each human soul from the first moment of its existence. And this of

39. *Conv.* III, x, 2; cf. I, iv, 3; xi, 3.
40. *Conv.* II, xiii, 6 (cf. III, iii, 11; IV, xv, 11); *Inf.* III, 18.
41. *Mon.* I, xii, 3-4.
42. See especially *Mon.* I, xi, 6, 11.

course implies – given Dante's Christian faith and his *implicitly* Thomist conviction that charity is the perfection and fulfilment of natural desire[43] – it implies that cupidity is contrary to charity and in fact leads to Hell. But Dante is – not perhaps surprisingly – most effective when he is analysing or 'imaging' the observable effects of cupidity in the soul. He sees it above all as an endless pursuit of things that do not satisfy; and they do not, he passionately held, because they cannot; because of the 'natural thirst' in man which only eternal life can slake.[44] This 'insight' is at the root of all Dante's thinking about man: so much must be said whatever we may think of its philosophical validity. It follows that cupidity is, in effect, a desiring merely to desire. And this indeed is how Dante seems to interpret the fall of Adam: in willing a freedom unchecked by reason and nature and the will of God, Adam in effect willed simply to will – or desire – endlessly and in vain; [45] and left such barren desire as his legacy to us all, an actual and effective psychic imbalance displayed in a perpetual outrunning of reason by appetition.

When, in *Paradiso* VII, Dante treats explicitly of the Redemption he draws on more usual metaphors to describe the condition that Christ came to cure: 'the human race lay sick'; [46] but in the next line, I suggest, we hear the more directly Dantean note: *giù per molti secoli in grande errore*, where the last word surely retains from the Latin original some of the sense of 'wandering, going astray'. But if man, the 'divine animal',[47] was going astray, it was as impelled by this inborn everlasting desire of the divinity in whose image he was made – driven without rest by the terrible force of 'that bowstring', *quella corda*, which is the Power that created his soul *in* joy, *mossa da lieto Fattore*, and therefore only *for* joy.[48] Created in the fullest sense, an immediate effect, *sanza mezzo*, of the eternal Love, man is a direct image of that Love and so must eternally desire its Object. 'Your life', as Beatrice says,

---

43. Cf. *Summa Theol.* 1a, 60, 5. Since writing this essay, however, I have come to take a rather different view of the point at issue here; see below, chapters 10 to 12.
44. *Purg.* XXI, 1-3.
45. *Par.* VII, 25-27.
46. *Par.* VII, 28.
47. *Conv.* III, ii, 14.
48. Texts directly referred to: *Par.* I, 118-26; *Purg.* XVI, 88-90; cf. XXV, 70-75; *Par.* IV, 124-32; XXVIII, 108.

> ... vostra vita sanza mezzo spira
> la somma beninanza, e la innamora
> di sé sì che poi sempre la disira.[49]

'Your life the supreme Goodness breathes out directly, and makes it in love with himself, so that henceforth it always desires him.' The challenge of Dante's poetry is precisely and entirely in this statement.

49. *Par.* VII, 142-4.

4

ST. THOMAS AND DANTE

The legend of Dante's 'Thomism' arose from the fact that a main component of his culture is obviously 'scholastic', and that until not so very long ago the authentic thought of St Thomas had not been clearly differentiated from its general scholastic background. A poet writing within a few decades of St Thomas's death, and showing a great respect for him, and delighting to reason, even in verse, about form and matter, act and potency and so on, seemed plainly a 'Thomist'; and when this designation began to be questioned there were not wanting those who went on insisting on it for the greater glory of the Dominican Order or of Catholic culture,[1] which was thought to have reached its apex in the work of Aquinas. But now all that has changed. Since the pioneering labours of Bruno Nardi[2] and Gilson's brilliant book[3] it has become increasingly evident that Dante cannot be called a Thomist in any strict sense of the term as denoting a body of doctrine characteristic of St Thomas.

However there is, I think, a qualified sense in which one may speak of the poet's Thomism, and which it is one purpose of these notes to indicate. But first a little more should be said about the question in general; and here I may be allowed to bring myself briefly into the picture. When, some years ago, I undertook to write the article 'Tommaso d'Aquino' for the *Enciclopedia Dantesca*,[4] I

1. I have in mind particularly the work of two Dominicans and one Jesuit: M. Cordovani, O.P., in *Xenia Thomistica*, III, Rome, 1925, pp. 309-26; P. Mandonnet, O.P., *Dante le théologian*, Paris, 1935; and G. Busnelli, S.J.'s learned but very tendentious commentary on the *Convivio* in the 'Edizione Nazionale' of D's works, Florence, 1934-37.
2. For a full bibliography of Nardi's writings down to 1954 see *Medioevo e Rinascimento: Studi in onore di B. Nardi*, 2 vols., Florence, 1954, pp. 907-27. Nardi's chief studies in this field since 1955 are collected in *Dal 'Convivio' alla 'Commedia'*, Rome, 1960, and *Saggi e note di critica dantsca*, Milan-Naples, 1966.
3. *Dante et la philosophie*, Paris, 1939 (Eng. tr. *Dante the Philosopher*, London, 1948).
4. Published at Rome by the 'Istituto della Enciclopedia Italiana'. It will consist of six volumes, five of which had appeared by the end of 1976.

naturally set about reading or re-reading all the relevant texts, beginning with Dante. My task, as I saw it, was twofold. First, on the
abstract doctrinal plane – comparing ideas with ideas – I had to try
to decide how far Bruno Nardi had been right in his lifelong effort
to detach Dante from Aquinas by expounding the poet's philosophy
as a variant on the Neoplatonist tradition, with traces (especially in
the *Monarchia*) of Averroism. Nardi was a very great scholar, but I
had learned long ago to keep a wary eye on his polemical temper; he
was too irascible a man to be always a fair debater; especially
perhaps when his opponent happened to be a priest. However, the
result of my resumed researches was to confirm, for me, Nardi's
general negative contention – that Dante's universe was not the
Thomist one. The differences were too distinct and deep to allow
any other conclusion: differences in cosmogony – regarding, especially, the creation of matter, and the role of the angels in the formation of the sublunary world and their relation to the heavenly
bodies;[5] and differences in anthropology touching the soul-body
relationship, and the process of human generation, and the 'end' of
human life considered as mortal and terrestrial.[6] Moreover it
became clearer to me than ever before (though I would like to be
clearer still on this) that the *unity* of this Dantean world is poetic
rather than philosophical. Analysed philosophically it turns out, I
think, to be a rather uneasy synthesis of Neoplatonist and
Aristotelian elements. But as the 'matter', precisely, of poetry it is
unified by a double 'drive' of tremendous power, expressing two
aspects of one extraordinary human soul: an intellectual drive
towards understanding that culminates in the *Paradiso*; a moral-
political drive towards the establishment of justice on earth,
predominant in the *Inferno* and the *Purgatorio*.

The other part of my task was, of course, to relate Dante to
Aquinas in and through the historical context of the poet's life from
1265 to 1321. His philosophical education began, he tells us, not
long after the death of Beatrice in 1290, when he began to frequent

5. *Par.* XXIX, 22-4, 34-6. On angelic influences on the sublunary world see (to begin
with) *Par.* II, 112-38, VII, 121-41: on angels and the heavenly bodies. *Par.* XXIX,
37-45.
6. On this crucial matter see E. Gilson, *Dante et la philosophie*, op. cit., pp. 100-199, and
my own essay 'Religion and Philosophy in D.' in *The Mind of Dante*, ed. U. Limentani,
Cambridge, 1965, pp. 47-78,

'le scuole de li religiosi' in Florence; [7] by which he presumably means that he attended courses given by the Dominicans at S. Maria Novella and doubtless also by the Franciscans at Santa Croce on the other side of the city. This relatively late start in philosophy (he was over twenty-five and married) [8] had an immediate effect on his lyric poetry but its chief fruits were the great works written after his exile from Florence (1302), the *Convivio* in Italian prose, the *Monarchia* in Latin, and of course the *Divine Comedy*. As for theology proper, the first evidence of Dante's giving it really serious attention is Books II-III of the *Monarchia*, which can hardly have been composed before 1310. Dante knew the Vulgate Bible extremely well but, this apart, I would say that the firmest elements in his mature culture were literary and philosophico-scientific, not theological. It may even be misleading to speak of the *Comedy* as a theological poem, though of course it contains much theology and certainly reflects in various ways the influence of St Thomas. But this influence does not seem to me primarily *doctrinal*. I would prefer to describe it as primarily a 'cultural' and moral influence — giving each of these terms a sense to be defined presently.

Guelf Florence in the 1290s was a thriving commercial centre and closely linked politically with France and the papacy; but it had no university and the echoes that reached it of contemporary philosophical and theological debate at Paris and Oxford must have come largely through the two great international Orders of the Friars; and their interest in that debate had by now become, to a marked degree, a matter of *esprit de corps*. For a major controversial issue was the teaching of the Dominican master who had died in March 1274. The half-century, covering most of Dante's life, between that date and the canonisation of Thomas in July 1323, was perhaps the most troubled period in the history of Thomism; and from the early 1280s the Franciscans were increasingly identified, as a body and even officially, with the anti-Thomist cause. And as action leads to reaction, and the ideas of a genius may quick-

---

7. *Conv.* II, xii, 7. On Italian Thomism in Dante's time the best general study is still perhaps M. Grabmann's *Mittelalterliches Geistesleben*, I, Munich, 1926, pp. 332-391. See P. O. Kristeller, *Le thomisme et la pensée italienne de la Renaissance* ('Conférence Albert-le-Grand' 1965), Montréal-Paris, 1967, pp. 41-125; and with particular reference to Dante, C. T. Davis, 'Education in Dante's Florence', *Speculum*, 40 (1965), pp. 415-435.

8. Dante's statement in *Conv.* II, xii, 7 can however be taken with a pinch of salt; he shows signs of having some philosophical culture in poems written before 1290.

ly become a party-line, so by the turn of the century the doctrine of
brother Thomas (still of course uncanonised) was being imposed by
authority on all Dominican teachers and students.[9] What Dante
thought, or later came to think, of this deplorable rivalry between
the two Orders appears obliquely but magnificently in *Paradiso*
X-XII, in the lovely dance of the Sages in the Solar Heaven, where
Thomas sings in praise of St Francis and Bonaventure of St
Dominic;[10] but neither here nor elsewhere does Dante express any
judgement on Thomism as such. And by this I mean that he never
either (1) says that he is for or against Thomism in general, or (2)
identifies any particular philosophical or theological position as
'Thomist' and then states his opinion of it. This is to say that Dante
took no part in the current debates about Thomism as a system. He
always used his sources freely, selecting what suited his immediate
purpose, as a tool to help him clarify his own very personal vision of
life. The only master he persistently tries to have on his side is
Aristotle.

I grant that on some fundamental matters Dante speaks *prima
facie* like a Thomist: angels, for him, are wholly non-material; [11]
man has only one substantial form, the rational soul; [12] intellect is
pre-eminent over the will.[13] As to these points (and others might be
adduced) Dante probably was influenced, directly or indirectly, by
St Thomas; but from the way he enunciates them it is impossible to
be sure (at least as regards the first two) that he did not think he was
also following, say, St Albert the Great — some of whose writings
he knew very well, as Nardi pointed out long ago.[14] In any case it is
hardly likely that Dante distinguished between Albertinism and
Thomism with the subtlety of a modern medievalist; as Gilson says,
'suivre Albert le Grand sur un point n'était sans doute pas pour lui se
séparer de saint Thomas'.[15] Dante venerated both men and when he

9. I refer to legislation of the General Chapters of the Order in 1278, 1279, 1286 and
1313; see *Monumenta Ord. Fr. Praed.*, ed. Reichert, I, pp. 199, 204, 235; II, p. 64. A
brief but well-documented account of the late 13th century controversies over Thomism is
in F. J. Roensch, *Early Thomistic School*, Dubuque, Iowa, 1964, espec. pp. 1-27, 170-199.
See also the excellent survey by C. Fabro in *Enciclopedia Cattolica*, XII (1954), col.
281-285.
10. See below, pp. 120-36, 'The Celebration of Order: *Paradiso* X.
11. *Parad.* XXIX, 21-36; *Conv.* III, vii, 5.
12. *Conv.* III, iii, 5; *Purg.* IV, 1-12; XXV, 61-75.
13. *Mon.* I, v, 4; *Par.* XXVIII, 106-111.
14. *Saggi di filosofia dantesca*, Città di Castello, 1930, pp. 67-78.
15. *Dante et la philosophie*, op. cit., p. 158, n. 1.

meets them in paradise he is at pains to emphasise their closeness one to the other; he has Thomas introduce Albert as 'my brother and my master'; and he has Albert, Thomas and Siger of Brabant standing side by side as (so at least it seems to me) the three greatest Aristotelians of their century.[16] But we need not see in this an expression of Thomism in a precise sense of this term. Far more probably it expresses Dante's sense of the debt that Christian thought in general owed to Aristotle. If he had to leave the Philosopher down in Limbo — for reasons, by the way, not exclusively theological — he could beatify his influence; he could show sheer rationality enjoying glory. Hence he has Thomas compliment Siger on his expertise with the syllogism,[17] and Thomas himself gives a little lecture on the value of distinctions.[18] There was an extremely tough vein of rationalism in Dante and this gave him a special sympathy with the Christian Aristotelianism of Albert and Thomas.

But the rare reader who comes to Dante with 'ears accustomed to Thomist language', as Gilson puts it, will meet with surprises; with a *materia prima* apparently created in the beginning devoid of form;[19] with angels far more involved than those in the Thomist system with the heavenly bodies;[20] what is more important, with that drastic division of human life under 'two final ends' (*duo ultima*), corresponding respectively to man's nature as mortal and as immortal, which is set out at the end of the *Monarchia*[21] and reappears implicitly, I would say, in those Noble Pagans in the poet's Limbo whom St Antoninus, O.P., was later to find so unacceptable.[22] And then there is the negative aspect of the question. What is precisely most distinctive and original in Thomist metaphysic and anthropology seems to me but faintly, if at all, reflected in Dante's system: the distinction between essence and ex-

16. Cf. E. Gilson, op. cit., p. 263.
17. *Par.* X, 136-138.
18. *Par.* XIII, 109-142.
19. *Par.* XXIX, 22-24.
20. *Par.* XXIX, 37-45 — where Dante seems to say that *all* the angelic Orders are *essentially* movers of this or that heavenly 'sphere'. This goes far beyond St Thomas's position in *Contra Gentiles* II, 92. It is interesting to note that the Dominican Robert Kilwardby, St Thomas's contemporary and critic, was still further from Dante on this point; he saw no reason to think that any of the angels were star-movers; see M. D. Chenu in *Mélanges Mandonnet*, 'Bibliothèque Thomiste XIII, Paris, 1930, I, pp. 191-222.
21. *Mon.* III, xv, 5-6.
22. See A. Renaudet, *Dante humaniste*, Paris, 1952, p. 124.

istence in creatures and their identity in God; the notion of *intellectus agens* as the distinctive function of human intelligence. Dante never so much as mentions the agent intellect and though he uses, once, the distinction between *esse* and *essentia*, this use is quite marginal and incidental.[23]

Doctrinally then there is not much to be said for calling Dante a Thomist. Nevertheless Gilson was plainly right to say that Dante '[a] profondement admiré et aimé saint Thomas'.[24] So the question is, how we should define, and explain, that admiration and love. After all, Dante also admired and loved Aristotle, Virgil, Boethius, Cicero, St Bernard: what distinguishes the motive and manner of his regard for St Thomas? A fine subject for a book which no one has written! But if I were to try to write it I would begin by distinguishing, in the poet's devotion (the expression is not too strong) to 'il buono frate Tommaso',[25] two basic motives: (a) gratitude to the Aristotelian scholar, the author of the commentaries, and (b) esteem for the thinker as a model of intellectual probity and finesse. And I would show that the former attitude appears chiefly in the *Convivio* and the latter above all in cantos X-XIII of the *Paradiso*. Let me briefly illustrate what I mean.

(a) For a layman and a non-academic Dante had a very extensive knowledge of Aristotle's writings (the *Poetics* being a notable exception). The *Convivio* alone contains some 80 references to Aristotle, nearly all of them naming some particular work.[26] Now an examination of these references gives solid grounds for holding that Dante frequently studied Aristotle with and through the commentaries – or, better, 'expositions' – of Aquinas. True, there are, in the *Convivio*, only two explicit mentions of St Thomas in this connexion, at II, xiv, 14 and IV, viii, 1; but in a good many other cases an implicit recourse to the Thomist 'exposition' is, I think, more or less clearly discernible; and in six cases which I have examined [27] a careful comparison of the *loci* in Aristotle to which Dante seems to refer (in a Latin version of course) with the corresponding 'exposi-

23. *Epist.* XIII, 53-61.
24. *Dante et la philosophie*, op cit., p. 118.
25. *Conv.* IV, xxx, 3.
26. Among these references are 34 to the *Nicomachean Ethics*, 10 to the *De Anima*, 8 to the *Metaphysics*, 7 to the *Physics*, 6 to the *De Coelo et Mundo*, 2 to the *Politics*.
27. II, iii, 2; xiii, 6; xiii, 18; IV, viii, 6; xi, 9; xiii, 8. There is a similar case in *Quaestio de aqua et terra*, 75.

tion' of Thomas (or in one case, at IV, xiii, 8, with *Contra Gentiles* I, 5) show that the poet's quotation or paraphrase is much closer to the latter than to the former. The commentary he made most use of — and it is the only one he explicitly cites — was that on the *Nicomachean Ethics*; but he certainly also knew those on the *Physics* and *De coelo et mundo*, and probably those on the *Metaphysics* and *De anima*.[28] Dante's literary culture depended, of course, on other sources, and there were aspects of his scientific, philosophical and even theological culture that owed as much or more to other masters.[29] But his formation as an Aristotelian came principally through St Thomas — with Averroes perhaps a good second (see *Conv.* IV, xiii, 8; *Monarchia* I, iii, 9; *Quaestio de aqua et terra*, 12).[30]

(b) What is particularly interesting, however, about Dante's admiration for St Thomas is that it goes to the *moral* component in the saint's thinking; it carries the strong suggestion that this man's extraordinary intelligence was only the other side of extraordinary goodness. The term Dante picks on to denote this double quality is 'discrezione'; which in the immediate context, at *Convivio* IV, viii, 1, means the rational power of seeing the relations between things, and so of discriminating and drawing distinctions,[31] but in its wider context in the book this passage connects with a number of others which all turn on a contrast, both intellectual and moral, between 'discretion' and its consequence 'reverence' on the one hand, and 'presumption' with its consequences 'irreverence' and 'insolence' (*tracotanza*) on the other.[32] And both the denunciations and the recommendations are supported by appeals, explicit or implicit, to St Thomas. And this repeated recourse to Thomas in connexion with the same general theme is the more impressive in that elsewhere in the *Convivio* he is only mentioned twice[33] (though again, in one of

28. See note 26 above.
29. To St Albert, Avicenna, Alfraganus, Ptolemy, for example, for natural science; to the *Liber de Causis* (the Thomist commentary on which Dante shows no sign of having read) for neoplatonist tendencies; to the Pseudo-Denys and Bonaventure for aspects of angelology and trinitarian theology.
30. Dante had a great respect for Averroes (cf. *Inf.* IV, 144) but rejected his monopsychism, *Purg.* XXV, 61-66.
31. Dante has raised the question whether, in refuting the Emperor Frederick II's opinion on 'nobility', he had been guilty of 'irreverence'. So he defines 'reverence'. It is a 'fruit' of 'discrezione', which in turn is identified with the kind of knowing that St Thomas had called 'proper to the reason', i.e. 'ordinem ... unius rei ad aliam cognoscere'. *In X libros Ethicorum Expositio*, I, lect. 1. This is the passage referred to in *Conv.* IV, viii, 1.
32. Compare *Conv.* IV, v, 9; viii, 1-5; xiii, 8; xv, 12-13.
33. II, xiv, 14; IV, xxx, 3.

these cases,[34] as pronouncing on the *moral* aspect of the intellectual life). It seems clear then that in Dante's mind, as he wrote the *Convivio*, the figure of St Thomas was associated in a special way with *discrimination*, conceived as a quality both intellectual and moral though rooted specifically in the human reason whose task it is to 'discern the relations between things'.[35] For Dante Aquinas both represents and justifies the properly *human* use of intelligence which is 'intelligere componendo et dividendo ... quod est ratiocinari' (*Summa theol.* 1a, 85, 5).

The same twofold theme reappears, subtly and splendidly developed in *Paradiso* X-XIII. Indirectly these cantos sum up all that Dante personally owed to Aquinas; directly they present him as the image and synthesis of a special kind of saintly intelligence – the saintliness of the good friar in the Dominican way of being a friar –

> Io fui de li agni de la santa greggia
> che Domenico mena per cammino
> u' ben s'impingua se non si vaneggia (X, 94-6) [36] –

and the intelligence of the good theologian according to the way of doing theology that gives full place and honour to reason. The motif of sanctity appears especially in Thomas's tribute to St Francis (reciprocated in Bonaventure's to St Dominic in canto XII) and in his critique of unworthy Dominicans, in XI, 40-139; while the motif of intelligence appears in Thomas's being the spokesman of the first circle of Christian scholars and sages (X, 91-138), but more particularly in the recurrent stress – evidently intended as characteristic – in his three discourses[37] on the need for and the beauty of rational discrimination, measure and sobriety of judgement, the stress which reaches its climax in the last words Thomas speaks in the *Commedia*, the great closing passage of canto XIII. Thomas speaks all through as 'a logician and a great clerk',[38] because that is how Dante saw him and saw the value of his example. Hence the admonition that opens the second discourse: 'e qui è

---

34. II, xiv, 14.
35. See note 31 above.
36. 'I was a lamb of the holy flock that Dominic leads along a path where you fatten well if you don't waste time'.
37. In *Paradiso*, X, XI, XIII.
38. *Conv.* IV, x, 6. In their context the words refer, a bit ironically, to the Emperor Frederick II.

uopo che ben si distingua' (XI, 27).[39] Hence the praise of Siger of Brabant (X, 133-8), for whatever else Dante may have intended in making Aquinas honour his former adversary, he certainly meant to show theology giving due honour to philosophy and particularly to the properly human activity of logical reasoning ('sillogizzò invidiosi veri', X, 138;[40] cf. *Summa theol.* la. 58, 3). Hence the significant word 'discreto' in Bonaventure's concluding compliment to Thomas: '... l'infiammata cortesia/di fra Tommaso e 'l *discreto* latino' (XII, 143-4).[41] Hence above all the three great distinctions which guide and govern the discourses in cantos X and XIII: that of orders and functions in the Church and in the *studium* (X, 94-138; XI, 28-42); that of the creative Word and secondary causes (XIII, 52-78); that of the two orders of intellectual excellence, the speculative and the practical, the latter being represented supremely by Solomon who has practical knowledge of the highest kind, the wisdom of the good ruler, 'regal prudenza' (XIII, 91-108). Hence, in conclusion, the vehement recommendation already noted of 'distinguishing' – of the need to be grounded in the 'art' of thought and the weighing of evidence before one can safely pronounce on deep matters (XIII, 109-42). Incidentally, it is by no means unlikely that, in making his Thomas exalt his Solomon in the way he does, Dante is reading a lesson in political science to the theologians of his time – is cunningly using the theologian he most admired to uphold his *own* rather extreme view of the independence of the civil power with respect to the ecclesiastical; the view which led the *Monarchia* to be condemned by the Church in 1329,[42] eight years after Dante's death, and placed on the Index in 1554, where it remained until 1881.

It is worth remembering that Dante wrote the *Paradiso* before the canonisation of St Thomas which took place, of course, in July 1323, nearly two years after the great poet's death. It is also worth noting that within fifteen years of Dante's death his love for Aquinas, and all his published praise of him, did not save him from

39. 'and here we must carefully distinguish'
40. 'he reasoned out truths that brought him ill favour'
41. 'the flaming courtesy of brother Thomas and his well considered speech'
42. This is well attested. Boccaccio adds, and we have no reason to disbelieve him, that the *Monarchia* was publicly burned at Bologna by order of the Cardinal Legate (*Trattatello in laude di Dante*, c. 24). See *D.A., Monarchia*, 'Edizione Nazionale', ed. P. G. Ricci, Milan, 1965, pp. 3-4.

bitter Dominican hostility. Between 1327 and 1334 Guido Vernani, O.P., of Rimini wrote his violent attack on the *Monarchia*; [43] and in 1335 the Provincial Chapter of the Roman Province, meeting at Florence (of all places) strictly forbade all the brethren, young or old, to study the *Commedia*.[44]

43. *De reprobatione Monarchiae*, ed. N. Matteini, Padua, 1958. On Guido Vernani see also T. Kaeppeli, O.P., in *Quellen und Forschungen aus italienischen Archiven und Bibliotheken*, XXVIII. 1937-38, pp. 107-146.
44. *Monumenta Ord. Fr. Praed. Hist.*, XX, *Acta Cap. Prov. Provinciae Romanae* (1243-1344), ed. T. Kaeppeli and A. Dondaine, 1941, p. 286.

5

DANTE'S VISION OF GOD

T he nineteenth-century cult of Dante — of which we are the heirs — was already active and productive long before the modern historical study of his scholastic background really got under way. Nor has this study fully caught up yet with contemporary work on the poet. Despite the spade-work of Bruno Nardi, Busnelli and others, and the brilliant essay of Gilson,[1] there is still no commentary on the *Divine Comedy* that would satisfy a specialist in medieval philosophy or theology. Such specialists are doubtless inclined to overrate their own importance; yet, certainly, Dante's poetry and the scholastic formation of his mind are so closely interrelated that either aspect of his personality may lead one into the other, and indeed must do so for any but the superficial reader; and this even apart from those general questions about the relation of poetry to abstract thought to which the study of the *Comedy* tends to give rise.

With such wider issues I am here not directly concerned, though I cannot touch my subject at all without implying them. Let me begin by remarking that, Dante's abstract thought being what is roughly called scholastic, his poetry may illuminate as nothing else could do one aspect of the thing connoted by that adjective, I mean the dynamic quality in medieval thought which found its formula in St. Anselm's phrase (itself an echo of St. Augustine) *fides quaerens intellectum*.[2] For if this formula, properly understood, is simply

1. Nardi was certainly the outstanding worker in his field: for a full bibliography, see his *Saggi sulla cultura veneta*, etc., ed. P. Mazzantini, Padua, 1971. G. Busnelli, S.J. is best known for his monumental though tendentious edition of the *Convivio*, Florence, 2 vols., 1934 and 1937. The essay of Gilson, referred to, is *Dante et la Philosophie*, Paris, 1939. Reference is also due to R. Palgen, for his *Ursprung und Aufbau der Komödie Dantes*, Graz (Styria), 1953; and to J. A. Mazzeo, *Structure and Thought in the 'Paradiso,'* Cornell Univ. Press, 1958.

2. *Proslogion*, PL 158, col. 225: cf. St. Augustine, *De Trinitate*, XV, 2,2; PL 42, col. 1058; and many similar texts cited by E. Gilson, *Introd. à l'étude de S. Augustin*, Paris, 1943, ch. 1.

Christian and not narrowly medieval, it has never perhaps been more thoroughly applied than by the great intellectuals of the thirteenth century or more rendered *imaginable* than in the poetry of Dante. And conversely, a little familiarity with scholastic thought may greatly assist us to understand what Dante was being, so to say, dynamic about in his poem – which, let us remember, represents a voyage, a movement, and two thirds of it an upward movement, and one third of it a spiral soaring into an intellectual zenith which drew the more powerfully the more closely it was approached:

> Perchè appressando sè al suo disire,
>   nostro intelletto si profonda tanto,
>   che retro la memoria non può ire.[3]

Here, in the very opening of the *Paradiso*, a note is struck which we shall hear right on to the end. It is a movement that we are following, 'appressando sè'; and of desire, indicated in its term, 'disire'; and a desire that is suddenly deepened, as we read, by the significant word 'intelletto.' It is desire for knowledge; and as we read on the perspective becomes apparently endless,

> . . . si profonda tanto,
>   che retro la memoria non può ire . . .

which is a hint already that this intellectual movement is no ordinary acquisition of knowledge; it will go so deep that memory cannot follow it. Where then will it go? And what sort of object is it pursuing, if we must allow that this is at the same time something to be known ('intelletto') and yet never remembered ('la memoria . . .'), that is to say, always forgotten? Is this not a contradiction? For, surely, forgetting pre-supposes a moment at least of remembering; it is a failure of a recollection, that must exist before it can begin to fail. Yet here the recollection, we are told, never actually exists: '. . . non può ire.' What sort of memory then is this? Not, certainly, that retention of the past which the term usually denotes; for here the past, as such, is irrelevant. The movement of the *Paradiso*, as Dante means us to understand it, is clearly not mere reminiscence, the recalling of events in past time; though, equally clearly, that is how he represents it in the fictional narrative of his voyage. For he writes

3. *Paradiso*, I, 7-9: 'for, as it approaches the end of its desire, our mind goes so deep that memory cannot follow'.

in the past tense. He has visited heaven and is now attempting to say what he saw there. The poem is *given* as reminiscence. But the event it recalls was intellectual, and precisely under this aspect it cannot now be fully recalled. It is forgotten, or half-forgotten, not as past, but as intellectual; not, obviously, because it happened a long while ago, but because it was a particular sort of experience – whether in time or out of time does not matter for the moment. What matters is that the experience was too great for the mind's power of retention, and so of apprehension after the event, and so of 'memory.' The use here of this term invites us to take the horizontal (so to say) movement back along the time-sequence as symbolic of a vertical (so to say) movement of intellect into eternity. And perhaps for some of my readers (for such as those 'few' whom the poet expected as readers of his *Paradiso*:-

> Voi altri pochi che drizzaste il collo
> per tempo al pan degli angeli . . . .[4])

it was not necessary to labour this point. They will have already recognized the Augustinian and metaphysical resonance of that 'memoria.'[5]

The *Paradiso*, then, begins with a statement of desire, and it ends with one of fulfilment. Between these are all the movements, pauses and recommencements which make up the narrative of the voyage; spaced out and made imaginable by the structure of the physical heavens, themselves all contained within, and in some sense adumbrating, the ultimate, purely spiritual Empyrean heaven, the

> ciel che più de la sua luce prende.

Now at this last heaven Dante only arrives in canto XXX; and at the direct vision of God only in canto XXXIII; and this vision itself is presented in stages, as a gradual though intensely active process occupying nearly a hundred lines; themselves preceded by the fifty-line preface of St. Bernard's prayer. This marked gradualness of Dante's approach to the final vision is highly characteristic, but in any case it was virtually a technical necessity.

---

4. *Par*. II, 10-11: 'You other few who've already looked up to the Angels' food' . . .
5. Cf. *De Trinitate* XI, 3, 6, XIV, *passim; Confess*. X, 1-26. For St. Thomas's synthesis of Augustinian and Aristotelian thought on this matter see *QQ de Veritate* X, 2, 3; *Summa Theol*. 1*a*, lxxix, 6, 7.

The *Paradiso* had to have thirty-three cantos, and even a Dante could hardly have filled so much space with a single vision, particularly with one that by definition was ineffable. But there was also another factor making for gradualness. It is not, I hope, impertinent to point out that the Dante self-described in the *Paradiso* was not yet dead; his experience is shown as an interlude in his mortal life – which the poet, writing *post eventum* has now resumed. In the *Inferno* and the *Purgatorio* it was repeatedly stressed that the protagonist, Dante, was a live man walking among the dead; or, more precisely, a still embodied soul briefly and miraculously visiting the world of souls that are temporarily disembodied by death.[6] And in this respect the voyager's condition is the same in the *Paradiso*, though, since the fact is here less stressed, we may forget it or not consider its consequences. Now one of these is that Dante could take liberties with his subject-matter which otherwise he could not have taken or only taken with a risk of doctrinal unorthodoxy which we have no reason to suppose he was prepared to take. For had his fiction taken the form of a flight to heaven *after death*, Dante could hardly have ignored the very strong theological tradition that between Purgatory and the beatific Vision there were no intermediate stages. It is true that this point was not officially defined as Catholic dogma until fifteen years after the poet's death; but it was already undoubtedly the normal view; and we may be helped to understand Dante's distinctively poetical handling of the paradisal material if we recall that definition of 1336. It is contained in Benedict XII's Constitution *Benedictus Deus*, and the relevant words are as follows: 'By our Apostolic authority we define that the souls of all the saints, deceased after the Passion of our Lord Jesus Christ, ... in whom, when they died or shall come to die, nothing remained or shall remain to be purified, and likewise of all those who have needed or shall need such a purification after death ... that all these souls, immediately after death or after the said purification, in the case of those who need it, and even before the resumption of their bodies ... have been, are and shall be in heaven, in the heaven of heavens and the celestial paradise ... and that they have seen and shall continue to see the divine essence in an intuitive and face to face vision, no creature intervening in the manner of an

6. E.g. *Inf.* VIII, 27, 84-85; X, 58-60; XV, 46-47; XVI, 32-33; XXIII, 88-96; XXIX, 94-96; XXXII, 91. *Purg.* II, 91-92; III, 94-99; V, 4-9; VIII, 58-60; etc.

object (*nulla mediante creatura in ratione objecti visi se habente*); but rather that the divine essence itself immediately, nakedly, clearly and openly manifests itself to them; and that they thereby enjoy the said divine essence (*eadem divina essentia perfruuntur*) and ... are by it truly beatified (*sunt vere beatae*) and possess life and repose eternal."[7]

This official declaration is the term of an interesting theological development which must be glanced at later: here it may serve to support my assertion that Dante's method in the *Paradiso*, his way of presenting the vision, would not have been doctrinally orthodox if it had not pre-supposed that his heavenly vision was experienced before death. Consequently — from the orthodox standpoint — such a vision before death had to be conceivable. By representing himself, in the *Paradiso*, as still alive the poet could avoid the immediate transition from Purgatory to the beatific Vision; he was now free to expand his poem through those thirty-two preliminary cantos. But what about the thirty-third canto? Did that make sense to theology? Was the experience it describes — a direct vision of God granted to a man before death — was this conceivable in Christian terms? To answer this question we may turn to the notion of 'rapture' or ecstasy, *raptus*, as this is analysed by St. Thomas in the *Summa theologiae*.[8]

For St. Thomas, who here as elsewhere merely resumes and elucidates the Christian tradition, the term *raptus* denotes the highest form of prophetic knowledge. Prophecy, he says, extends 'not only to future events in the human world, but also to divine things'; and to the latter, not only as they are presented to all Christians in the articles of the creed, but also as they may be presented to privileged souls in a kind of vision, itself a special effect of that gift of the Holy Spirit which is Wisdom. And this effect of the Spirit is *raptus*, which itself has degrees, the highest conceivable being a purely inellectual (i.e. supra-sensible), but necessarily only transitory, sight or glimpse of the divine essence. This highest form of *raptus*, though always possible in theological theory (as St. Thomas goes on to show) was naturally regarded as extremely unusual; indeed only two men,

7. Denzinger Schönmetzer, *Enchiridion Symbolorum*, 34th ed., 1967, no. 1000. For the proximate background to *Benedictus Deus* see D. Douie, 'John XXII and the Beatific Vision,' *Dominican Studies*, III, 2, 154-74.
8. 2a 2ae, clxxv, 1-6.

Moses and St. Paul, the first great teachers of the Jews and Gentiles respectively, were generally supposed to have been granted it. And St. Paul in particular, in view of the experience mentioned in 2 *Corinthians* xii. 1-4, became the traditional example of *raptus* in its highest degree. Now this has an important bearing on the *Divine Comedy*. We all remember the voyager's timid protest to Virgil at the beginning of the journey: 'I am no Paul, I am no Aeneas'; and that Virgil's answer assured Dante, implicitly, that in some sense he was indeed to be an Aeneas and even — with the hint already given of the 'beate genti' who are beyond Virgil's own experience — a St. Paul.[9] That same hint is recalled and confirmed early in the *Paradiso*, in an evident allusion to the *locus classicus* of 2 *Corinthians*, and again in cantos XXVI and XXX.[10] Dante, then, is clearly taking St. Paul's experience as proto-type of his own: as his descent into Hell recalled that of Aeneas (*Aeneid VI*), so his ascent into heaven is given as analogous to that of St. Paul. Theologically speaking then, it too is a *raptus*; and particularly in respect of the final visions of the Empyrean heaven (cantos XXX to XXXIII).

Touching the vision of God, as the form of the eternal life promised to believers, Christian tradition held two points as axiomatic: that it was a 'grace' beyond the reach of unaided human nature, and that once attained it brought perfect bliss. On a third point — the question whether the divine essence is seen directly by the blessed in heaven or only through some similitude or 'theophany' — there had been, as we shall see, some disagreement among theologians, but the matter was virtually settled by the mid-thirteenth century in favour of the doctrine of intuitive immediacy as defined by Benedict XII in the document quoted above. The supernatural character of the vision implied *a fortiori* that it was supra-sensible; but of more interest here is the theory of the 'light' (*lumen gloriae*) imparted by God to the created intelligence in order to bring it beyond its natural limits into the act of the final vision. It

---

9. *Inferno* II, 10-42; I, 118-22.
10. *Par.* I, 73-75. 'If I was only that in me which You created last, You know . . . who with Your light did raise me.' Cf. 2 *Cor.* xii. 2: 'whether in the body or out of the body, I know not, God knows . . . .' What is 'last created' is the human rational soul, cf. *Genesis* ii. 7 and *Purg.* XXV, 67-75. The other texts referred to as allusions to St. Paul's are direct allusions only to the vision on the road to Damascus (*Acts* ix. 1-19): *Par.* XXVI, 10-12, and XXX, 49-51; but it seems reasonable to extend their reference to the Apostle's vision-experience in general, and so to his *raptus*.

is this light, 'luce viva,' which greets Dante on his ascent into the
Empyrean, and of which he says with a sublime simplicity:

> Lume è là su che visibile face
> lo creatore a quella creatura
> che solo in lui vedere ha la sua pace — [11]

where the contrast of 'creatore' and 'creatura' is, I suggest, in significant harmony with the conclusion to which the western Church was
moving through the thirteenth century, namely that the basic reason
for postulating this *lumen gloriae* at all was the immediacy of a vision
whose object would be the divine essence itself. For if God's essence, and no mere 'similitude,' was to be directly intuited, then
somehow the creature would have to receive into its apprehension
the Creator himself. Any lesser, any created form could be nothing
more than a likeness of God, a 'theophany'; and this being excluded, there was no alternative but to say that God himself informed
the created intellect as both its idea and as the object known in this
idea. But how could a finite being be thus in-formed, indwelt, immediately, by infinite uncreated Being — except it were somehow intrinsically disposed to this, raised, as St. Thomas says, with a rare
touch of feeling, *in tantam sublimitatem?* And this intrinsic disposition is the *lumen gloriae.*[12]

In the *Paradiso* Dante's sight of the divine essence is, we have
noted, transitory; he will return to the mortal world after it, like his
prototype St. Paul. But in the Thomist theology of vision the tran-
sience of St. Paul's *raptus* (and therefore, we may say, Dante's also)
is its only difference from the truly final beatific Vision. The
supreme degree of *raptus* also is a sight of God's essence and
therefore requires that supernatural 'light of glory,' without which,
said St. Thomas (discussing precisely this question of the manner of
St. Paul's vision), 'the divine essence cannot be seen by any created
intellect.' But the theologian adds that, in the particular case of the
raptus, the light of glory would affect the intellect, not as an indwell-
ing form, but as a sort of passing disturbance, *per modum cujusdam
passionis transeuntis.*[13] And this last phrase might serve as an epitome

---

11. *Par.* XXX, 100-102. 'A light is there above, which makes the Creator visible to the
creature that finds its peace only in seeing him.'
12. *Summa theol.* 1a, xii, 1, 2, 4, 5.
13. *Summa theol.* 2a 2ae, clxxv, 3.

of the *Paradiso*, provided we add that the disturber is God as seen, and that the disturbance is utter bliss.

Bliss; the fulfilment of all desire. Let me repeat the end of the tercet last quoted:

> . . . a quella creatura
> che solo in lui vedere ha la sua pace.

But here a contrast suggests itself with what has been said of the supernaturalness of the vision – with that gulf between all created natures and God which compelled the theologians, committed to the view that the heavenly vision was direct and unmediated, to introduce the *sine qua non* of the *lumen gloriae*. For Dante's term 'pace,' concluding with some emphasis the tercet, connotes an intense desire. 'Pace' is a very strong term in Dante, and it usually connotes (apart from its use in political contexts) an ultimate fulfilment of desire.[14] But then the question arises, what is this desire in created natures for a supernatural fulfilment? How can nature desire what is beyond nature? This question indeed is suggested already in the *Comedy*; very clearly at the opening of *Purgatorio* XXI,

> La sete natural che mai non sazia
> se non con l'acqua onde la femminetta
> samaritana dimandò la grazia . . . . [15]

or again in *Paradiso* II,

> La concreata e perpetua sete
> del deiforme regno . . . .[16]

or again, by implication, in canto VII,

> Ma vostra vita sanza mezzo spira
> la somma beninanza, e la innamora
> di sè sì che poi sempre la disira.[17]

14. 'Pace' in the sense of erotic fulfilment, *Rime* CIII, 78 (and implicitly perhaps *Inf.* V, 99): in the sense of fulfilment of intellectual love, *Convivio* 3, 6, 8 and 3, 13, 3-7. In *Purgatorio* and *Paradiso* 'pace' always or nearly always means the bliss of heaven, especially in the sense of fulfilment: *Purg.* XXVII, 115-17; XXVIII, 93; cf. XXI, 17, XXVI, 54, XXX, 9; *Par.* III, 85, IV, 117, XXX, 102; cf. X, 129, XXXI, 111.
15. *Purg.* XXI, 1-3: 'The natural thirst which is never slaked save with that water the little Samaritan woman asked for'.
16. *Par.* II, 19-20: 'The concreated, perpetual thirst of the God-formed realm'.
17. *Par.* VII, 142-4: 'But your life the supreme Goodness himself directly breathes forth, so filling it with love of himself that it desires him ever after'.

For do not all such texts imply that a desire for paradise, the vision of God, is *natural* to certain creatures, at least to

quelle c'hanno intelletto ed amore? [18]

Yes, without a doubt that is the implication; and certainly too these texts contrast with (I would not say contradict) certain other texts in the *Convivio* and the *Monarchia* which seem to lend support to the thesis that there is a fundamental difference of outlook between those more secular works and the *Divine Comedy*.[19] With that issue, however, I am not at present concerned; nor (need I say?) with the difficult theological questions that lurk in any statement about a natural — innate in our nature — human desire for union with God. Let us grant that Dante allows such a desire in some sense — and indeed that is putting it mildly; and that Catholic theology allows it in some sense too.[20] Moreover, the *Divine Comedy*, though it all pre-supposes such a desire, never raises it explicitly as a problem to be solved by argument, as it does, for example, raise free-will and creation as problems. On the one hand Dante states, implicitly, the supernaturalness of the Vision; on the other he shows it, explicitly this time and emphatically, as the fulfilment of natural desire. But this latter point requires some further consideration, especially touching the intellect's desire for truth.

It is a commonplace that the thirteenth-century thinkers had a great confidence in the power of reason. But it would be a mistake to think of this only, or even primarily, as a confidence in ratiocination, in dialectic and the syllogism. It was this certainly, but, underlying and pre-supposed to the confidence in the *ratio*, was confidence in the *intellectus*. Now these terms do not denote two powers, but two modes of activity within the same power — *ratio*, the mind's discursive procedure from point to point, *intellectus* its resting, or its capacity to rest, in a point acquired, i.e. understood, in a truth actually apprehended.[21] Speaking therefore of the mind as *in*

18. *Par.* I, 120: 'those endowed with intellect and love'.
19. *Con.* 3, 15, 6-10; 4, 13, 6-9; *Mon.* I, 3 *passim* and 4, 1; III, 15, 6-7. Referring to 'the thesis etc.,' I have chiefly in mind Bruno Nardi; see his polemic against Gilson (and Barbi) in *Nel mondo di Dante*, pp. 221-28, 235-45. I discuss aspects of this matter in cc. 10 and 12 below.
20. See A. Finili O.P., 'Natural Desire,' in *Dominican Studies* I, 4, pp. 313-59; II, 1, pp. 1-15; V, pp. 159-84.
21. *Summa theol.* 1a, lxxix, 8-10.

via, 'provando e riprovando,' as Dante says, the scholastics might prefer the term *ratio*; but speaking of its deepest orientation, as to its proper and final fulfilment in the actual vision of truth, in truth's 'dolce aspetto,' as Dante says in the same place[22] – here the scholastics preferred the nobler term *intellectus*. And with all their differences in detail the thirteenth-century Schoolmen (with perhaps a few notable exceptions) saw in this fundamental orientation of *intellectus* to truth the sign of an affinity in the human mind to truth absolute and entire, such that, short of the vision of God, in whom all questions would find their truest answer, the mind simply could not rest. Let Aquinas speak here for all: 'From a knowledge of effects arises a desire to know their cause; thus philosophy began as a search for causes. Hence the desire for knowledge, which is natural to intellectual beings, cannot rest until, the natures of effects being known, that of their cause is also known. It follows that if spiritual beings acknowledge God as cause of all that they see, their natural desire will remain unfulfilled until they see the nature of God himself.' Again (in terms which remind one of the fourth canto of the *Paradiso*) the theologian continues: 'Nothing finite can satisfy the intellect's desire: I mean, that whatever finite object it apprehends, it strives after something greater; just as with lines and numbers the mind goes on adding to infinity. Now in being and power every creature is finite. Therefore, intellect, of its nature, does not rest in the knowledge of created natures, however great these may be, but must tend always towards an understanding of the infinitely great substance which is God.' And finally, this noble homage to the intellect, so moving in its controlled ardour: 'Whence I conclude that the final bliss of spirits is not to be found in such knowledge of God as they may gain from their own natures (as created effects), since their natural desire must lead them ever on to the divine nature itself. Whence too it is clear that in nothing else than in intellectual activity is our ultimate bliss to be looked for, since no other desire soars so high (*tam in sublime ferat*) as the desire of intelligible truth. All our other desires, whether of pleasure or anything else that man may long for, can find rest in other things. But this desire will not rest, except it reach the supreme principle and maker of all things, God . . . . Let them blush then for shame

22. *Par.* III, 1-3.

who seek the bliss for man – so noble a thing – in lesser
objectives.'[23]

In all this, not *ratio* but *intellectus*, in the sense already indicated,
is evidently the main theme. Seeking the clearest sign in man of a
capacity for union with God, St. Thomas finds it in the appetite for
truth, in that basic orientation of conscious being as such to union
with being in general, and so with Being unqualified and absolute,
God. This thoroughgoing intellectualism is of course
characteristically Thomist. The schools represented by St. Bonaventure or Scotus saw the will as superior to intellect and love to
knowledge. Yet these more 'mystical' metaphysicians too were intellectualists in their own way; as in general was all western thought
of that age. As also was our poet; indeed, though I would not call
Dante, without much qualification, a Thomist, I would agree that
his doctrinal affinities were with the school of Aquinas rather than
with any other.[24] But, once granted the profound aspiration of
Dante's mind towards intellectual union with God, we can, I think,
usefully distinguish in his work two ways in which this aspiration to
that end is articulated through the means to it. I would call these
ways the argumentative and the interpretative, respectively.

The argumentative way – the way, predominantly, of *ratio* –
runs from point to point in a dialectical movement of question and
answer, where each answer solves a particular problem, the solution
then raising a new problem requiring a new answer. It is the process
– to adapt Dante's own simile – of truth seeding or breeding truth
by way of questioning, of enquiry, of 'dubbio.' The great statement
of this procedure comes near the end of canto IV, in the exclamatory interlude between two questions about the human will:

> Nasce per quello, a quisa di rampollo
> a piè del vero il dubbio . . . . [25]

The passage is a kind of metaphorical paradigm of the entire course
of the *Paradiso*, as far as canto XXIX. Now the movement that it
represents could go on, one might suppose, to infinity; because each
of the questions it successively raises yields, when answered, only a

23. All three texts are from the *Contra gentiles* III, 50; cf. *Par*. IV, 115-32.
24. For the Thomist influence in Italy in Dante's time see M. Grabmann, *Mittelalterliches
Geistesleben* I, pp. 332 ss; III, pp. 197-212.
25. *Par*. IV, 130-31: 'Because of this [desire], doubt springs like a shoot at the foot of
truth'. 'This' (the desire mentioned in l. 129).

particular aspect of truth: one truth about free-will, another about the redemption, another about creation, and so on. Each answer satisfies for the moment, brings a moment of contentment, an 'essere contento,' to use a favourite word of Dante's, in this sense, which harks back to the *Convivio*[26] ; but that moment could, evidently, never be final on these terms. But it is not left on these terms. For in the same lyric interlude the poet suddenly alters and deepens the perspective; he introduces the notion, not now of a series of limited truths juxtaposed, but of a series of *widening* truths, each included by the one beyond it, until a truth is reached.

> di fuor dal qual nessun vero si spazia.[27]

And this last truth, since it leads no further, is infinite, at least with respect to the questioning mind: since no more questions remain to be asked, it includes all possible answers. It can limit the series, being itself unlimited. So the poet exclaims:

> Io veggio ben che già mai non si sazia
> nostro intelletto, se 'l ver non lo illustra
> di fuor dal qual nessun vero si spazia.
> Posasi in esso come fera in lustra,
> tosto che giunto l'ha; e giugner puollo:
> se non, ciascun disio sarebbe frustra.
> Nasce per quello, a guisa di rampollo,
> a piè del vero il dubbio; ed è natura
> ch' al sommo pinge noi di collo in collo.[28]

Such, in outline and suggested in imagery, is the way of rational argument towards the final vision. I say 'towards' only; for as explicit in the *Paradiso*, while it starts in canto I, this way does not ex-

---

26. See especially *Con.* 3, 15, 3; and in the *Paradiso* I, 97, IV, 72, XVIII, 18, 112, XX, 74, XXII, 30, XXXII, 134.
27. *Par.* IV, 126: 'outside of which there's no truth'.
28. *Par.* IV, 129-32 'I see well, our mind is never sated unless that truth enlighten it outside of which there is no truth. There it rests, like a beast in its lair, as soon as it gains it; and it can gain it, else every desire were aimless. Because of this, doubt springs like a shoot at the foot of truth; and it's nature itself, urging us on to the Summit from height to height.'
Note the strong stress on the naturalness of the desire for ultimate vision. Line 129 recalls *Con.* 3, 15, 3-4 which is Dante's clearest statement of the ultimateness, among human desires, of the truth-appetite – itself recalling *Nicomachean Ethics* X, 7; cf. St. Thomas's commentary *in loco* (ed. Leonina, pp. 587-8), *Contra gentiles* III, 50, *Summa theol.* 1a, xii, 1.

tend beyond the discourse on creation in canto XXIX.

On the other hand what I call (for want of a better term) the interpretative way goes right on to the end, because it consists essentially in a passing through symbols to substance, through intermediary appearances to reality. Its most brilliant expression perhaps is the transformation scene in canto XXX, where the river of light and the living sparks or gems – those 'umbriferi prefazi' – change gradually into the great white rose. But the full meaning of this way is only revealed in canto XXXIII; for only here at last does Dante pass beyond all intermediaries. Only here – after Bernard's prayer and Mary's – is the pilgrim alone with his God. Now what he writes at this point is of course poetry, a work of art; based no doubt on some high intellectual experience, but not necessarily – need I say? – on a real sight of God's essence such as tradition ascribed to St. Paul in *his* rapture. Yet what Dante is trying to represent *as if* it had occurred is precisely that ultimate sort of rapture –

> . . . tanto ch' i' giunsi
> l'aspetto mio col valore infinito.[29]

It is a direct contact, and so the end of all images and even of all concepts –

> Da quinci innanzi il mio veder fu maggio
> che 'l parlar nostro, ch' a tal vista cede,
> e cede la memoria a tanto oltraggio.[30]

And again:

> O quanto è corto il dire e come fioco
> al mio concetto! e questo, a quel ch' i' vidi,
> è tanto, che non basta a dicer 'poco.'[31]

And yet this 'poco' he must use for all it is worth, passing on from images – light and melting snow and the Sybil's leaves and Argo's shadow – to the great universal concepts 'il vero,' 'il ben,' 'il fine di tutt' i disii,' 'l'amore'; and then back to imagery, with the moving

---

29. *Par.* XXXIII, 80-81: '. . . till I reached and saw the Infinite Good'.
30. *Par.* XXXIII, 55-57: 'From then on my vision surpassed our speech, which fails at such a sight, and memory too fails at such excess'.
31. *Par.* XXXIII, 121-23: 'O how scant is speech and how feeble to my conception! and this, to what I saw! . . .

circles representing the Trinity and the final flash of lightning: and all this because he is a poet whose task is expression. And the repeated statement that he cannot express what he saw, or even what he thinks he remembers that he saw, is, of course, part of the expression; for his whole aim is to suggest an experience beyond art (the external, poetic word) and indeed beyond thought (the inward, conceptual word or 'memoria').[32]

And here we are reminded once more of St. Augustine and of that chapter in the *Confessions* where the saint relates his conversation with his mother at Ostia shortly before her death; and which seems an effort to represent essentially the same experience as Dante tried to convey. 'And so we came to our own minds, and passed beyond them to the region of never-failing plenty where Thou feedest Israel forever with the food of truth, where life is Wisdom by which all these things come to be ... and the Life itself never comes to be, but is as it was and shall be evermore; because in it is neither past nor future but present only, for it is eternal; for past and future are not eternal. And as we spoke and yearned after it, we touched it for an instant with the whole force of our hearts. And we sighed ... and then heard again the babble of our own tongues, wherein each word has a beginning and an ending. Far unlike Thy Word, our Lord ....

We were saying then: 'If the tumult of the flesh were hushed; hushed the shadows of earth, sea, sky; hushed the heavens and the soul itself, so that it passed beyond itself, not thinking of itself; if all dreams were hushed and sensuous revelations and every tongue and sign; if all that comes and goes were hushed. These all proclaim to him who has ears to hear, We made not ourselves, He made us who abides forever; but suppose that, having delivered their message, they held their peace ... and that He alone spoke, not by them but by Himself; and that we heard His word, not through any tongue of flesh or angel's voice, not in the thunder, nor through any similitude, but His own voice, whom we love in these creatures; suppose we heard Him with no intermediary at all. And now we reached out and with swift thought touched on the eternal Wisdom that abides above all things. And suppose that this moment endured, and all other modes of vision were removed, and this alone ravished

32. *Par.* XXXIII, 52-145.

and absorbed the beholder ... might not the eternal life be like this moment of understanding for which we sighed? Is not this the meaning of, Enter thou into the joy of thy Lord?' [33]

Clearly the pith of this famous text is a longing to pass from relative being to the absolute, from the derived to the Original. And the connexion of these terms is not analysed but contemplated, in a meditation moving around it from one pair of opposites to another – passing-away and stability, time and eternity, effects and their cause, signs and the signified. In Dante too we find these contrasts; but in the *Comedy* especially the last one, the passage through signs or symbols to substance. And this was natural in a poet whose self-assumed task, 'figurando il paradiso,' it was to make spiritual order imaginable.[34] Images had to be Dante's starting-point; a system of signs that both hid and half-revealed a reality 'chiuso e parvente del suo proprio riso.' [35]

Had I space I would dwell at this point on that theological development concerning the immediacy of the beatific Vision, to which allusion has already been made and which has been made accessible in an excellent study by H. F. Dondaine.[36] It has to do with a semi-agnostic influence, transmitted from Greek sources (chiefly St. John Chrysostom and Denys) to the West in the tenth century through Scotus Erigena, and with the western reaction to it at the end of the twelfth century and in the first decades of the thirteenth. In essence the 'Greek' theory – itself, in Chrysostom, a reaction against Eunomian semi-rationalism – was a denial that the Deity could ever become, even for the angels or the blessed in heaven, the direct object of a creature's knowledge. Reverence for the divine majesty required, on this view, a distinction between God's substance and his glory. The latter only could ever be seen by creatures; the former forever remaining essentially mysterious or unknown, except to God himself. 'Theophany' as a name for God's glory, for his greater or less self-manifestation to creatures, was given currency in the West by Erigena's versions of the Pseudo-Areopagite. Some Latin theologians were tempted by this

33. *Confessions*, IX, 10.
34. *Par.* XXIII, 61-63; cf. XXX, 22-33.
35. *Par.* XVII, 36.
36. H. F. Dondaine, O.P., 'L'objet et le "medium" de la vision béatifique chez les théologiens du XIIIe siècle,' in *Recherches de Théologie ancienne et médiévale*, XIX (1952), pp. 60 ss.

'Greek' view, but its eventual rejection by the Church was a certainty once its terms were clearly understood: it could not be squared with St. Paul and St. John,[37] let alone with Augustine. Already censured by the university of Paris in 1241,[38] it was finally ruled out by Benedict XII in 1336, in the definition quoted above. Between these dates it got no serious support in the West, though indirectly no doubt, and through the authority of Denys, it had some effect on theological thought, for example on Q 12 of the *Prima pars* of the *Summa theologiae*, where (article 7) St. Thomas explains how, since God's knowability is infinite, no creature, even granted the *lumen gloriae*, can ever completely comprehend it: *nullus intellectus creatus potest Deum infinite cognoscere.*[39] And with this balanced view Catholic theology has remained satisfied. By the blessed God is both known immediately, beyond all intermediaries, and at the same time he remains incomprehensible in the sense of not completely known.

As for the *Paradiso*, most of it describes 'theophanies,' in the sense indicated; while Dante more than once echoes, in his own way, the doctrine of God's ultimate incomprehensibility, also in the sense indicated.[40] But I hardly think he was directly influenced by the 'Greek' current that has been mentioned.

In conclusion I want to suggest two interrelated aspects of Dante's representation of the final vision which seem to me characteristic. Let me call them the 'causal-assimilative' and the 'cosmic' aspects.

1. Dante persistently stresses the idea of causation: great artist that he was, he saw reality as *productive*, he saw *making* everywhere. Now to make anything is to cause, and to make it absolutely — where the alternative is simply non-existence — is to create. To create is to cause with nothing, no material, presupposed. And only God can do this, but this emphatically God can do. Moreover — and here is Dante's stress — the effect of any causing is some degree of resemblance; effects as such are like their cause. If then effects are thought of in activity or movement, they appear as moving

37. Chiefly I *Cor.* xiii. 12 and 1 *John* iii. 2.
38. *Chart. Univ. Paris*, No. 128 (Paris, 1889).
39. 1*a*, xii, 7*c*.
40. But with a special stress on the mysteriousness of the divine *will*, in its particular decisions: thus in *Par.* XI, 28-30; XX, 118-20, 134-35; XXI, 91-99; XXIX, 17; XXXII, 61-65. In a more general sense, XIX, 52-57.

resemblances; and the whole cosmos as a moving resemblance to its Creator.[41] Now such a thing may be thought of in two ways, extrinsically or intrinsically. A cloud's shadow is a moving resemblance of the cloud, but the movement only affects the resemblance extrinsically; the resemblance itself is not in movement towards the cloud. But plant a seed, and the movement that follows, the growth of the young plant, is towards an increasing resemblance to the parent plant. It is intrinsic to the likeness, which itself is moving, itself is developing. And this difference becomes still clearer when mind and consciousness enter; for then the effect's assimilation to its cause is by way, not only of material growth, but of knowledge also; and the movement is, to this extent, more interior. A human child grows towards its parents by knowing them, and into society generally by knowing it; knowledge being an immanent interior union with the object known.

These ideas — if not explicitly in these terms — I find everywhere in Dante; and particularly in his thought about the relations between God and creatures. 'The chief desire of anything,' he says, 'and the first given it by nature, is to return to its originating principle.'[42] Here is the assimilation of effect as such to cause as such. And where the causing is unmediated, the consequent trend to assimilation will be at its strongest. Hence the rational soul of man, 'breathed out' by God immediately ('sanza mezzo'[43]), not only resembles God *ab origine* more than anything in the physical world (which comes into being through secondary causes) but it also must tend, of its nature, to a certain direct and immediate assimilation to the divine nature; and this through its proper and innate capacity for knowledge. Its nature tends to a God-assimilation by direct knowledge of God; the immediacy of its origination from God being the measure of the force of its essential impulse to return to him.

> ma vostra vita sanza mezzo spira
> la somma beninanza, e la innamora
> di sè sì che poi sempre la disira . . . .

41. Cf. *Par.* I, 103-08; which recalls *Convivio* 3, 2, 5; 3, 7, 2; 3, 14, 2-3; cf. *Monarchia* I, 8.
42. *Convivio* 4, 12, 14.
43. *Par.* VII, 142-44; 'but your life the supreme Good breathes out directly, making it in love with himself, so that it desires him ever after'; cf. *Purg.* XXV, 70-75. cf. note 17.

Thus for Dante the assimilation-movement is governed by the concept of cause; more precisely, he sees the relation to the 'final cause,' the term *ad quem*, as above all a consequence of the relation to the 'efficient cause,' the term *a quo*. Doubtless all Christian theology sees the end of creatures as some sort of assimilation to God; but Dante's personal stress falls on an assimilation to God as Producer and Creator; and this not so much in the creature's representing God by its own causal power as in its knowing God as its source. Man's end is then especially a direct knowledge of God as *power*, as creative source of being, and of intellectual being in particular. So it is in the final canto of the *Paradiso*. After St. Bernard's prayer to Mary, and Dante's prayer directly to God (lines 1-39, 67-75) the vision itself is then stated in a succession of alternated exclamations and precise descriptions. The latter fall into three graded divisions, each corresponding to a stage in the voyager's approach to the completest possible sight of the nature of God. Yet to the end God is still seen in relation to the creature: first, explicitly, as source of the whole cosmos (lines 85-90); then in his triune nature, and so, implicitly, as the exemplar-cause of intellectual being, self-knowing and self-loving (lines 114-20, 124-26);[44] and finally as united with human nature by the Incarnation (lines 127-32). And this last is the final point before the 'lightning flash' which closed both the canto and the *Commedia*. And it is, I suggest, significant that in its utmost reach Dante's mind should touch precisely God as Man, the union of the Second Person with 'our image' (130-38). True, the final object represented as seen is not God as *causing* man, but it is emphatically *man in God*. The causal line which Dante follows back to its source in God could not reach, in fact, all the way; because at the end Dante had to pass beyond all effects, at least as media of the vision. Yet, in another way, one effect — human nature — is there at the very end. This is in virtue of the Incarnation; and any Christian might therefore, representing the beatific Vision, have represented Man in God; but Dante's insistence on this point — he gives it no fewer than twelve lines — seems a clear indication of the stress that I am concerned to point out — the stress on the link between God and

---

44. That this is the implication (especially of *Par.* XXXIII, 124-26) cannot be proved, but it may be felt by any reader, familiar with the extraordinary consistency of the whole body of Dante's work — who compares, for example, *Convivio* 4, 2, 18 and *Purg.* XXV, 70-75 with the *Paradiso* 'descriptions' of the Trinity — including *Par.* X, 1-3 and XIII, 52 ss.

creatures and so on God's power manifested *ad extra*, whether simply as causing creatures or as causing one created nature, man's, to be
nothing less than God's own nature by the Incarnation of the
Word.

2. If, as I have suggested, his poetic nature predisposed Dante to
see causal power everywhere, and to stress it in his theology, that
nature also involved an extreme sensitivity to beauty; and this both
in the detail of visible forms and in their total cosmic coherence.
Dante had, as it were, a painter's eye for colour, a sculptor's for
shape and a most delicate ear for musical harmony; but to the sensible order of things in general – as systematized by the science of his
time and above all by astronomy – his response may most appropriately be called *poetic*, if this term can denote a certain interplay
of sense and intelligence issuing in a vivid imaginative apprehension
of being in general. This apprehension in Dante was both delicately
detailed and extraordinarily wide-ranging: witness the wonderful
astronomy-poetry of the *Paradiso*.

We should expect this cosmic feature, so to call it, of Dante's outlook to affect his representation of the vision of God; and so indeed
it does; and this, I suggest, briefly, in two ways. For the cosmos is
brought into that vision both on the side of the object and on the
side of the subject: Dante both sees it *in* God and it becomes one
with him as seeing God. He sees it in God: let me recall the lines
already alluded to:

> Nel suo profondo vidi che s'interna,
>   legato con amore in un volume,
>   ciò che per l'universo si squaderna;
> sustanze e accidenti e lor costume,
>   quasi conflati insieme. . . .[45]

And the cosmos is one with him as he sees God. Already in the
Convivio, in a text that is fundamental for his philosophy, Dante had
presented the soul's natural love of God as a kind of natural union
with the universe. Love is 'spiritual union,' and this 'union' with the
Creator implies and requires a certain union with his manifestation
which is the cosmos. God, so the argument runs, 'most naturally

---

45. *Par.* XXXIII, 85-89: 'In its depth I saw, gathered into it, bound by love in one
volume, the scattered leaves of the universe; substances and accidents and their modes, as
though fused together.'

loves being,'[46] and therefore so does the human soul, God's likeness; and therefore, since the soul's being depends on God, 'it naturally desires and wills to be united with God in order to strengthen its being. And since the divine goodness is manifested through the varieties of goodness in nature and reason, it is natural for the human soul to unite itself with these, and the more swiftly and strongly the more perfectly it is aware of them . . . .' This intimate linking of the two unions — with God and with creation — reappears implicitly in other places; but nowhere, I think, more clearly than in the final lines of the *Paradiso*. With the final flash of vision the poet's memory failed, but this at least he knew — that then his 'desire and will,' like a wheel turning evenly, was moved by

l'amor che move il sole e l'altre stelle.[47]

Postscript. I wrote this essay 18 years ago. Were I now (1977) to write a fresh study of *Par.* XXXIII, I would give more heed to the imagery, especially to the wonderful lines 94-6 evoking the Voyage of the Argonauts; on which see R. Hollander's comments in *Dante's Allegory in the Commedia*, Princeton Univ. Press, 1969.

---

46. Dante refers here to the *Liber de causis*, presumably to Prop. IV, *Prima rerum creatarum est esse, et non est ante ipsum creatum aliquid* (Lectio IV in St Thomas's Commentary); but he obviously alters the meaning of the text by omitting the limiting adjective 'created': cf. the Busnelli-Vandelli ed. of the *Convivio*, Vol. I, p. 268 (Florence, 1934). *Conv*, 3, 2, 7-8.
47. *Par.* XXXIII, 145; 'the love that moves the sun and the other stars'.

6

THE CANTO OF THE DAMNED POPES:
INFERNO XIX[1]

As evil is only a negation or perversion of goodness, so in Dante's *Comedy* the vision of evil, the *Inferno*, presupposes forms of goodness which appear in the rest of the work. So it is very clearly with *Inferno* XIX; the vision here of the Church as corrupt and senile presupposing that of the Church still young, ardent and confident, the Apostolic community that the closing cantos of the *Purgatorio* will evoke and the *Paradiso* explicitly recall.[2]

Dante's ideal of the Church must be left to emerge, indirectly and in part, from my comments on our canto; but his attack on the Church of his day calls for a few preliminary remarks on its place in the *Inferno* and its historical context.

It may be recalled that the damned popes in this canto exemplify a subdivision of *frode* — cunning, deceit, guile — and that *frode* in the *Inferno* is one of the two ways in which *malizia* operates, the other being *forza*, violence. *Malizia* then works through fraud or force, the way of the crook and the way of the thug; and the crook's way is the worse, because in him reason, man's specific gift and quality, is degraded. Hence it appears lower down in hell, cantos XII to XVI

1. In preparing this paper on *Inf.* XIX, I made especial use of the following studies of the canto as a whole: the commentaries of Natalino Sapegno (Dante, *La Divina Commedia* ... Firenze, 1955-1957) and Hermann Gmelin (*Die Göttliche Komödie. Kommentar.* 3 v. Stuttgart, 1954-1957); Edoardo Sanguineti, *Interpretazione di Malebolge* (Firenze, 1961), pp. 35-57); Paolo Brezzi, 'lectura' on canto XIX, in *Nuove letture dantesche* (Firenze, 1968), Vol. II, pp. 161-182; Antonino Pagliaro, *Ulisse: ricerche semantiche sulla Divina Commedia* (Messina-Firenze, 1966), Vol. I, pp. 253-309. I have not seen Paul Renucci's study of the canto, 'Le chant XIX de l'Enfer,' in *Bulletin de la Société d'Etudes Dantesques*, XIII (1964), 7-20.

On Dante's anticlericalism, see Jacques Goudet, 'L'Anticléricalisme chrétien de Dante et de Manzoni,' in *Revue des études italiennes*, N. S., XIV (1968), No. 2, pp. 117-147. Goudet finely distinguishes what is specifically 'medieval' about Dante's hostility to the clergy.

2. In the *Paradiso* Dante's chief touchstone for judging the Church is the example of the Apostles: cf. XVIII, 115-136; XXI, 127-142; XXII, 88-93; XXVII, 10-66; XXIX, 109-114.

being occupied by the violent, and XVII down to XXXIV, at the
bottom, by deceivers: first, in Malebolge (XVIII-XXX) by those
whose victims had no claim on them apart from common humanity;
and then in Cocito (XXXI-XXXIV) by those deceivers who were
also traitors. There are difficulties about the details of this overall
arrangement, but what I want to stress here is the central concept of
Dante's hell, the common motive and fundamental evil disposition
which he sees at work in all his thugs and all his crooks: *malizia*.
And what is *malizia*? The answer is given in Virgil's defining it, in
canto XI, by the effect it aims at bringing about, which is 'ingiuria'
– 'D'ogni malizia ... ingiuria è il fine' (XI, 22-23). *Ingiuria* I
would render as 'injustice,' taking this in a broad sense, and define
its basic presupposition as the belief that all reality, and in particular
human reality, is the product of divine Power, Wisdom, and
Goodness, and is therefore sacred. *Ingiuria* is the violation or
profanation of the goodness, the holiness in things and in man as
manifestations of God. Evil, for Dante, is in essence the will to
destroy or degrade that goodness. Therefore the ethic of the *Inferno*
is implicitly religious, and it becomes explicitly so where God, as the
object attacked by *ingiuria*, is explicitly envisaged – as in the
blasphemies of Capaneo and Vanni Fucci, the pride of Satan, and
the abuse of a sacred office by Popes Nicholas III and Boniface
VIII and Clement V in canto XIX, and by Boniface again in
XXVII.

So much on points of general structure. But what Dante
specifically charges these popes with is the sin technically called
Simony, the buying or selling (but in their case the selling) of
'spiritual things,' that is, in the first place of sacraments, the vehicles
of divine grace entrusted to the Church, and secondly of offices and
ministries connected with the sacraments. In fairness to the papacy it
has to be said, and with emphasis, that in the early Middle Ages, the
popes had been the leaders of the fight against simony in the
Church, of the effort to keep its specific activities in this world disinterested and clean. For the great reforming popes of the eleventh
century, and on into the twelfth, simony was a detestable effect of
the Church's subjection, in practice, to the feudal system and the
powers of this world: bishops bought their pastoral office from the
king or baron who disposed of such things.[3] But that movement of
reform proved, in a sense, only too successful. For, once the Church

had achieved a certain freedom from secular control, she began to be excessively controlled, on the administrative and economic level, by her own 'spiritual' head, the pope. In this sense the papacy was corrupted by an increase of power. And yet, from another point of view, it was corrupted through weakness. For through the twelfth and thirteenth centuries the Church's struggle to maintain independence of the secular power involved her ever more deeply in political manoeuvre and conflict; and on this level the papacy, besides tending to be in a false position, was relatively weak. The Papal State was politically and militarily no match for the new national kingdoms arising in Europe — for France in particular.[4] This helps to explain the rather feverish opportunism and expediency that bedevilled papal policies from the mid-thirteenth century on.

In any case, by the early fourteenth century the papacy found itself in a very dangerous situation, and not politically only, but spiritually; its moral authority was gravely impaired. And Dante was well aware of this, of course. But he was not at all disposed to see in the popes' political difficulties an extenuation for what he regarded as their crimes. On the contrary, he was disposed both by temperament and by circumstances to an extreme severity. His temperament can speak for itself. The circumstances I allude to were, first the interventions of Boniface VIII in Florentine affairs at the turn of the century, leading to the bitter conflicts that resulted in the poet's own exile; and then, a weightier factor, Dante's growing conviction that the official Church of his time was disastrously and culpably off course. The very law of its being, the example and teaching of Christ, had, he thought, been so systematically flouted by the Church's rulers that by now they were virtually in a state of apostasy. So at least he seems to say in the *Comedy*.[5] Yet the poem is certainly not heretical, as Catholics understand the term. Let us say that he belonged to the Catholic 'left' of his time. More precisely, Dante's later writings, the *Comedy*, the *Monarchia*, and the political

3. On the idea of simony and the history of the attitude towards it of the Catholic Church, see: *Dictionnaire de théologie catholique* ... (Paris, 1899-1950), Vol. XIV, cols. 2141-2160; *Lexikon für Theologie und Kirche* (2nd ed.: Freiburg, 1957-1965), Vol. IX, cols. 774-776; *Enciclopedia cattolica* (Città del Vaticano, 1948-1954), Vol. XI, cols. 642-646; Denziger-Schönmetzer, *Enchiridion Symbolorum* ... (32nd ed.; Freiburg, 1963), under Index at p. 869.
4. Daniel P. Waley, *The Papal State in the Thirteenth Century* (London, 1961).
5. I have especially in mind such texts as *Purg.* XXXIII, 34-35, and *Par.* XXVII, 22-24.

letters, show deep affinities with that revolutionary evangelical
movement which swept through the western Church in the
thirteenth century and which drew its immediate inspiration from
St. Francis — in whom Jesus himself seemed to have been reborn —
and much of its ideology from the prophetic writings of Joachim of
Flora. This was chiefly a Franciscan movement, led by the so-called
'Spiritual' party in that Order; and its more extreme positions, in
particular the dichotomy between the spiritual Church and the carnal Church, were to be condemned by John XXII in 1318.[6] The
details of Dante's connection with this movement are obscure. What
is certain, and relevant here, is that some of its characteristic ideals
and aspirations are apparent in everything said of the Church and of
Christian history in the *Comedy*. But they first come right to the fore
in *Inferno* XIX, in the form of an indictment of the Holy See for in-
fidelity to the Gospel. This theme will reappear twice, on a large
scale, in the *Comedy*: in *Purgatorio* XXXII and in *Paradiso* XXVII.
What most obviously distinguishes our present canto is the comic
element, the way religious polemic is translated here into mockery
and burlesque. It is worth noting too that the judgment on the
papacy is pronounced here by Dante himself, while in the *Purgatorio*
he leaves this to Beatrice and in the *Paradiso*, as a climax, to St.
Peter.

The canto opens abruptly with a cry, in effect a call to attention
underlining the seriousness of the theme. There follows a narrative
section (vv. 7-45) preparing for the main dramatic action in verses
46 to 120; which is then rounded off quietly with a return to
narrative (vv. 121-133). The main dramatic section itself falls into
two parts: the representation of the damned popes (down to v. 87)
and then Dante's verdict on them. A link between these parts is
supplied by the brilliant stroke of verses 52-87, whereby the direct
encounter with Nicholas III serves as an indirect encounter with
two of his successors whose damnation is still to come; and this also

6. On this movement as a whole, in relation to Dante see R. Manselli, 'Dante e l' "Ecclesia
Spiritualis",' in *Dante e Roma* (Firenze, 1965), pp. 115-135. The ample bibliographical
notes provided by Manselli can serve as a way into the study of the 'movement' as a
whole. For English readers perhaps the best general introduction is still the scholarly and
readable work of Decima L. Douie, *The Nature and the Effect of the Heresy of the Fraticelli*
(Manchester: The University Press, 1932). See also Gordon Leff, *Heresy in the Middle
Ages: The Relation of Heterodoxy to Dissent, c.1250-1450* (Manchester: The University
Press, 1967), Vol. I, pp. 51-255; Charles T. Davis, *Dante and the Idea of Rome* (Oxford:
Clarendon Press, 1957), pp. 239-243.

provides a basis for the generality of the indictment contained in Dante's speech beginning at verse 90. Corresponding to this dual narrative pattern is a certain duality in the dominant tone, this being predominantly 'comic' down to verse 87, whereas the concluding indictment, though it begins ironically, quickly becomes straight reproof and denunciation.

The six-line opening apostrophe, 'O Simon Mago,' etc., with its deliberately disjointed syntax, effects an abrupt break in the narrative, marking off, emphatically, this canto from the preceding one. At the same time it defines the sin that is now to be dealt with; and this, first by naming its prototype – Simon Magus who tried to buy from the Apostles the power given them by the Holy Spirit (Acts, 8:14-24); and there may well be an intended contrast with that other Simon, Peter the first pope – and then by expressing the sin itself in the complex metaphor of verses 2-4. Traditionally the Church was the bride of Jesus Christ, and this image (one very dear to Dante) was sometimes extended to the Church's relation to Christ's vicar, the pope. Thus to traffick with the Church's 'sacred things,' 'le cose di Dio,' is like forcing a woman into adultery and harlotry at once. The harlot image will return in this canto, and then again, greatly elaborated, in *Purgatorio* XXXII.

Verses 7 to 30 set the scene for the action, showing us the third ditch of Malebolge, following Dante's usual narrative procedure and with his usual extraordinary visual precision; the mind's eye here is drawn persistently towards one dominant image, the movement of upturned burning feet to and fro over the *bolgia* floor. But the description is twice interrupted: first, by a second apostrophe, 'O Wisdom supreme' . . . , addressed to God himself and strongly underlining, by implication, both the impiety and the deep absurdity of simony;[7] and then by the sudden autobiographical digression of verses 16 to 21. These last two tercets are difficult, both because the literal sense of verse 18, and so too of verse 20, is disputed, and also

7. Simony is very directly a crime against *order*, as reversing the order of means to ends by which material things are for the sake of spiritual, and not *vice versa* (hence, of course, the 'topsy-turvy' imagery freely used in this canto); and being against order, simony is against divine Wisdom, the proper cause of order. Thus the implications of this tercet, 'O somma sapienza' etc., coincide with those of the opening of *Paradiso* X: the appearance of the term 'arte' in both passages is most significant; though evidently there is this nuance of difference, that *Inf.* XIX, 10, gives this term to the general *effect* of God as Wisdom whereas *Par.* X, 10, applies it to God himself as Wisdom, i.e., the Son or Word, the object of the Father's delighted contemplation – 'Guardando nel suo Figlio' etc.

because the intention behind the emphatic concluding verse 21 is not clear. The verse seems to convey a hint that there is more in the whole passage than meets the eye – more than a mere illustration or simile. I have not space for a full discussion, so I will merely summarize the chief disputed points and propose the interpretation that seems to me the most plausible.[8]

The chief difficulty, as regards the sense, is 'per loco d'i battezzatori' in verse 18. 'Battezzatori' could be either the plural of 'battezzatore,' one who baptises, or the plural of 'battezzatorio,' a place for baptism, a font. In favour of the first sense are most of the old commentators and many modern ones. Dante would then be comparing the holes in the floor of the *bolgia* to cavities arranged around the baptismal font at Florence, in which the priests stood while actually baptizing Florentine infants; and in that case, since such cavities would obviously not themselves contain water, the 'one' whom Dante says he rescued 'not many years ago' (vv. 19-20) could not have been drowning, so that 'v'annegava' would presumably only mean 'was suffocating inside it,' which is philologically at least possible. The other interpretation, that 'battezzatori' means the actual fonts, has the strong support of the early 'Ottimo' commentator who gives a fairly detailed description of the Florentine Baptistery (for the benefit, he says, 'especially of *forestieri*,' that is, non-Florentines), adding that the effect of Dante's having broken one of the fonts was still visible when he, the 'Ottimo,' wrote.[9] Chiefly on the strength of this testimony I am inclined to think that 'fonts' are meant, and consequenty to render 'v'annegava' as 'was drowning.' On the wider issue – whether

---

8. For the reading of verse 18 I follow G. Petrocchi's critical edition, *La Commedia, secondo l'antica vulgata* (Milano, 1965): 'fatti per loco d'i battezzatori.' Those familiar with the controversy over verses 16-21 will see that on the whole I am following A. Pagliaro in his 'Lectura Dantis Scaligera,' *Il canto XIX dell'Inferno* (Firenze, 1961); cf. his *Ulisse, op. cit.,* Vol. I, pp. 292-309; also Lucienne Portier, ' "E questo sia suggel ch'ogn'uomo sganni" (*Inf.* XIX, 21),' in *Bulletin de la Société d'Etudes Dantesques,* XI (1962), 45-46, and André Pézard in his translation of Dante, *Oeuvres complètes . . .* (Paris, 'Bibliothèque de la Pléiade,' 1965), p. 998. It will be plain too that I am left unconvinced by the purely symbolic interpretation offered by Susan Noakes in her learned article, 'Dino Compagni and the Vow in San Giovanni: *Inferno* XIX, 16-21,' in *Dante Studies,* LXXXVI (1968), 41-63. This article contains many good things, but as a thesis it all hangs on the premiss that the action of 'breaking' which Dante records in v. 20 was not literal but only metaphorical. Yet it seems to me that the circumstantial way in which Dante speaks of his action is such as to make the literal sense antecedently more probable.

9. See Giuseppe Vandelli: 'I "fori" del "bel San Giovanni",' *Studi Danteschi,* XV (1931), 55-66.

Dante here is doing more than merely illustrate a detail in his story by reference to an outside object — I think that, in its context, this passage undoubtedly has further implications and undertones. There is, first, the peculiar force of the allusion to 'il mio bel san Giovanni.' The Florentine Baptistery is one of the chief points of emotional convergence in the *Comedy* : [10] the sacred centre of Dante's homeland, where he had been christened and where he longed to be crowned, in the end, as a Christian poet, the sign and focus of his triple loyalty to his city, his art, and his Church (and we must stress, in the present context, 'his Church'). The allusion, moreover, to baptism is clearly appropriate in this canto on the profanation of the 'things of God,' as is the image of the confessor further down (vv. 49-51). But I think it fairly probable also that verse 21 contains a half-veiled defiance of an anticipated charge of irreverence towards the Church. As we shall see later, Dante expects this accusation — and how could he not? — and he may well have already been accused of irreverence for breaking that font 'not many years ago.' Certainly he is stressing here his good reason for having broken it (v. 20), and this may well be a reference to an accusation of that sort and at the same time carry the implication that the attack he is now about to launch on the popes is equally free from irreverence.

But I ought at least to mention another interpretation I heard recently in a lecture in London, developing a suggestion put out some years ago by Leo Spitzer.[11] On this view, the relative pronoun 'questo' in verse 21 does not refer to the action recalled in the preceding line — 'I broke' etc. — as an event in Dante's personal life (which is how I prefer to understand it) but as a kind of parable expressing symbolically the whole meaning of the present canto. Dante's breaking the stone font to save a human life would be an allegory of his 'breaking' the rock of the papacy, the Petrine rock, insofar as this had become oppressive and deadly for the spiritual life of mankind. As an interpretation of the images involved, taken in themselves, this seems to me plausible; but also a trifle far-fetched when tested by linguistic and grammatical analysis of verse 21 in its adjacent context.

10. The chief texts are, of course, *Paradiso* XV, 134-135; XXV, 7-12.
11. The lecture was the first of the Barlow Lectures on Dante for 1969, given by Mr. J. A. Scott. The article by Spitzer (used also by Miss Noakes and discussed by Pagliaro) is the first of 'Two Dante Notes' in *Romanic Review*, XXXIV (1943), 248-262.

Verses 31 to 45 are the immediate preparation for the central act
of the canto, but a deliberately gradual preparation, the main
emphasis in which falls on the unity of Dante and Virgil, their
perfect mutual understanding – to the point, it would seem, of their
exchanging a smile or two; for surely there is a trace of shared irony
in the little dialogue of verses 31-39, especially in the malicious zest
of Dante's question – 'sì cruccia . . . guizzando . . . più roggia fiam-
ma succia' – and in Virgil's very dry last line (36). But of course the
agreement of the poets goes far deeper than shared amusement, and
when this motif is resumed, and very persistently, at the canto's
close, the only sentiment remaining will be a gentle grave concord.
The unity, in any case, of Virgil and Dante is a vital factor in this
canto; for Christianity gone rotten is an offence to reason. The main
action that starts at verse 46 divides, as I have said, into two chief
phases. The first might be entitled, 'the Disclosures of Pope
Nicholas'; the second, beginning at verse 88, is Dante's judgment
on the contemporary papacy in the light of those disclosures. The
structure is dialectical in the sense that the judgment is a conclusion
drawn from premises supplied by Nicholas. But it is worth noting
that it is not Dante who begins the judging and condemning.
Nicholas' two speeches, the abrupt outburst of verses 52-57, and
the longer speech beginning at verse 66, are full of sharp acrid moral
comment – first, on Boniface VIII, verses 55-57 ('Se' tu sì tosto di
quell'aver sazio' etc.), then on himself, verses 70-72 ('e veramente
fui figliuol de l'orsa/ cupido sì' etc.) and finally, and still more grim-
ly, on Clement V, verses 82-84 (. . . 'verrà di più laida opra/ . . . un
pastor sanza legge . . .'). Indeed Nicholas, in his rather base way,
seems to be more preoccupied with morality than any of the other
major self-exposers in the *Inferno*, except perhaps Vanni Fucci. It is
precisely as a moral delinquent that he brands himself and his
fellow-popes. Yes, his fellow-popes; what he exposes is a *series*, a line
of evil men, one succeeding the other in the same high office and in
a similar abuse of it. Stuck head downwards in his hole, Nicholas
appears as but one link in an evil chain forever moving steadily
downwards; below him are those who, in his own words, 'went
before' him in simony; above him, moving ever closer in time, are
the shadows of other evil men who, one by one, will take the place
which he now occupies in the same horrible moving chain. We
begin to realize that Dante's image of the friar confessor in verses

49-51 is more than mere simile: sin really *is* being confessed, though without hope of absolution, and – as a further paradox in the whole topsy-turvy situation, both physically and morally 'upside down' – though the normal roles are reversed and here it is the layman who judges the priest, the successor of those to whom Christ had said: 'Whose sins you shall forgive, they are forgiven.'

But the whole scene is a careful depiction of abnormality and perversion. The papacy was founded on Peter the Rock, and here the popes are planted head down in 'pietra livida,' livid stone, symbols of contradiction of the sacred order they abused; and the rock is 'livid', calling to mind by contrast that block of bright diamond under the feet of the enthroned Angel of the Church in *Purgatorio* IX, the Angel who carried the keys of the sacrament of Penance and lets Dante into Purgatory. And whereas at Pentecost the fire of the Holy Spirit had come and flamed like tongues on the heads of the Apostles, here it is the grotesquely upturned feet of false Apostles that are aflame.[12] A kind of Anti-Church is being depicted.

Let us now run through this central action from the moment when Virgil sets Dante down on the floor of the *bolgia* (vv. 44-45). The poets are now standing beside the hole from which protrude, kicking madly, the two burning feet which had attracted Dante's special attention. Stooping down to the mouth of the hole (the stoop is given in the simile of the friar confessor inserted here), Dante calls to the sinner, at the same time reminding him of his odd position: 'Speak if you can.' At once from out of the hole comes a cry of astonishment: 'Is that you already, Boniface?'; followed by a curt testy 'aside' and then the long jeering question of verses 55-57. And all is now clear – for us if not for Dante as a character in his own play. The sinner knows that Boniface VIII is to be damned, and to this particular hole, and has jumped to the conclusion that this new arrival is he, although Boniface was not due to arrive – and hence the astonishment – for another three years and more. We are now, let us remember, in the spring of 1300. Pope Nicholas had died in August 1280; Boniface will die in October 1303. Be it noted in passing that verses 55-57 reflect a common belief, shared by Dante, that the forceful and resourceful Boniface had bullied his predecessor, St. Celestine V, into resigning the papal throne to make

12. Another intended stroke in Dante's caricature is probably 'si piangeva con la *zanca*' (v. 45), as E. N. Kaulbach has shown in *Dante Studies*, LXXXVI (1968), 127-135.

way for himself.[13] The Fair Lady is of course the Church. We can skip the half-humorous exchange between Virgil and Dante that follows, only noting the delightful 'quasi scornati' in verse 60.

When the voice comes again from the hole it is almost volubly informative. It tells us that the speaker was a pope (v. 69); and we note that the words 'I was clothed with the great mantle' will be deliberately echoed in the canto parallel to this in *Purgatorio*, where another pope, Adrian V, whom Dante meets there among the penitent avaricious will speak of 'il gran manto.' Then, fiercely punning on the name, the speaker declares himself an Orsini and a nepotist, that is, Giovanni Orsini, pope as Nicholas III from 1277 to 1280. The next two tercets add that he was a simoniac, and one of a line of such sinners who are being thrust down successively into the rocky floor, the next one due to arrive being, as we now know, Boniface VIII, pope from 1294 to 1303; and this glance into the future is ominous of further prophecy to come. But besides all these facts, the voice reveals something else: a character. There are greater characters in the *Inferno*, but none more vividly presented than this fretful, sharp-tongued, irascible priest — who is presented, let us remember, only through his voice, he is never *seen*. It is notable how the shifts of tone in this speech successively light up different facets of a personality: the irritation in verse 54; the savage glee, in the following tercet, over the sins of Boniface; the peevish wail of 'Dunque che a me richiedi?' followed by the quick change to jesting self-mocking wit in verses 70-72, and thence to the harsh objectivity of the next six verses; and finally the sudden 'lift' from the racy humorous colloquialisms of verses 79-81 to the menacing gravity of 'che dopo lui verrà di più laida opra/di ver' ponente un pastor sanza

13. G. Villani, *Cronica*, VIII, 5-6, Cf. Bruno Nardi, 'Dante e Celestino V,' espec. pp. 316-318, in *Dal 'Convivio' alla 'Commedia,'* (Roma, 1960). Michael Wilks, in *The Problem of Sovereignty in the Later Middle Ages* ... (Cambridge: University Press, 1963), p. 497, n. 2, refers, 'for a survey of contemporary opinion,' to W. Ullmann, 'Medieval Views concerning Papal Abdication,' in *Irish Ecclesiastical Review*, LXXI (1949), 125-133; and notes that 'the outcry against Celestine's resignation was largely a propaganda weapon in the contest between the Colonna and Boniface VIII, but it served to bring up for discussion the whole nature of the papal office.' Naturally, the 'Spiritual' Franciscans tended to reject Celestine's resignation, though it was defended by the great Olivi (see *Archivium Franciscanum Historicum*, XI [1918], 309-373): it was rejected, e.g., by the anonymous author of the *Liber de Flore* (see H. Grundmann in *Historisches Jahrbuch im Auflage der Görres-Gesellschaft* ... XLIX [1929], 33-91) and by Ubertino da Casale, *Arbor Vitae Crucifixae Jesu* (Venice, 1485; phototype ed., Torino: Bottega d'Erasmo, 1961), v, cols. 7-8. See also Arsenio Frugoni, *Celestiniana* (Roma, 1954), pp. 95-100; Douie, *op. cit.*, pp. 43-44, 56-57.

legge,' with the rest to the end of the speech. It is brilliant characterization, a small *tour de force* of satiric drama.

Yet what does it tell us of the real Nicholas III? Little enough, no doubt. To the historian it will seem hardly more than a one-sided summary of memories and gossip that were circulating in Italy at that time and are recorded, for example, but more critically, by the chronicler Giovanni Villani: [14] memories of a rather wordly pope whose nepotism had been notorious — but whose more defensible policies seem to have been as unappreciated as they were in effect unsuccessful. But these policies had one overriding and not discreditable aim, to reassert the independence of the Holy See against the French power in Italy represented by the masterful Charles of Anjou, king of Naples and Sicily since his victory — as champion of the Church — over Frederick II's son Manfred in 1266. Nicholas as a cardinal had been leader of the anti-French party in the Curia, and as pope he used every means at his disposal, and he was not overscrupulous, to check and reduce the power of Charles. It is then rather curious that Dante, who detested and feared the French power in Europe, should have been so hard on this pope. Perhaps as a Florentine he bore Nicholas a grudge for his interventions in Tuscany.[15] Perhaps as a political anticlerical he was repelled by this pope's designs over the Romagna. More probably he seized on the nepotism of Nicholas as a particularly clear sign of the moral decline of the papacy (rather as Villani had done).[16] And then he was also perhaps, after all, attracted as an artist by the idea of having a fairly recent pope in his hell who could prophecy, from the right chronological distance, the damnations of Boniface VIII and Clement V, those inevitable reprobates. Compared with these two, anyhow, Nicholas is a minor figure in the *Comedy* — a voice from the past to illustrate a thesis and serve as a weapon. The more present enemies were Boniface and Clement; especially the proud, gifted, violent Boniface whom Dante had met face to face in Rome in the autumn of 1301, and for whom he may even have felt a certain

14. G. Villani, *Cronica*, VII, 54. See Waley, *op. cit.*, chap. vi, on the character and policies of Nicholas III; also Steven Runciman. *The Sicilian Vespers: A History of the Mediterranean World in the Later 13th Century* (Cambridge: University Press, 1958), pp. 182-190.
15. This is P. Brezzi's explanation, in *Nuove letture dantesche, ed. cit.*, pp. 171-172, on the authority of Leonardo Bruni; but it is a mere hypothesis.
16. D. P. Waley remarks: 'There was an unspiritual zeal about Nicholas III's family policy ... which had the flavour more of what was to follow than of what had come before' (*op. cit.*, p. 189).

grudging admiration.[17] But the role of Boniface in the *Comedy* is too big a topic to be explored here: enough to remark that he stands out in the poem as the corrupt priest *par excellence*, 'the Prince of the new Pharisees,' the very embodiment of the Church's betrayal of Christ; and that in taking this one-sided and extreme view of Boniface, Dante was of course at one with other Catholic reformers of his time like the Franciscans Jacopone da Todi and Ubertino da Casale — though, unlike Ubertino, Dante never identifies Boniface with Antichrist. As for Clement V, though he receives the hardest judgment here (v. 82), the reason may be rhetorical as much as anything; on the whole, he is a remoter figure in the *Comedy* and no less despised than hated — hated as the 'Gascon' who betrayed the noble Emperor Henry VII [18] and despised as the servile tool of Dante's transalpine *bête noire*, the French king Philip the Fair (vv. 84-87).

This king, as we know, had challenged the papal authority over the matter of the taxation of the French clergy. The resulting conflict, one of the turning points in Church history, brought Boniface VIII to his grave, a broken man. He was succeeded by the conciliatory Dominican Boccasini, Benedict XI, who died, however, within a year of his election, in July 1304. After a long interval, and much tension between the pro- and anti-French parties in the Curia, the Archbishop of Bordeaux, Bertrand de Got, became pope as Clement V, in June 1305. Clement, as a then subject of the king of England, was a compromise choice; but his election was to prove another gain for France; and though Avignon, where he established the Curia in 1309, lay outside the domain of the king of France, the papacy remained, for the rest of Clement's pontificate, firmly under French influence. An intelligent man but sickly and uninspiring, Clement could only struggle, rather feebly, to make the best of a bad situation. He died on April 20, 1314, and this date brings us back to our text; for verses 79-84 contain a prophecy that Clement V will die less than twenty-three years after the encounter of Dante and Nicholas III in hell; that is, before 1323, since Dante journeyed through hell in the spring of 1300. What Nicholas actually says — to give the gist of it — is that he has been for a longer

---

17. Dino Compagni, *Cronica*, II, xxv (cf. iv and xi). See A. Frugoni, 'Dante e la Roma del suo tempo,' in *Dante e Roma, op. cit.*, pp. 73-96.
18. *Paradiso* XVII, 82; cf. XXX, 142-148.

time *half*-buried in the rock than Boniface will be. Now Nicholas
has been like this for twenty years. In three and a half years' time —
in October 1303 — Boniface will arrive and take up the same position, pushing Nicholas underground; but will himself remain half-
buried for less than twenty years, for within that time Clement V
will arrive and bury *him*. In themselves these are sordid details but
they raise an important question, which however I do not propose
to discuss here: the date of the composition of the *Inferno*. For clearly, on the face of it, they seem to imply that about half of the *Inferno*
must have been written after Pope Clement's death in April 1314;
which on other grounds would seem implausibly late. But, patently,
for our present purpose it does not really matter whether, in composing this canto, Dante knew that Clement was dead or only
reckoned that he would be before a certain date. The point has
nothing to do with the canto as poetry.

So to the poetry let us return. We have reached the point — verse
88 — where Dante draws his conclusions from all he has seen and
heard in this *bolgia*. The indictment that follows, if not perhaps the
most moving statement in the *Comedy* of his case against the rulers
of the Church, is the most complete one; more so even than the invective of St. Peter in *Paradiso* XXVII. In essence it is a simple
case: the Church has been corrupted by the desire for money and
possessions, in a word, by cupidity — *cupidigia, cupidità, avarizia* —
and by the political ambitions that this desire involved. But here in
Inferno XIX the main stress falls on the lust for material possessions.

The reasoning behind this indictment is set out with all logical
rigour in the Third Book of the *Monarchia*, especially chapters x
to xiv, where all that is said on his topic in the *Comedy* finds its
equivalent in analytical prose; while in a very different style it is
summed up once again in the great Letter to the Italian Cardinals,
written in the summer of 1314. Both of these prose texts should be
studied by whoever would get below the surface of Dante's
Catholicism and understand how a real belief in the Church and
reverence for the papacy could go hand in hand with the freedom of
thought and speech that he claimed and used. I would refer particularly to chapters iii and xiv of *Monarchia* III; [19] the former text
to compare with verses 100-101 of our canto, the latter as a gloss

19. In the critical edition (Milano, 1965) by Pier Giorgio Ricci in the Edizione
Nazionale of Dante's works sponsored by the Società Dantesca Italiana.

especially on verses 90-96. In that chapter iii, then, Dante is preparing the ground for what was to be his major prose critique of the
Church authorities; and the point to note is how warily he does this,
how carefully he wards off in advance the inevitable charge of impiety and insubordination; exactly as he again does in our canto, at
verses 100-104 (and probably, as I think, already at verses 19-21).
Of course the *Monarchia* is an entirely different kind of work from
the *Comedy*: it aims at rational persuasion. And the Third Book is
aimed at persuading antagonists whom Dante professes to respect.
For among the upholders of the thesis that he is out to destroy, the
thesis that the Church has supreme *political* authority on earth and
that the civil power, and specifically the Empire, has authority and
jurisdiction only through and from the Church, among the upholders of this clericalist or papalist view, Dante expressly distinguishes those who adopt it out of pure good faith, out of a
genuine 'zeal for the Keys,' as he puts it, out of 'zeal for Mother
Church' and a sincere conviction that any other position would be a
betrayal of the Catholic faith. And addressing himself only to such
worthy adversaries as these, Dante begins by insisting that he too is
moved by a sincere zeal for Mother Church ('la reverenza de le
somme chiavi'); and so concludes his preface declaring that his argument will be only with such as these, that his one aim is to show
them a truth which they do not yet see, and that he approaches both
his argument and his adversaries with all due reverence: 'cum quibus
illa reverentia fretus quam *pius* fillius debet patri, quam *pius* filius
matri, *pius* in Christum, *pius* in Ecclesiam, *pius* in pastorem, *pius* in
omnes cristianam religionem profitentes, pro salute veritatis in hoc
libro certamen incipio.' [20] Six times in one sentence that almost
untranslatable word *pius*, adduced like a pass-word, a certificate of
his right to speak on this subject at all. And it was not mere policy,
much less timidity, that made Dante so guarded. It was, quite simply, that he was 'pius in Ecclesiam,' he really did revere the Church;
and he thought in his candour that it was precisely the sincerity of
his reverence that gave him the right to speak with apparent
irreverence.

The other phrase I want to cite from the *Monarchia* occurs
towards the end of the work, in the course of a direct refutation of

20. *Monarchia* III, iii, 18.

the 'papalist' thesis that the Emperor got his authority to rule only through the pope (which, applied to the civil power generally, was implicitly the thesis of Boniface VIII in the famous Bull *Unam Sanctam* of 1300).[21] Thus the immediate context of the words I shall quote is an argument about jurisdiction; but implied in it is the burning issue which the 'Spiritual' Franciscans of that time so persistently raised and which predominates in canto XIX of the *Inferno*: the issue that focussed on the question whether the Church, in the sense of the clerical body, the pope, and the hierarchy, was obliged to practise evangelical poverty. Dante's own views on this matter were perhaps not so extreme as those of some of the 'Spirituals'; but that is a nuance we do not need to define. They were severe views, in any case, and based, of course, on the words and example of Christ himself. This was usual; but the way in which Dante formulates the authority, for the Church, of Christ's example is characteristically energetic and of great importance for an understanding of the opening lines of the speech we are examining, the splendid ironic question in verses 90-93. Basically, the reason why, for Dante, the Church cannot be a *political* authority is that her Founder chose to renounce all such authority, declaring to Pilate (appropriately): 'My kingdom is not of this world.' [22] And similarly, the reason why the Church ought to be poor — and even radically propertyless — is that Christ was extremely poor and called his Apostles to a like poverty.[23] And his example has the force of law, indeed, where the Church is concerned, of a law of nature: 'Forma ... Ecclesie nichil aliud est quam vita Christi, tam in dictis quam in factis comprehensa: vita enim ipsius ydea fuit et exemplar militantis Ecclesie, presertim pastorum, maxime summi, cuius est-pascere agnos et oves.' [24]

This great text is the best single gloss on *Inferno* XIX. For it would be to interpret this canto too narrowly to see it merely as directed against simony in the technical sense. It is that, but also more than that. Dante is not merely objecting to the spiritual distortion involved in putting sacraments up for sale; or rather he is denouncing in this particular priestly sin the deeper and more com-

21. *Enchiridion Symbolorum*, ed. Denzinger-Schönmetzer, 32nd ed., 1963, no. 873.
22. *Monarchia* III, xiv, 5.
23. *Ibid.* III, x, 14-17.
24. *Ibid.* III, xiv, 3.

prehensive evil that it implies, the evil symbolized – crudely, but so effectively! – in the head down posture of the popes and their flaming feet. One way of pointing to this deeper evil is to say that in these priests the Church is shown as having lost the sense of her own identity; for of her very nature the Church is an aspiration towards an end *beyond* this present world, towards Christ now risen from the dead and in glory, whereas these churchmen lived only for mortal and temporal ends. In them the Church is travestied. Their simony was merely the expression and bringing to light of a radical inversion of values, a substitution of what the Bride of Christ is *for* by what she precisely is *not* for. From a different angle the same point is put, in his terse way, by St. Thomas, when he explains that it is always wrong to sell a sacrament, because it is a vehicle of grace, and it is against the nature of grace to be given otherwise than freely: 'gratiae . . . rationi repugnat quod non gratuito detur.' [25]

To turn back now to our text, the indictment that begins at verse 90 is a kind of oration, and like all such passages in the *Comedy* it has a close-knit rhetorical structure, while at the same time it achieves an effect of urgent and passionate spontaneity. It falls into two movements, each preceded by a pause, a sort of hesitation: the first at verse 88, 'Io non so' etc., and the second at the wonderfully effective 'break' in verses 100-103. In style and diction the whole piece is very simple and direct, except that the biblical image of the harlot seated over the waters (vv. 106-108) is a bit overworked in the tercet that follows – the only infelicity I find in this speech. In the first part or movement, as I called it, Pope Nicholas is addressed individually in the second person singular; in the second it is the corrupt papacy in general that is addressed – the pronouns changing to the plural, 'vostra' and 'voi' – this wider perspective having been opened up by the strong and stately verse 101 alluding to the keys of St. Peter; while the 'hesitation' conveyed in this and the preceding verse serves as a springboard for the renewed polemical movement that follows, the direct onslaught of 'chè la vostra avarizia il mondo attrista' etc. Thus the indictment gathers force as it proceeds, though always in dependence on that appeal to the examples of Christ and the Apostles back in verses 91-96. The renewed attack, from verse 104 on, is delivered in three successive blows

25. *Summa theologiae* 2a2ae. 100, 2.

of increasing weight. The first is a *sententia*, the generalized moral judgment which thuds home with the two heavy gerunds in verse 105: 'ché la vostra avarizia il mondo attrista/calcando i buoni e sollevando i pravi.' The next blow – reinforced by yet another recall to the New Testament – is in the long contemptuous verb 'puttaneggiar' which dominates verse 108. The third blow – delayed a moment by verses 109-111 – comes straight from the shoulder with the first verse of the following tercet; a direct accusation of the worst crime in the religious order, idolatry: 'Fatto v'avete dio d'oro e d'argento.' Finally, all is rounded off with another apostrophe, the third of the canto, 'Ahi Costantin.'

A few words are in order on this short sad address to Constantine.[26] Its function is to set the indictment of the popes in

---

26. In the following paragraph I limit myself to a broad exposition of Dante's view of the Donation as an historical disaster, without going into the particular questions so sharply raised by B. Nardi, in *Nel mondo di Dante* (Rome: Edizioni di Storia e Letteratura, 1944), pp. 109 ff, and again in *Dal 'Convivio' alla 'Commedia,'* ed. cit., pp. 238-257; namely, whether Dante had ever read the text of the Donation, and precisely what, in his view, Constantine had 'given' to the Church. The latter question is of course the more important one; and Nardi's answer to it entails a certain interpretation of the phrase 'quella dote' in our canto, verse 116. According to Nardi, Dante thought that Constantine had originally intended the 'donation' in a sense to which no exception could be taken, either from the point of view of the Empire or from that of the Church; he intended, that is, to concede temporal power to the Pope 'non tanquam possessor, sed tanquam fructuum pro Ecclesia pro Christi pauperibus dispensator' (*Mon.* III, x, 17), he himself retaining possession in the full sense ('immoto semper superiori dominio,' *ibid.* 16). Thus Dante, in Nardi's view, limited 'la portata della donazione da lui (Constantine) fatta alla Chiesa' (*Dal 'Convivio' alla 'Commedia,'* p. 242); and this would explain two things: (a) the fact that Dante persistently *excuses* Constantine (*Purg.* XXXII, 138; *Par.* XX, 55-60; and cf. 'sua pia intentio,' *Mon.* II, xi, 8); and (b) that in *Inf.* XIX, 116, he calls the Donation merely a 'dote' ('. . . pare evidente che Dante, ignorando il tenore esatto della *donatio*, . . . l'ha interpretata nel senso di una "dote" che Costantino avrebbe formato per il sostentamento degli ecclesiastici e per i bisogni dei poveri,' *Nel mondo di Dante*, p. 146). Now, whether or not Dante had actually read the text of the Donation, Nardi's view of what he thought Constantine originally intended to give to the Church does not stand up to criticism. The arguments against it are marshalled by Pagliaro in *Ulisse*, I, pp. 281-289, and may be summarised in three points. (I) The image of the 'dote' in *Inf.* XIX, 116, merely continues the metaphor of the Church as Spouse (vv. 3 and 55-57); there is no reason to see in it an implicit definition of the *kind* of gift Constantine gave the Church; especially in view of the total absence of the 'dowry' image in the demonstration of the illegitimacy of the Donation *Mon.* II, x. (2) Dante does not in fact limit the 'portata' of the Donation in *Mon.* III, x: Nardi's linguistic argument to show that he does can be refuted by closer analysis of the texts (Pagliaro, *op. cit.*, espec. p. 284, n. 19: and cf. G. Vinay, ed., *Monarchia* (Firenze, 1950, pp. 246-247, n. I). (3) As for the 'pia intentio' ascribed to Constantine by Dante, this is sufficiently explained as 'quella che la tradizione voleva, cioè il sentimento di filiale riconoscenza' for the great benefit received by the Emperor from Pope Silvester (Pagliaro, p. 285); while the 'forse' inserted in *Purg.* XXXII, 138, would seem to allude to the suspicion, voiced by some of the Imperialist party, that the Donation, as a payment for baptism, was an act of simony. And one might add that even if Dante, in *Purg.* XXXII, was willing

historical perspective, to point to an important cause of the evils denounced that lay outside the will of this or that individual pope, and indeed of the whole papal line, being located in the bad decision of an Emperor – traditionally the first who was also a Christian, Constantine the Great. By his famous 'Donation' Constantine was supposed to have handed over to the Roman Pontiff political power over the West. The Donation is of course a ninth-century forgery, but Dante did not know this, and he thought it the most disastrous political error ever committed, for its effect had been to confuse the spheres of activity of the two powers to whom God had entrusted the government of mankind. Dante's historical vision was essentially the western medieval one which saw all history converging on two successive points: first on Rome and then on Christ. Or again, one might say that for him human history proceeded as two distinct but not, in principle, opposed movements: a horizontal movement, so to say, bringing people and nations together into the Pax Romana, and a vertical movement bringing human beings and God together in the Incarnate Logos. And these two movements entailed two distinct spheres of activity and jurisdiction: that of the Empire and that of the Church. Such was the divine design for mankind. But human malice and folly had disrupted the sacred order, confusing the two spheres of activity and authority. The fault lay chiefly with the Church which had tried to usurp on earth the functions of the State; but the way to that usurpation had been opened by Constantine's disastrous error. Again and again Dante returns to this point, with grief and fury, in his mature works: in the *Monarchia* III, x; here in *Inferno* XIX, and again in canto XXVII; in *Purgatorio* XXXII; and finally in *Paradiso* XX. There could be no peace on earth, he thought, and no reform of the Church, except by reversing the entire historical process which the Donation had started; except by Caesar's reclaiming what was his, so that the Church might freely attend to her proper business, the Kingdom of God. And because

---

to entertain the suspicion that Constantine's part in the business was simoniacal, he had withdrawn the suspicion in *Par.* XX, 55-60, where, as Pagliaro says, the *donatio* 'oltre a essere ispirato da una pia intenzione, era in sè anche un "bene operar" ' (*op. cit.*, p. 286). For a learned and balanced account of the Donation as a factor in Church history down to the eleventh century, see Y.M-J. Congar, *L'ecclésiologie du haut moyen âge* ... (Paris: Editions du Cerf, 1968), pp. 198-202. Congar's judgment on the Donation is not so far from Dante's own – "un des faux qui a fait plus de mal à l'Eglise: elle a en effet favorisé une évolution de l'idéologie papale dans un sens de puissance politique et d'allure impériale.' He provides a full bibliography.

the clergy as a body were set against so radical a *volte face*, Dante became politically an anticlerical.

A further point to note, in this speech of his, is the difference of tone and attitude adopted in the two parts into which it falls. Dante begins on an ironic note, 'Deh, or mi dì,' and though the tone is of course serious, it is also conversational, with the poet offering the pope an argument for his consideration. Nicholas is hardly in a position for cool reasoning, but Dante has a good case and can take his time, before drawing, at verse 97, his merciless conclusion: 'Però ti sta, chè tu se' ben punito,' with the cruel jest that immediately follows and which refers to the part that Nicholas was widely supposed to have played in bringing about the revolt of Sicily against Charles of Anjou in 1282, the so-called Sicilian Vespers. Rumour had it that the pope had been bribed with Byzantine gold to give his support to the great anti-Angevin conspiracy organized by King Peter of Aragon's agent, the famous John of Procida. The story of the bribing is dubious and in any case Dante, as I have remarked, was not a discerning or fair-minded judge of Nicholas III's policies regarding Charles of Anjou.[27] His gibe is well turned, but sounds spiteful.

But then Dante finds his truer voice and the invective mounts *crescendo* by the stages already analyzed. And now the tone too has changed, becoming assertive, oracular, prophetic. Not that reasoning is eclipsed altogether; verse 105 condenses all the argument required to support the moral judgment in the preceding line. It is worth noting, by the way, that this judgment has to do with simony under its *social* aspect; the society directly envisaged being of course the Christian society of the Church, while the 'matter' that the sin of simony directly bears on here is not any sacrament as such, but rather the pastoral offices and ministries. So I would interpret these two lines as saying, in effect, that the papal 'avarizia' (a wider term in Dante than our 'avarice,' it means the uncontrolled desire for possessions) that this 'avarizia' has spread a gloom, a depression, a general loss of confidence through Christendom inasmuch as the faithful have come to expect that their spiritual pastors will usually be careerists who have paid for their appointments. The popes are

27. On this matter, see Villani, *Cronica*, VII, 54 and 57; S. Runciman, *The Sicilian Vespers, op. cit.*, Chapters xii and xiii; D. Waley, *The Papal State in the Thirteenth Century, op. cit.*, Chap. vi; Pagliaro, *Ulisse*, 1, p. 278.

sinners, that is to say, against what the scholastics called distributive justice, the virtue of the good ruler who knows how to deal out responsibilities and rewards through a given society in view of the common good.[28] In this perspective, then, the judgment in verses 104-105 bears on a form of corruption that might be found in any society and has nothing to do as such with the Church. It springs from Dante's general study and experience of politics; and indeed, considered from this point of view, might just as well have been pronounced in other parts of the *Inferno*. At least this item in Dante's indictment, otherwise so full of specifically Christian allusions, must have been readily intelligible to the sympathetically attentive Virgil.

I conclude my remarks on this speech, and on the canto as a whole, with a few words on a significant feature of its language, the way Dante, while ringing the changes on terms denoting money and material possessions, returns with a certain persistence to the same expression, 'gold and silver.'[29] This expression is taken from the Bible and its repetition — it occurs three times — is a factor in the markedly biblical flavour of the canto as a whole. The Simoniacs, in the opening cry, are those who prostitute sacred things 'per oro e per argento,' which, fifty verses on, in the first thrust at Boniface VIII (v. 55), become 'aver,' possessions, and this word is repeated in verse 72, in the concrete sense of money kept in a purse. Then, in the first half of Dante's final speech, we get the three synonyms, 'treasure,' 'gold and silver,' and lastly the clinching term 'money,' 'moneta.' The chief biblical texts so far recalled are, in the first place, Our Lord's charge to the Apostles (Matthew 10:8-9 and parallels): 'Freely have you received, freely give. Take no gold or silver or copper in your purses'; and then Peter's answer to the beggar at the Temple gate in Acts 3:6: 'Silver and gold I have none, but what I have I give you: in the name of Jesus of Nazareth, get up and walk.' But when the phrase is used for the third time, associating avarice with idolatry (v. 112), the echoes come rather from the Old Testament, from the Psalms and Isaiah and Hosea, from all that ancient polemic against idolatry which Christianity sanctioned and presupposed; but most directly no doubt from the words of Hosea: 'Of

28. See St. Thomas Aquinas, *In libros Ethicorum Aristotelis expositio*, V, lect. 4-6; *Summa theologiae*, 2a2ae. 61, 1-4.
29. See E. Sanguineti, *Interpretazione di Malebolge, op. cit.*, 61-63.

their silver and gold they have made idols' (8:4).

It is within this fierce biblical tradition, descended from the Prophets and sanctioned by Christ himself and all primitive Christianity, that we have to set *Inferno* XIX. That is the line and tradition to which it belongs, the great Judaeo-Christian tradition of religious anti-materialism, anti-Mammon; the tradition so vigorously continued into the Middle Ages by the reforming popes of the eleventh century, by St. Bernard in the twelfth,[30] and by the Franciscan enthusiasts of the thirteenth.

The canto ends quietly, as I have said; and with a renewed emphasis on Virgil's agreement with the Christian poet. He carried Dante 'right to the top of the arch' that joins this ditch with the next. There he sets him gently down, 'where another valley was disclosed to me.'

30. Especially in the *De Consideratione ad Eugenium Papam*, I-IV (*S. Bernardi Opera*, III: *Tractatus et Opuscula*, ed. J. Leclercq and H. M. Rochais, [Rome: Editions Cistercienses, 1963], pp. 393-466). See W. Williams, *Saint Bernard of Clairvaux* (Manchester: University Press, 1935; reprinted 1952), Chap. xi.

7

THE HUMAN SPIRIT IN ACTION:
PURGATORIO XVII

C anto XVII is exactly at the centre of the *Purgatorio* numerically: sixteen cantos precede it and sixteen follow. But in the action of the *cantica* as a whole its place is less central, because the *Purgatorio* moves rather slowly at the beginning. What may be called Purgatory proper only begins with Dante's admission by the key-bearing Angel at the end of canto IX: it then extends over the next eighteen cantos (X to XVII) composing the main central section of the *cantica*, the account of Dante's progress up the seven terraces where the seven major vices are successively purged away: pride, envy, anger, sloth, covetousness, gluttony, lechery. Of these eighteen cantos ours is the eighth. When it begins Dante and Virgil are just about to leave the third terrace, that of anger; when it ends, they have reached the top of the stairway leading up to the next terrace above it, that of sloth. At this point night has already fallen, Dante's second night on the Mountain, and Virgil has already begun a major doctrinal discourse which will continue, in fact, well into the next canto. This discourse ended, Dante will have a brief encounter with the slothful on the fourth terrace. He will then fall asleep (end of XVIII) and have his dream of the Siren (the beginning of XIX). Only after waking from this dream will he at last set foot on the fourth terrace; whence, however, he will quickly pass on up to the next circle, that of the covetous.

In terms of place and time, then, this is a canto of transitions. It starts on the third terrace and ends high on the stairway up to the fourth; it begins a little before and ends a little after sunset. The transition from terrace to stairway comes at verses 64-69, that from evening to night at verses 70-78. Virgil's discourse begins at verse 91 and goes on to the end. Thus the canto falls into three parts: verses 1-69, describing Dante's experiences from the moment when he and Virgil begin to emerge from the dark fog of the terrace of

Anger to when they start to climb the stairway; verses 70-90, a short linking passage about the setting of the sun and the two poets' consequent halt for the night at the top of the stair; verses 91-139, Virgil's discourse on love and its perversions. Leaving these last sections for the moment, we can subdivide the first one again into three. Verses 1-12 are introductory; verses 13-39 describe a wholly interior event, the three images of Wrath that enter Dante's mind at this point and complete his experience of the terrace of anger which he is about to leave behind; then verses 40-69 describe his and Virgil's encounter with the Angel of Gentleness at the foot of the stairway.

This brief outline may have already indicated that canto xvii is not, in the ordinary sense, at all dramatic. There are no human encounters; no one is met except an angel; and the main stress is on *interior* events taking place in the mind imagining and reasoning. If there is drama here it is a specimen of what Francis Fergusson has called Dante's drama of the mind. Two powers of the mind are shown in action successively; that of forming images and that of discerning truth. The former, the imagination, appears as a wonderfully mobile yet radically passive response to stimuli that remain largely hidden, mysterious; the latter, the reason, is shown, in the last fifty lines of the canto, as entirely concentrated, actively, on its proper work of clarifying concepts. And the special quality of the canto is to be looked for, I suggest, precisely in the balance and contrast of these two complementary activities.

To turn to the beginning: 'Remember, reader ...' This address to the reader, abruptly opening the canto, is intended, obviously, to convey with all possible freshness and immediacy a visual experience. And how well it succeeds! – we are at once, in imagination, on a path over high hills shrouded in mist and cloud. The instrument the poet plays on is our memory; his material, the similarities of ordinary experience. Already at the end of the previous canto Marco Lombardo, bidding farewell to the poets and turning back into the fog of his terrace, had registered the sharp visual experience which is now elaborated: the white glow that Marco had noted shining through the fog now becomes, as the clouds thin out and become transparent, the delicately appearing disk of the sun showing faintly through the mist. We should note the sensitive word-placing – 'in the mountains' in verse 1 arousing an attention which the vivid 'a mist caught you' then satisfies; and similarly *spera* 'disk' in *enjambement* with *del sol*, etc., in verses 5-6. The quasi simile, exploiting the natural interchange of memory and imagination, is completed in the third tercet with the extremely felicitous *e fia la tua imagine leggiera/in giugnere*; where *leggiera* 'light', standing for ease of apprehension, is itself suggestive of the airy mountain scene evoked. Then verses 8 and 9 and the following tercet brings us back to the poet himself as he comes out of the mist and at once looks outwards and downwards with a glance that sweeps back from the westering sun to the great zone of shadow now gathering around the base of the Mountain.

The effect of all this rapid word-painting has been to make the external objective scene vividly present – the mist clearing away, the sun drawing down to the horizon, the mounting zone of darkness. But now, at verse 13, with a sudden shift of perspective in the reverse direction, our attention is switched to the poet's consciousness itself as successively filled by three images of Wrath: one from classical myth, one from the Old Testament, one from Virgil's *Aeneid*. But the point to stress is not so much the subjectivity of this new experience as its abnormality. It is subjective as *not* being an effect of the normal process of image-forming which, starting in sense-perception of the external world, terminates in phantasms preserved in memory – like that mountain scene which the poet's art has just evoked in our memory, so that in imagination ('la tua imagine,' v. 7) we might 'be' with him at this moment of his journey, seeing with him with our inward eye, but as it functions in an ordinary normal way. The three images of Wrath now arising are not however of this kind. What makes them different is not clearly enunciated, but only suggested. Certainly they occur in the image-forming faculty, the 'imaginativa' of verse 13 (where some such noun as 'potenza' is understood). But their source is not normal sense-perception (vv. 16-18); a sign of this being their power sometimes, 'tal volta,' so to seize on and absorb the soul as to render it for a time unaware of even violent external impressions (vv. 13-15). I say a sign rather than a proof of this because I do not think one need understand Dante to be proposing such ecstatic absorption as evidence, in any given case, that a preternatural source of imagery is at work in the soul. That would involve a *non sequitur* which there is no reason to ascribe to him (cf., for example, *Purg.*

IV, 1-12). The image here of a man absorbed in thought while
trumpets blare around him is poetic rhetoric. But the suggestion in
verses 16-18 of a preternatural source of the three 'visions' that
follow is doctrinally as well as poetically important, and it calls for
some elucidation. A doctrine of the imagination is presupposed here
which allows for a distinction between two modes of working of
this faculty, a normal working and an abnormal one, an ordinary
and an extraordinary.

For his theory of imagination in its normal working Dante
depends chiefly on Aristotle (*De Anima* III, 3). On this view images, *phantasmata*, are the end-product of a movement of change, a
movement that begins in the external senses – in the eye as modified
by a visible object, in the ear as affected by a sound. As Aquinas puts
it in his commentary on the *De Anima*: 'actual sensation is a being
moved by a sensible object,' and this movement in turn starts
'another movement which, as it proceeds from sensation, must
resemble sensation [for] that which, being moved, moves another,
must cause a motion similar to its own, and this leads him
[Aristotle] to conclude that imagination is a sort of movement caused by the senses in their act of sensing. It cannot exist without sensation nor in insentient beings' (*Comm.*, lectio VI, on III, 3; §
658-659). An image, then, on this view, is the inward end of a psychic movement that begins in the bodily senses. A further most important point concerns the relation of images to the intellect. On the
Aristotelian view, which Saint Thomas followed, there is no
thought and understanding for human beings without images; they
are the necessary 'matter' from which the mind draws out its ideas.
This doctrine was accepted by Dante. In his prose *Convivio*, speaking of the limitations of human thought he says: 'Owing to the
defect of the faculty whence our intellect has to draw out whatever
it apprehends – this faculty, namely, imagination [*la fantasia*] existing in a bodily organ [*è virtù organica*] – it follows that our mind
cannot rise to the knowledge of beings that are wholly non-material;
for with regard to such things imagination is no help at all, nor can
it be' (III, iv, 9). And the same doctrine is repeated implicitly in
Paradiso IV, 40-42: 'Così parlar conviensi al vostro ingegno,/però
che solo da sensato apprende/ciò che fa poscia d'intelletto degno'
(and cf. X, 43-48).

But in the medieval cosmos human nature was the meeting point of two worlds, the world of matter and the world of spirit; and as man had his spiritual inferiors in the universe, the levels of the animate and inanimate material world, so he had his spiritual superiors, the angelic hierarchies, and above all of course the Deity itself. The thinkers of that time commonly saw no reason why, even from a strictly philosophical point of view, these higher spiritual realities should not at times actively affect the workings of the human psyche, and more particularly the imagination. This attitude was reinforced of course by religion, and particularly by the belief in prophetic inspiration, a belief more or less common to all the three great monotheistic traditions that held the Bible, or parts of it, to be divinely inspired — Judaism, Christianity, and Islam. And so far as Christian theology was concerned, the study of prophetic inspiration, exemplified in the Old and New Testaments, positively demanded a theory of the human imagination as open to influences from higher powers. Such influences were thought of as working, not in place of the natural image-forming faculty, but, presupposing this, by the formation of images in a greater or less independence of external sensation; thus Saint Thomas will say, 'sometimes by divine power phantasms are formed in the imagination which are more expressive of divine things than those which we receive naturally from the sensible world' (*Summa theol.* 1a, 12, 13).

Now it is certain that Dante in the *Comedy* applied this concept of religious inspiration to his own case, either in the sense that he thought that in actually writing the poem he was inspired, like a prophet, or at least in the sense that he made his poem's protagonist to be so inspired. For our purpose it is only necessary to admit that supernatural inspiration occurs, intermittently at least, in the story we are reading. And it occurs of course explicitly here. The literal sense, however, of verses 16-18 remains a little obscure. Certainly in verse 16 we are told that the mechanism of normal imagining was not at work in the three visions that follow. We are then told (vv. 17-18) that these were the effect of a light 'that is formed in heaven,' being produced either by this light 'of itself' or by it as 'guided down' into Dante's psyche by the will of some spiritual agent. Probably by this 'heaven' where the light is formed is meant one of the physical spheres of the medieval cosmos whose power to initiate movements in the human soul has been admitted by Marco Lombardo in canto XVI; while I think it likely that the 'will'

alluded to in verse 18 is that of an angel or group of angels, conceived as movers of such a sphere; so that Dante would here be saying
that his imagination had now come under the influence of a higher
spiritual power working through the physical heavens.

The images of Wrath formed in Dante's imagination as he issues
from the fog of the Angry are in symmetrical correspondence and
contrast with the images of Gentleness which came to him, equally
unbidden and mysteriously, as he was about to enter that fog at the
end of canto XV. There were three images then, as there are three
now: then two figures from the New Testament, Mary and Saint
Stephen, framing one from classical legend, Pisistratus; now two
from classical legend, Procne and Amata, framing one from the Old
Testament, the death of Haman as recounted in the book of Esther.
What distinguishes these new visions of Wrath is a greater subtlety
in the way their actual formation in consciousness is represented.
Poetically what counts most here is the way the images are described as emerging. The first one, that of Procne – the woman
transformed into a nightingale in the macabre fable which Dante
read or misread in Ovid – appears only as a shadowy fleeting im-
print traced on his mind (vv. 19-21). But then suddenly the powerful figure of Haman 'falls' into the 'high fantasy.' The verb *piovve*
'rained down' used as a metaphor comes, incidentally, from the
love-lyric vocabulary, especially Cavalcanti's. But we note how
Haman's entry on the scene, 'falling' from above, contrasts with
that of the third figure, Lavinia, daughter of Amata and sister to
Turnus, who rises from below, ascending into vision (vv. 31-34);
and how, as a further variation, Lavinia arises weeping; and how
her wailing lament at her mother's suicide is heard for a full four
verses (36-39), in strong contrast with the silence of the group that
gathered round the crucified Haman (28-30). And we note finally
how the vanishing of these last two images is differently rendered –
the first with the simile of a bursting bubble (31-33), the second
with that of sleep broken into when a light falls on the sleeper's closed eyes (40-43).

A point of great interest in all this passage is the way the changes
are rung on terms denoting the act or faculty of imagination. At
verse 7, as we have seen, 'la tua imagine' renders the ordinary image-forming faculty. Next, the exclamatory 'O imaginativa' (13) an-
nounces the intervention of a supernatural influence. Then, after a

return to 'imagine' at verse 21, the powerful expression 'l'álta fantasia' (25) evokes almost explicitly the inspired state of the poet's mind — as it will do only once again in the poem, and then close to its absolute climax, only four lines from the end of the *Paradiso* ('a l'alta fantasia qui mancò possa'). At verse 31 we have 'imagine' once more, followed three lines later by 'visione' with its more mystical overtones; and then the sequence is rounded off quietly, almost prosaically by 'l'imaginar' at verse 43. So persistent a circling round one semantic field cannot be fortuitous. It signifies, surely, a deliberate intention to represent the image-forming faculty in action, and this in a variety of ways.

A psychological, quasi-scientific intention of this sort seems indeed to continue through the next dozen verses (43-54); only what is now explored is no longer states of imagination but the visual perception of externals. The third and last image of Wrath breaks and dissolves like a dream and Dante comes to himself, awaking from a kind of sleep of the senses under the shock of a great light striking on his face (43-45); and this light is the radiance of the Angel of this Circle, the Angel of Gentleness who is awaiting the two poets near the foot of the stairway that leads up to the next terrace. And a voice from within the radiance invites them to ascend: 'qui si monta.' The Angel's brightness is overwhelming; Dante has returned to the use of his bodily senses only to find himself here too confronted by a wonder, a kind of miracle, a walking sun. But as Virgil goes on to tell him (55 ff.), the very excess of light here has the quality of a sign: the Angel, concealing himself, like the sun, in his own light, is enacting, visibly and audibly, that selfless love which Christ commanded : 'Do to others as you would be done by.' But especially characteristic, I think, is the simple phrase (59) 'he who waits to be asked.' The true giver gives unasked, for he gives freely and asking is itself a sort of payment, as Seneca observed in a phrase that Dante quotes in the *Convivio* (1, viii, 16) and echoes in his canzone on Liberality, *Doglia mi reca*: 'nothing is bought so dearly as that which has to be begged for.' To see another's need and wait for him to express it by asking is, in a sense, to sell one's gift, it is not to *give*, in the full sense, at all.

But now, with a glance at the setting sun, Virgil has recommended haste (vv. 61-63). So they turn up the stairway, and as they turn a light wind touches Dante's face as from a beating wing, and the

Angel's voice is heard again, pronouncing the seventh Beatitude, 'Blessed are the peacemakers.' Then in the exquisite tercet that follows (70-72) we have one last glimpse of the darkening sky before the poets are halted for the night at the top of the stair. And how lovely in its naturalness and simplicity, after so much preternatural bedazzlement, is this glimpse of the last rays of light fading far overhead and the stars beginning to come out. Not till half-way through the next canto will the sky again be noticed, when, at the close of Virgil's discourse, Dante, who has been rapt in thought as he listened, becomes suddenly aware of the moon going up the night sky 'like a burning bucket' (XVIII, 76-81).

It is the end of the second day on Purgatory. By the law of the Mountain all movement upward stops at nightfall. Dante, halted at the top of the stairway, listens for a moment, but no sound comes from the terrace just above him; so, eager as usual not to waste time, he turns to Virgil for further instruction (79-84). Virgil briefly defines this new circle; it is where a too slack love of the good is corrected (85-87). But the definition itself calls for explanation; for, as involving already the notion of something, 'il bene,' the good, which both demands to be desired and measures the desire it demands, it implies a whole system of ethics. And so Virgil launches into his great discourse (91 ff.).

This discourse, which, as I have said, continues well into the next canto, is in effect an exposition of the foundations of ethics from the standpoint of natural reason and philosophy. Virgil, of course, is not a Christian; he speaks as a sage full of experience and wisdom, but aware of his human limitations. The nearest parallel in the *Comedy* to this speech, especially to this part of it, down to the end of our canto, is the discourse, also pronounced by Virgil, in *Inferno* XI. There he expounded the moral system of Hell in terms of one radical evil, *malizia*, injustice; here he explains the system of Purgatory in terms of a sevenfold perversion of one radical good, which is love, *amor*. The very orderly, logical construction of the two passages is similar, though the style is drier in *Inferno* XI. Each proceeds deductively from the general down to the particular, in virtue of certain basic preliminary distinctions. Each in effect is a kind of lecture, aimed above all at rational persuasion.

The basic idea presupposed here is that of love, viewed in relation to morality; and the basic aim is to reduce morality to a form of loving — or more precisely, so far as this canto is concerned, the aim is to show that immorality, wrongdoing, sin, is nothing but the various ways in which the radical impulse called love can be corrupted or perverted. Love itself is not defined, but clearly it is being taken in the widest possible sense. Already in classical Latin *amor* had a wide trans-sexual sense, which Christian theology soon appropriated and further expanded: enough to recall a great phrase from the *Confessions* of Saint Augustine, *amor meus, pondus meum,* 'my love is my weight; thereby I am borne, whithersoever I am borne.' From the scholastics, Dante's masters, the term got a finer precision and its width of reference was clarified by the technique of analogy. Thus Aquinas identifies *amor* with the natural *appetitus* or desire which inclines every conceivable being towards the perfection appropriate to its nature. And so *amor* came to express the dynamic factor in the cosmos, variously realized on all levels of existence; a dynamism which derived from and variously manifests the absolutely primal subsistent love which is simply the Creator himself. 'God is love,' Saint John had said, and this Christian word expressed, for Saint Thomas, a metaphysical necessity too; for the summit of being could not be conceived of as *not* delighting in being and goodness; and such delight is just what the term love ultimately means. This is the thought behind verses 91-92.

But verse 93 introduces a distinction which will govern, in fact, the rest of the discourse: 'either natural or rational.' It is vital to realize what this does *not* mean. It cannot mean that some beings love *only* in a natural way and others *only* in a rational way. For the love that is 'naturale' in a thing springs from that thing's *natura*, and every conceivable thing — including the Deity — has its proper *natura* or essence; and with this and because of this it has the inclination proper to it which, as Aquinas says, is its natural appetition or love (*S.T.* 1a, 60, 1). Thus appetition, *amor*, in this primary sense, spans all being. But some beings, humans for example, are endowed with mind; and in these the natural drive, 'amor naturale,' takes effect, in part at least, through a conscious awareness and deliberate choice of the objects that are actually loved. So that in such beings, as well as 'natural love' there is 'rational love'; whereas in beings not endowed with mind, the subhuman world, there is only the 'natural' instinctive love. The distinction, then, of these two loves is not, as it were, between x and y but between x and x + y.

So much for love considered as the dynamic factor in all things, without reference yet to the question of right or wrong. But this moral question is precisely the relevant one in Purgatory ; so now we see Dante locating the division between right and wrong precisely within the field of action of the second love, 'amor d'animo,' rational love, x + y. This he does, in a general way, in verses 94-96; and then, in the two following tercets (vv. 97-102), he draws out his ethical point more explicitly. The natural love as such cannot go wrong; it springs directly from nature which itself springs directly from God. It is God's product, primarily; his product *in* this particular man, beast or plant: to say that *it* could go wrong would be to find fault with God (cf. *summa* 1a, 60, 1 ad 3). Wrongness, then, can come into the universe only through the plus factor added by a creature's mind, only through love working through conscious choice. Evil begins only at the point where mind begins. This is stated as self-evident; only the *modes* of this going wrong are assumed, here, to need explanation (vv. 95-102). How can love, appetition, desire in fact go wrong? Only three ways are possible, logically. Either a bad *object* is desired; or a good object is loved *badly* — that is, either it is not desired *as much* as its goodness merits, it is desired too little; or it is desired *more* than its goodness merits, it is desired too much. Now the love of an evil object is what is involved, as we shall see, in pride, envy and anger; while insufficient desire for the good is sloth, and excessive desire for good gives rise to the three remaining vices, covetousness, gluttony and lust. This distinction of a defective and an excessive desire entails, obviously, the notion of a measure; and the measure involved is stated in verses 97-98. The 'first good,' the being who has goodness absolutely, namely God, cannot be loved too much, but only too little, as by the slothful. Therefore excessive love only arises with respect to 'secondary goods' (98) — the good things of the created world through which God attracts the soul towards himself, but which the soul, by a perversion of its 'rational love,' may treat as ends in themselves, inflating them into idols.

The following tercet, verses 103-105, rounds off this first basic part of the discourse with a statement which will be picked up, implicitly, and drawn out in canto XVII. Right and wrong, says Virgil in effect, is always in the end a matter of what you love and how you love; all morality is ultimately erotic. This idea has a long tradition behind it, and notably the influence of Augustine, but it is also an entirely characteristic utterance, as the whole *Comedy* testifies.

The rest of the canto only adds precision and detail to the teaching already sketched out. We have seen that sin is always a perversion of love, and this in three ways: either you love what is bad, or you love something good too little or too much. Under these three heads the seven major vices are now classified, it being assumed, apparently, that this will amount to a complete, if summary, account of moral evil, at least as the philosopher sees it. But let us not assume too readily that this is a complete picture of evil as Dante saw it — I mean Dante the poet, not Dante the character in the poem now listening to his master half-way up the Mountain. Virgil speaks in character and this Dante listens in character, but the creator of both characters, the poet, is outside and above them. Especially with regard to verses 106-117 is this distinction called for, where Virgil says that you cannot desire evil for yourself or for God, but only for your neighbour, and where he reduces pride simply to an offence against one's fellowmen. You want to excel, to stand out in some way; but you can't do this, it seems, if others are excelling also, in the same way; so you strive might and main to prove them your inferiors, to 'put them down'; and that, simply that, says Virgil, is pride. Well, doubtless it is; but from the standpoint of Christianity, indeed of any genuine religion, there is more to pride than that. What Virgil has left out is simply the religious dimension. The intolerance of human rivals — Virgil's essential point — is a social effect of pride, a mere by product, from the religious point of view, for which pride consists, essentially, not in not tolerating rivals, but in not tolerating *superiors*, and above all the superior who is one's Maker. That was the sin of Lucifer — rebellion against his Maker (*Inf.* XXXIV, 35). And Virgil had seen Lucifer, down in Cocito, but he had not, I think, perfectly understood what he saw. There were extremes of evil in Hell that Virgil could not comprehend, as there will be extremes of repentance in the Earthly Paradise that he cannot foresee. There is a certain innocence, even naiveté, about the Virgil of the *Comedy* which is part of his charm and also of his credibility. How could this gentle humanist understand the deep negativity of spiritual pride? He is on firmer ground with sloth (127-132), also a negative sin, to be sure, but one only rather remotely – 'confusedly' – involving relations with God. Nor can one fault him as far as he goes on the positive sins of excessive love (133-137). In fact, this is too negative a commendation, for what Virgil says or implies on these sins by excess is very pregnant indeed, and I must not end this *lectura* without some attempt to elucidate it, however briefly . Let us pause then on verses 127-129 and 133-135.

I have already hinted that I would not apply to these two tercets the kind of qualification I have applied to Virgil's definition of pride, since in their case I see no clear difference between the poet's thought and the words of the character in his poem. Whereas Virgil's *dicta* on pride will in some sense be corrected elsewhere in the *Comedy*, what he says in these six verses will only be expanded and clarified. They express, unquestionably, Dante's mature mind. But what exactly do they say? They say in effect, I think, three things: first, that implied in all human desires there is one basic common aim – happiness, *felicità* (127-128, 134); second, that the objective reality which is thus drawing us through our desire for happiness, all the time and through all our faculties, is in fact God, for happiness is only found, in the end, in experiencing God; and third, that this 'drawing' us is effected by God's acting on us at a remove, as it were, for he draws us only through signs or adumbrations of himself, which are the forms of goodness we apprehend in nature or in ourselves. So much in general.

Now let us glance at two phrases in particular, and first at verse 127: 'Everyone confusedly apprehends a good,' etc. On anlysis this would yield the meaning that the soul on earth is vaguely aware indeed of some possible perfect joy, but does not distinctly see any thing or object in which such joy is to be found; hence its knowledge of the joy itself is indistinct or 'confused.' To adapt a scholastic distinction which Dante is certainly presupposing here, the soul has an inkling of perfect *beatitudo* or bliss; it does not see the *res*, the divine object which alone can confer *beatitudo*, since that lies outside and beyond it, *extra animam*, and indeed beyond the reach of its natural powers, *supra naturam*. And this may help us with the other tercet, verses 133-135. The subject here, 'another kind of good,' *altro ben*, includes everything except God, all creatures; and their difference from God is just what the sentence states. Not being God, they cannot confer perfect joy, *felicità* (134), and this because they are not 'the good essence itself' — where 'essence' has quasi-adverbial force, the sense being 'that good thing which is good essentially, *per se*, and not through merely participating in goodness.' This is Platonist language, but here Dante is certainly thinking in that great tradition. What merely partakes of goodness is good in some limited finite way. The infinite transcendent Good partakes of nothing, it simply is what it is, total goodness as such and of itself. And precisely as such it, and it only, can fulfill the desire of the creature endowed with reason; for reason as such is open to the infinite and cannot be satisfied, ultimately, with anything less. This last point will be the lesson of the *Paradiso*. I cannot presume this to be self-evidently true; but I have not space now for further explanations.

So we end our brief survey of this oddly disjointed but rather beautiful canto: beautiful especially perhaps in its variety; wherein so much of the human spirit has been shown us, successively, in action: the wonder of human imagination; memory and visual perception; the lucid gravity of reasoning.

8

THE CELEBRATION OF ORDER: *PARADISO* X

L et me begin with the concept of beauty, which the old philosophers defined by essential properties: wholeness (*integritas*), due proportion, and a certain 'clarity'.[1] And so Dante thought of beauty, but it is relevant to note in his allusions to it a stress on the second factor, the interrelation of parts in a whole. Thus in the *Convivio* (I, v, 13) we read: 'A thing is called beautiful the parts of which answer to one another in a right sort of way, so as to make a pleasing harmony. Thus a man seems beautiful if his limbs are well-proportioned, and we call a song beautiful when the voices producing it are interrelated as art requires they should be.'[2] Here beauty is associated with art, and this too is relevant to my theme, as we shall see. But still more so is the stress on proportion, harmony, intrinsic order; for I find in the idea behind these terms the key to the long and intricate section of the *Paradiso* which begins at canto X and continues to canto XIV, and describes the heaven of the Sun.

The note of *order*, in the wide sense of interrelation, is struck at the opening of our canto:

> Guardando nel suo Figlio con l'Amore
> che l'uno e l'altro etternalmente spira,
> lo primo ed ineffabile Valore . . .[3]

The Absolute, the creative source of 'all that moves through mind or space,' is itself a nexus of relations: the Father and the Son and the Spirit that proceeds from them — the Christian paradox of the triune

1. See, for example, St. Thomas, summarizing the neoplatonist tradition as it came to him through Dionysius the Pseudo-Areopagite: *Summa theol.* 2a2ae. 145, 2; cf. 1a. 5, 4 ad 1; 1a2ae. 27, 1 ad 3.
2. Cf. also *Conv.* III, xv, 11; IV, xxv, 12.
3. Quotations from the poem are cited in the critical text established by Giorgio Petrocchi, *La Commedia secondo l'antica vulgata* (4 vols.; Milano, 1966-1967).

God. But before we go further into the canto it will be useful, at this point, to glance at two structural features involved in it.

The first of these is the fact that all three main divisions of Dante's *Comedy* have a marked break at cantos IX-X: a kind of prolonged prelude comes to an end and there is an new beginning. So it is in the *Inferno* with Dante's entry into the City of Dis; so in the *Purgatorio* with his ascent to the circles of purification; so here in the *Paradiso* with the passage out of the earth's shadow – thought to terminate in the heaven of Venus (*Par.* IX, 118-119) – and Dante's ascent into the Sun. Symbolically, this exit from the earth's shadow is an important moment in the transcending of the limits of nature represented by this part of the *Comedy* as a whole; and is marked, solemnly, by this abrupt introduction into the theme of the poem of the supernatural mystery of the Trinity.

But more important for the meaning of this and the following cantos is another, less obvious structural feature peculiar to the *Paradiso*. This third *cantica* is all in a sense a discourse about God; but he is viewed in it under different aspects, with now one now another more in evidence; and I think that underlying these variations is a typically medieval pattern of ideas already traced out by Dante in the *Convivio*, ten years or so before he began the *Paradiso*. What it amounts to is that the contemplation of the Trinity by created intelligence is expressed in terms of the traditional division of the angels, the spiritual part of creation, into nine Orders composed of three Hierarchies. The highest Hierarchy contemplates especially the Father, the middle one the Son, the lowest one the Holy Spirit; and the physical effect of these contemplations is the revolving motion of the nine heavens of the material cosmos.[4] On arriving then in the heaven of the Sun, Dante enters the special province of that Hierarchy which has a special relationship with God the Son, the Word or Logos. Now each divine Person is contemplated by his respective Hierarchy under three aspects, corresponding to the three Orders which constitute the Hierarchy: as he is in himself, and as he is in relation to each of the other two Persons. Thus, of the second or middle Hierarchy, whose special 'object' is God the Son, the first Order, the Dominations, con-

---

4. *Convivio* II, v, 7-11. St. Thomas arranges the angelic Hierarchies and Orders on different principles (*Summa theol.* la. 108 *passim*). Dante's arrangement may have been suggested by St. Bonaventure (*In Hexaem.* xxi, 17; ed. Quaracchi, V, 434).

template him simply in himself, and so move the heaven of Jupiter (cantos XVIII-XX of the *Paradiso*); the second Order, the Virtues, contemplate the Son's relation to the Father, and so move the heaven of Mars (cantos XIV-XVIII); while the third Order, the Powers, contemplate the Son in relation to the Holy Spirit, and so move the solar heaven, which is precisely the one we are now entering (cantos X-XIV). And this has considerable importance for an understanding of this section of the *Paradiso*. It means that underlying all that is said and done in Dante's heaven of the Sun is the idea of the 'procession,' to use the theological term, of the third Person from the second, of the Holy Spirit from the Word, of subsistent Love from the Logos.' Hence the implicit theme of these cantos X-XIV is that 'order,' intrinsic to the Godhead itself, whereby intellectuality issues into love, knowledge into ecstasy; which, transposed to the human level, becomes the theme of ideal human *wisdom*, the co-inherence of intellect and love, which is precisely what the moving and singing circles of the solar heaven represent — that of Aquinas and his companions in canto X, who stand for knowledge begetting love, and that of Bonaventure and his companions, introduced in canto XII, who stand for love born of knowledge. And all this takes place against the backcloth of the sun, both light and fire. It is with this double chorus of sages, that 'the chief imagination of Christendom,' as Yeats called Dante, found perhaps his most telling image of ideal intellectual life, of an ideal culture; basically the same ideal, perhaps, as the Irish poet, with less assurance, aspired to:

> O sages standing in God's holy fire,
> As in the gold mosaic of a wall,
> Come from the holy fire, perne in a gyre,
> And be the singing-masters of my soul.[6]

So much by way of preface to a quick reading of our canto. It divides into four unequal parts: verses 1-27, declaring that the cosmic order reflects an order *within* the Creator, the Father, the Son, and the Spirit of them both; verses 28-81, describing, not Dante's ascent into the sun with Beatrice, for that was instan-

5. Cf. *Summa theol.* 1a. 27, 3; 36, 3 and 4.
6. 'Sailing to Byzantium,' stanza III, 1-4 (*The Collected Poems of W. B. Yeats*, Definitive edition [New York, 1956], pp. 191-192).

taneous, but what they saw on arriving there; verses 82-138, the speech of St. Thomas Aquinas, introducing himself and his eleven companions; and finally ten verses rounding off the canto with a simile that links the song of these souls to the liturgy of the Church on earth — which itself, in turn, is thus linked back, through the ordered diversity of the blessed, to the dynamic unity of the Godhead.

Turning back now to the opening verses, one notes as characteristic the way the celebration of a Christian dogma is at once related, as closely as possible, to the physical world. Theology combines with astronomy. The intricately ordered motions of the heavenly bodies are shown as the outward sign and expression of a pre-existing order in the Creator, which alone renders them intelligible. And the link between these two orders, the created and the uncreated, is given in the fourth tercet, verses 10-12, and precisely in the term *arte*, 'art,' which in verse 10 refers indeed to the visible cosmic order (we are invited to gaze at this), but in verses 11-12 — under the pronouns *la* (before *ama*) and *lei* — *arte* has changed or extended its meaning; it now refers directly to God the Son, the Logos. Such a reference is perfectly in line with the scholastic sense of the term *ars*, which is primarily a disposition (*virtus*) in the mind towards making things well (*recta ratio factibilium*), and then the *idea* of a thing to be made, and only in the third place things actually made, works of art, artifacts.[7] Here in verses 11-12 the sense intended seems to include both art as *virtus* and art as idea, but as transposed, by analogy, from the human level to the divine: the divine intellect, expressing itself in the eternal Word, which is its 'art', sees in this Word all that it then *re-expresses* as created beings existing in time. This analogy goes back to St. Augustine, who had called God the Son *ars quaedam Dei*; and the term is accepted by Aquinas, along with the cognate terms 'wisdom' and 'beauty,' as particularly appropriate to the Second Person.[8]

All this Dante leaves rather implicit; but not so the divine art in the sense of artifact, the visible cosmic order. This we are expressly

---

7. For the basic relevant concepts and vocabulary, see St. Thomas' *Summa*: art as intellectual 'virtue' directed to making, 1a2ae. 57, 3-4; 93, 1; 2a2ae. 47, 5; art in God as creator, 1a2ae. 93, 1; cf. 1a. 14, 8; the 'good' of art as consisting in the artifact 1a2ae. 57, 5.

8. St. Augustine, *De Trinitate* VI, 10 (PL, XLII, 931); St. Thomas, *Summa theol.* 1a. 39.

invited to contemplate (vv. 5-7), and at a carefully chosen point where *order* is especially manifest: the point of intersection of the sun's two movements, the diurnal and the annual (7-12). Here a minimum of Dantean astronomy cannot be avoided. (1) The sun's two movements. The sun goes daily round the earth from east to west carried by the rotation, ultimately, of the outermost heavenly sphere, the *primum mobile*. But it has also, with the other planets,[9] a yearly motion round the earth from west to east, under the signs of the Zodiac. (2) This annual motion from west to east is *oblique* with respect to the daily one (see verse 14 of our canto) because the axis of the solar heaven does not coincide with that of the earth; with the result that as the solar heaven revolves from west to east, the sun, which is set on *its* equator, turns in a path that is at an angle to the *earth's* equator. This oblique annual path of the sun is called the ecliptic. (3) From what has been said it follows that the sun's annual path, from west to east, along the ecliptic takes it from an extreme point south of the earth's equator (the winter solstice for us) to an extreme point north of it (the summer solstice) and then back again; thus crossing the equator twice a year, at the spring and autumn equinoxes. (4) This results in the changes of the seasons on earth, and in vastly more animal and vegetative life than if the sun were to be on the equator all the year round and not only at the equinoxes. Two further points and we have done with astronomy. First, since the sun's path is both east to west *daily* and, in effect, north to south *annually*, its yearly motion round the earth is in effect spiral – as noted in verse 32. Secondly, Dante arrives in the sun at the spring equinox (in fact a little past it) as noted in verse 31.[10]

Here then are Dante and Beatrice, having arrived from Venus at, he tells us, more than the speed of light (34-39). It is a world of wonders, and yet the preceding verses (28-33) evoke no wonderland but only the ordinary beneficence of 'Nature's greatest minister' – a usual glory for Italian eyes (and how this Italian loved it). The celebration of sunlight continues through the next three tercets, verses 40-48, though indirectly, for what is directly affirm-

9. For Dante the sun and the moon count as planets.
10. Figure to illustrate the preceding paragraph. AB – the Zodiac, CD – the axis of the solar sphere, XY – the ecliptic. See also Dante's prose description of the sun's movements, *Convivio* III, V. Further explanations in E. Moore, *Studies in Dante*, 3rd Series (Oxford: Clarendon Press, 1903, reprinted 1968), pp. 1-108; M. A. Orr, *Dante and the Early Astronomers*, 2nd ed. (London, 1956).

ed is the appearance of nuclei of light *within* the sun's radiance, a
thing unimaginable if, as verse 48 implies, all luminosity in our
world is measured by that of the sun. We note that the procedure
here, especially in verses 43-45, is a variant of a device often used in
the *Paradiso*, that of describing a thing by calling it indescribable.
Here the poet offers to our imagination lights within the sun, knowing that we cannot imagine them.

The first clear apprehension, by Dante and Beatrice, of objects in
the sun is conveyed in the dense and splendid tercet,

> Tal era quivi la quarta famiglia
>   de l'alto Padre, che sempre la sazia,
>   mostrando come spira e come figlia.
>   (49-51)

And now the body of the sun is becoming mere background to a
group of spirits seen within it, the 'fourth family' — the others being
the spirits met in the three lower heavens (cantos III-IX).

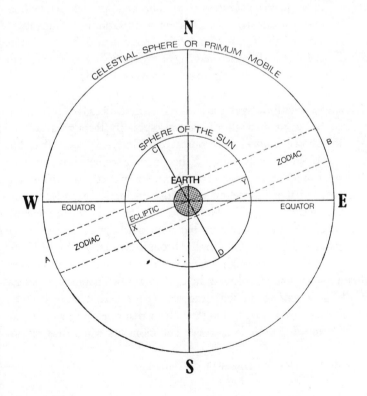

But not for another thirty verses is personal contact established with these solar spirits, not, that is, till verse 82, when one of them speaks to Dante. The poet is taking his time. The group has been visible since verse 40, and audible as a singing chorus since verse 73. So long a pause before conversation begins is unusual in the *Comedy* and is worth considering for a moment. It is clear, to start with, that the ten tercets from verse 52 to 82 divide into two 'actions.' Verses 52-63 show us Dante and Beatrice engaged in a sort of byplay, in momentary detachment from the souls, of whom nonetheless they are already well aware; after which, verses 64-81 bring those souls themselves more distinctly into view. The byplay, so to call it, is full of life and charm and perfectly 'in context'; but it is also perhaps more subtle than it seems. At the sight of the 'fourth family,' now majestically present (49-51), Beatrice reminds her companion to give thanks to God (Paradise can be so distracting), whereupon his eager mind plunges so deep into God that Beatrice 'went into eclipse, forgotten'; a beautiful *riposte* on his part — which she however immediately counters by a smile of approval so dazzling that his mind, for one moment all intent upon God, now finds itself divided between the Creator and this dear creature. To a puritan sort of piety this little scene may seem profane: here is a Christian poet who sees nothing wrong — even in heaven — in being distracted from God by a woman's beauty. But from Dante's Catholic point of view the situation is perfectly all right: first, because God can in any case be loved through a creature, especially through a saint — and the whole *Comedy* presupposes that Beatrice is just that for Dante; and secondly because of the poet's peculiar situation here and now, caught up as he is before death into the eternal life but not yet granted that life's deepest and most distinctive experience, the immediate vision of God.[11] This experience he will have in the end; the final canto will describe it; but until that climax, Dante, even here in heaven, knows God only through created *media* of some kind, and especially through Beatrice and the other blessed. Hence, unlike Beatrice and the blessed, he can always be distracted momentarily by such *media*; and will need, from time to time, to be detached from excessive absorption in this one or that one, to be recalled to the final aim of the whole journey. The moments when Beatrice, as

11. See ch. 5 in this book, 'Dante's Vision of God'.

Dante's guide, detaches him from herself are among the most exquisite in the *Paradiso*.[12]   .

This said, it would be easy to link up in detail the byplay contained in these ten verses, 52-63, with the negative technique and
procedures already noted. Dante's forgetting Beatrice in verses
59-60 is a step on what the theologians called the *via negativa*, the
way of renunciation; his then being brought back by her smile from
unity to multiplicity is a reminder that he is not yet at the end of
that way.

The next six tercets are a careful preparation for St. Thomas' intervention at verse 82. Distinguishing and combining visual and
aural impressions, they gradually build up a total complex image of
this group of blessed souls, the image conveyed in the beautifully
composed concluding sentence (76-81) with its balanced complementary similes of stars moving round the poles and of women
circling in a dance and singing as they dance, until for a moment the
music stops and they pause with it, waiting for 'the new notes.' This
gradual description, by analysis and synthesis, of a complex
sense-object is extremely characteristic. Notice how the concluding
synthesis is already adumbrated in verse 66, and that the items of
sight and sound which this verse combines are rendered separately
in the nine following verses, beginning with the lunar halo (67-69).

But it is time to pass on to the speech of St. Thomas, to which all
this has been leading; of which, however, the first thing to say is
that it cannot be adequately studied in a commentary confined to
the present canto; and this because it opens a series of great discourses — with two more by Aquinas, one by St. Bonaventure and
one by Solomon — which continue down to canto XIV and together
compose a single, many-sided intellectual statement, one of the
weightiest in the *Divine Comedy*. Here I limit myself, as to details, to
the speech of St. Thomas in canto X; adding only some general
remarks to indicate its wider significance in the context of the solar
heaven as a whole.

It is a speech of introductions, made by the south Italian
Dominican friar, the philosopher-theologian Thomas Aquinas, who
died in March 1274 and was declared a saint by the Church in

---

12. For example: XVIII, 20-21, XXI, 1-8, XXIII, 70-72, XXXI, 91-92; cf. *Purgatorio*
XXXII, 1-9.

1323, a few years after the actual writing of this canto.[13] Thomas
introduces himself, and then, one by one, his eleven companions; the
whole glittering circle. It is a company of sages — to borrow Yeats's
term — and as we read on three features of this sagacity or wisdom
gradually become clear. First, it is represented collectively by these
twelve spirits and by the parallel group of souls, led by St. Bonaventure, which will appear in canto XII. Secondly, within this collec-
tive, common wisdom we are meant to recognize distinct and
diverse aspects of wisdom, corresponding to the various figures in
the groups. Thirdly, it becomes sufficiently clear (though not stated
explicitly) that these different aspects of wisdom are distinguished in
relation to *society*, so that each one represents, in principle, one or
other function of the intellect in view of the common good; this being understood, of course, in the medieval Christian manner, as a
harmonious ordering of human life on earth, and in time, towards
the divine transcendant Good, through Christ and his Church.

But to get closer to Dante's intentions here it will be useful to
recall a phrase which St. Thomas is fond of quoting from Aristotle's
Metaphysics 'sapientis est ordinare,' [14] 'the wise man gives orders, it
is he who should command.' However, in his commentary on the
Ethics Aquinas takes the phrase in the sense of 'the wise man is *concerned* with order'; and this, he explains, because 'wisdom,' *sapientia*,
denotes the perfection of that rational power in us, *ratio*, which
perceives order in things. But wisdom is not only perceptive, it is
also — and here Thomas rejoins Aristotle — directive; it considers the
relation of means to ends. The wisdom, then, will be concerned with
the highest end, the end of the universe as a whole, and with the
means for its achievement. But let us have Thomas' words, from the
beginning of the *Contra Gentiles*: 'The end of anything is that intended by its first cause ... Now the first cause of the universe is
Mind ... therefore its last end must be the good of mind, which is
truth. Truth, then, is the ultimate purpose for which the universe ex-

13. On the early controversies around St. Thomas' teaching, see Frederick J. Roensch,
Early Thomist School (Dubuque, Iowa, 1964), pp. 1-27; E. Gilson, *The History of Chris-
tian Philosophy in the Middle Ages* (London, 1955), pp. 381-427; David Knowles, *The
Evolution of Medieval Thought* (London, 1962), pp. 291-300. On the canonisation of
Aquinas, see my *The Life of St. Thomas Aquinas: Biographical Documents* (London, 1959).
His influence on Dante is considered in detail in my article 'Tommaso d'Aquino' for the
Enciclopedia dantesca (6 vols.; Rome: Istituto della Enciclopedia Italiana).
14. *Metaph.* I, 2, 982a 18; St. Thomas, *In Met* I lect. 2, par. 42-43; In *Ethic.* I, lect. I',
par. 1; *Contra Gentiles* I, 1.

ists; and the principal concern of the wise man.' [15] This text was quite certainly known to Dante and it may well have been in his mind when composing this part of the *Paradiso*; which is all an effort to express, in argument and symbol, an order of relations which should govern the two distinctively human activities of knowing and loving : to show, or at least to suggest, the right relation of these (a) to each other, (b) to their last end, which is God, and (c) to the more limited, proximate ends of statecraft and natural philosophy. From a different angle we might, for our part, interpret Dante's intention here as an effort to render his conviction of the unity of intellect and life – that unity which Yeats (whom I quote again only because of the contrast he presents and implies) expressly denied in the sad phrase, 'Wisdom is the property of the dead.' [16] It is almost a definition of Dante to say that he was incapable of saying that.

Dante's teaching on the more limited ends within the general order scanned by wisdom is only implicit in this canto X; latent in the figures of Siger and of Solomon, the philosopher and the king; nor do the succeeding cantos do much to develop the hint (to which I shall return) contained in the former figure. But the significance of King Solomon's presence in this circle of sages will be brought out clearly in canto XIII, where St. Thomas, speaking for the third time, explains precisely in what sense Solomon was supremely intelligent (cf. X, 109-114): he knew exactly what *kind* of wisdom he needed, so as to be a 're sufficiente,' and he knew just *where* to go for it, as he showed by his prayer to God for light to distinguish between good and evil in the government of his people (1 Kings 3:5-15). And from God he only received the wisdom appropriate to his temporal task: human, earthly, 'regal prudenza.' Always, in Dante, to be wise is to discriminate and distinguish; to know the limits and circumstances which condition each particular use of intelligence. It is in line with this stress that, in canto XIV, Solomon, now in glory, now no longer a king, shows wisdom of a different kind, uttering heavenly theology (XIV, 34-60).

A wider view of the interrelation of knowledge and love emerges in these cantos through the contrasted and complementary figures of St. Thomas and St. Bonaventure; in whose speeches however – in

15. *Contra Gent.* I, 1.
16. 'Blood and the Moon,' stanza IV, 7, *ed. cit.*, pp. 232-234.

cantos XI to XIII — those activities are now shown rising beyond
natural philosophy and politics towards a union with the absolute
Source of all truth and goodness. That the two theologians are contrasted and complementary is clear enough: Thomas, a Dominican,
utters the panegyric of St. Francis (canto XI); Bonaventure, a Franciscan, that of St. Dominic (XII). But each is a critic as well as a
eulogist; for each saint, having sung the praises of the founder of the
other's Order, takes the holiness of that founder as a touchstone to
measure the corruption of his *own*. The whole symmetrical construction is in fact profoundly polemical. Through this dramatic device of
speeches of alternate praise and blame, Dante is charging the two
great Orders of friars — which, let us remember, had changed the
face of Catholicism during the half-century before his birth — with
betraying the very cause which they had both been founded to serve
and promote, the Dominicans in one way, the Franciscans in
another.[17]   For Dominic had been a cherub, luminous with
knowledge of God, and Francis like a seraph on fire with his love
(XI, 37-39): light and fire, knowledge and love, intellect and will;
but converging towards the same point, each an image in his own
way of the one incarnate Logos, who is Wisdom itself become man
for the love of men (XI, 106-108, XII, 67-75). But the followers
of both saints had betrayed them, neglecting their example; and
betraying them, had betrayed the Church. And this was apparent,
for Dante, in two ways: first, in a horrible confusion of ends and
means, so that the temporal was preferred to the eternal, cupidity to
charity — and in this respect the corruption of the Friars was only
that of the Catholic body as a whole, from the papacy
downwards;[18] and secondly, — and this was the two Orders' particular corruption — in their forgetting the basic identity in aim of
the two Founders. Dominic and Francis had worked with the same
end in view, 'ad un fine fur l'opere sue,' as Aquinas will say (XI,
42): but by the close of the century in which both saints died —
Dominic in 1221, Francis in 1226 — the division and rivalry
between their Orders had become a crying scandal. To a considerable extent this was a matter of doctrinal disagreements; the
effect in particular of the new line taken in philosophy and theology
by the Dominicans Albert the Great and Thomas Aquinas, which,

17. See E. Gilson, *Dante et la philosophie* (Paris, 1939, repr. 1953), pp. 242-252.
18. See ch 6 above, 'The canto of the Damned Popes: *Inferno* xix'.

as involving a decisive option for Aristotelianism, aroused stiff opposition from conservative theologians in the Augustinian tradition,
among whom Franciscan thinkers quickly took the lead. Between
about 1270 and 1310 the counter-attack on Thomism was largely
led by Franciscans: St. Bonaventure, Peter John Olivi, John
Pecham, Duns Scotus; the natural consequence of which was to
make the Dominicans rally round their great new teacher for
motives which had often little to do with a disinterested search for
truth; the insights of a genius became a 'party line,' the official dicta
of a school.[19] With this aspect of the matter, however, Dante is
much less concerned directly than with the harm done to the Church
by the split and strife between the two Orders; and in the heaven of
the Sun we see his effort to heal the division. He was fighting a
rearguard action; the future, immediately, did not lie with the
Friars.

Let us return now, briefly, to St. Thomas' speech in our canto.
An elaborately courteous introduction (verses 82-93) leads to the
presentations, occupying fourteen tercets, of himself and his companions. The style is pointed, elegant, epigrammatic; with a touch of
pathos in describing two of the souls, the philosophers Boethius and
Siger of Brabant, these being the only members of the group whose
deaths are mentioned. A more important difference appears in the
way emphasis is distributed so as to focus interest upon certain
figures in the circle: on Thomas himself, implicitly, as its spokesman,
on Solomon — 'the fifth light, the fairest of us all' — who gets two
full tercets, as do Boethius and Siger. These four then are the outstanding figures, St. Thomas, Solomon, Boethius, and Siger; a
theologian, a king, and two philosophers. Notice however that
theology as represented by Aquinas in a sense includes philosophy;
on the principle stated in the *Summa theologiae* and, as Dante well
knew, pretty thoroughly practised in it, that 'just as grace does not
destroy nature but fulfills it, so reason can and should be of service
to Christian faith.' [20] It is also in line with this notion of theology
that Albert of Cologne (97-99) and Peter Lombard (106-108) are
in the circle; the former as Thomas' fellow-Dominican and teacher
(and so placed next to him at his right),[21] the latter as author of the

19. See above, note 13 and ch. 4, 'St. Thomas and Dante'.
20. *Summa theol.* 1a. 1, 8 ad 2.
21. On Albert of Swabia, called 'The Great' (1206-1280), the works of Gilson and

standard text-book of the theological schools. With these we may
also connect Dionysius the Pseudo-Areopagite (115-117), not, certainly, as a 'scholastic,' but as a major authority in the schools and
also for Dante; [22] and then Richard of St. Victor (131-132), the
twelfth-century mystical theologian; [23] and finally perhaps the
Venerable Bede (131), though to Englishmen Bede is better known
as their first historian than as a biblical exegete. Thus we have six
representatives of various aspects of theology: Thomas, Albert,
Peter Lombard, Dionysius, Richard, and Bede. Of the rest, the en-
cyclopedist Isidore of Seville (131) need not detain us here; nor the
'little luminary' enigmatically described in verses 118-120 and
usually identified with the Christian apologist Orosius, but not in
any case a major figure. This leaves Gratian (103-105), Boethius
(124-129), and Siger (133-138). Gratian is the great canonist who
taught at Bologna in the mid-twelfth century. Obviously he stands
for legal wisdom in some sense; Dante had all the Latin respect for
and interest in law. But what are the 'two forums' to which Gratian
gave his support, thus winning approval 'in Paradise'? Most commentators have answered, 'the canon law and the civil law,' or as
Pézard asserts without argument, 'la justice religieuse et la justice impériale et civile.' But I think it far more probable that Gmelin is
right and that Dante is alluding to an important distinction which
belonged precisely to the canon law of the Church, the only law
Gratian was concerned with; the distinction between the inner
forum of conscience and the outer *forum* of ecclesiastical public
jurisdiction.[24] This was a crucial distinction for Dante, as is shown
by the episode of the Excommunicates in *Purgatorio* III; and he
could have found it without much difficulty in the works of
Aquinas.

Knowles, cited in n. 13, may be consulted to start with; also, for his influence on Dante,
ch. 4 above.

22. Cf. *Par.* XXVIII, 130 ff.; *Convivio* II, xiii, 5; *Epist.* XIII, 60.

23. Dante's only other allusion to this profound and fascinating writer is in *Epist.* XIII,
80.

24. Gmelin's interpretation, which I accept, was based on the thorough and persuasive
study by F. Brandileone in *Rendiconti dell'Accademia dei Lincei*, VI, 2 (1926), pp.
65-149. See H. Gmelin's note in vol. III of his Commentary on the *Divine Comedy*
(Stuttgart, 1957), p. 204; for A. Pézard's see his *Dante. Oeuvres complètes* (Paris, 1965), p.
1445. For relevant passages in Aquinas, see *Summa theol.* Supplement, 22, 1; 1a2ae. 96,
4; 2a2ae. 89, 7 ad 3; *In Sent.* IV, 18, 2, 2.

So we are left with the wise king and the two philosophers. The significance here of Solomon has been touched on already; let it suffice to add that his appearance, and still more his preeminence, in the group – he outshines even Aquinas (109) – is surely a deliberate surprise and is certainly highly polemical ; it has behind it Dante's passionate concern with politics, his belief (so vehemently upheld and defended in *Monarchia* III) in the high dignity and sacred autonomy of the civil power and in the vocation of the civil ruler as something utterly distinct from that of the priest or the intellectual.[25] As for Boethius, the honour done to him is a revealing touch but it poses no special problems: his *De Consolatione Philosophiae* was one of Dante's favourite books and is often echoed in the *Comedy*; and in his sad fate – 'martyrdom and exile' – the poet saw a sort of paradigm of his own.[26] The same is true, in a sense, of the fate of Siger, obscurely hinted at in verses 134-135 and 138. But wider problems are raised, as every Dantist knows, by the sudden and splendid tribute paid here to one of the most controversial, and enigmatic, figures of the thirteenth century. But for want of space I must limit myself to the barest essentials. Siger then, born in Brabant about 1240, was the most conspicuous figure in the Arts Faculty of the University of Paris in the 1260's and the 1270's; the chief spokesman of the movement – known, perhaps misleadingly,[27] as Latin Averroism – which tended to claim for philosophy an autonomous status independent of theology. He certainly, for a time at least, maintained, as a philosopher, positions incompatible with orthodox Christianity; and, he was very strongly opposed, both as a philosopher and as an interpreter of Aristotle, by St. Thomas – for whom however, and also for Albert the Great, Siger explicitly put on record his esteem.[28] In 1270 Aquinas, recently returned to Paris from Italy, attacked Siger, without naming him, in the masterly *Tractatus de Unitate Intellectus contra Averroistas*, a detailed refutation of monopsychism (i.e. that there is

---

25. Cf. *Par.* VIII, 139-148; *Conv.* IV, ix.
26. Cf. *Conv.* II, xii, 2, xv, I; *Monarchia* I, ix, 3, etc.
27. The phrase was coined by P. Mandonnet who wrote the first important work on Siger: *Siger de Brabant et l'averroisme latin au XIIIe siècle* (2 vols.; Louvain, 1908-1911). Further studies, especially by F. Van Steenberghen and B. Nardi, have partly revised and corrected Mandonnet's conclusions. For an able summary of the matter see Nardi's article in *Enciclopedia cattolica*, XI, col. 560-562.
28. 'Praecipui viri in philosophia, Albertus et Thomas,' *QQ. de anima intellectiva*, III (ed. Bazan, Louvain, 1972, p. 81).

one intellectual principle common to men, the individual man as such having no rational soul).[29] In December 1270 this and other averroistic theses — denial of free will and individual immortality, the eternity of the world, the negation of divine providence — were formally condemned by the bishop of Paris at the instance of the theological faculty of the University. But, as events were to show, influential theologians in the faculty were hostile to St. Thomas too. He was, in fact, fighting on two fronts. Convinced as he was that Aristotelianism, once separated from Averroistic interpretations, was perfectly compatible with Christianity, St. Thomas vigorously opposed Siger and his group. But at the same time the clear distinction he drew between the spheres of reason and faith, philosophy and theology, and his consistency in applying this distinction (for example to the problem of the eternity of the world or the demonstrability of the Christian mysteries) [30] together with certain theses of his own on matter and spirit and their interrelation in creatures — all this was extremely displeasing to theologians of more traditional views. And three years after his death they took their revenge, when in March 1277 the bishop issued a second and far more sweeping condemnation of unorthodox trends in the University: 219 theses were condemned, of which some fifteen are recognizably Thomist.[31] But already Siger's academic career was broken. Suspected of heresy, he was formally summoned to stand trial before the Inquisition in October 1276. Instead he fled to Italy, to appeal to the pope. He seems to have been in fact acquitted of heresy by Nicholas III (who became pope in 1280) but kept under house arrest in the papal Curia, only to be murdered, some time before the end of 1284, at Orvieto, by his servant: the end darkly alluded to here by Dante.[32]

Siger was a genuine philosopher, but only in our century has his work begun to be edited and studied. The early commentators on the *Comedy* are strangely ignorant about him. Yet for Dante, it is clear, Siger was a great and wise man and a hero: one of the lights

29. Critical ed. by L. Keeler, S.J., 2nd ed. (Rome: Apud Aedes Pont. Universitatis Gregorianae, 1957). There is a recent translation, *On the Unity of the Intellect against the Averroists* ... with Introduction and notes, by B. H. Zedler (Milwaukee, Wisconsin: Marquette University Press, 1968).
30. Cf. *De aeternitate mundi contra murmurantes* (1270-71): *Summa theol.* 1a. 32, 1.
31. Text in *Chartularium Universit. Paris*, I, pp. 543-555.
32. Siger's violent death is mentioned in *Il Fiore* (XCII, 9-11), a contemporary sonnet-sequence very hostile to the Dominicans, which some scholars (including G. Contini, whose opinion carries much weight) ascribe to the young Dante.

of the world. This is already remarkable; but the strangest thing, of course, is his position in the circle of *sapientes*, by the side of St. Thomas, his adversary on earth now singing his praises in heaven. What does this signify? In the first place, surely, a conviction on Dante's part similar to his conviction touching the divided Orders of the Friars, that what divided the contestants in each case was less important than something else that united them. So the good Franciscan and the good Dominican could be 'merry in heaven' together, as Thomas More hoped that *he* might be with the judges who sentenced him to death; and so also the good theologian and the philosopher. But what, in this case, was that 'something else' uniting, in Dante's mind, Siger and Thomas, bringing them together in the work of his mind, the poem? For of course this is not a question about the historical Thomas and Siger, except so far as historical reality offered a springboard for Dante's imagination.[33] In real life St. Thomas rejected Siger's Averroistic interpretation of Aristotle; as did Dante himself (see *Purg.* XXV, 61-75). But did Siger perhaps change in his later years, and incline towards Thomism? Would this explain St. Thomas' approval of him here? At least one eminent scholar — Fernand Van Steenberghen — has taken this view.[34] But even were it proved — which it has not been — that the 'real' Siger changed in this way, I personally would consider the point irrelevant to the Siger in the poem, the object of Thomas' praise; and would still regard the 'explanation' based on it as not only unnecessary but incomparably inferior, in its banality, to an alternative interpretation, one which the whole context suggests but is not easy to express — and I have not space for entering into subtleties. Briefly, then, I am persuaded that Etienne Gilson[35] is right, and that Dante intended his twenty-four sages to represent a harmony, *not* of doctrinal agreement, but of diverse aspects and functions reflecting the various ways in which mankind may participate in one divine Wisdom; and that he wrote this vision out, like everything else in the *Comedy*, 'in pro del mondo che mal vive,' as a sign and a model for Christian society on earth.[36] Thus his St. Thomas (with St. Albert and Peter Lombard) represents one kind of

33. See Gilson, *Dante et la philosophie*, pp. 265ff.
34. Especially in his edition of *Siger de Brabant d'après ses oeuvres inédites* (2 vols.; Louvain, 1931 and 1942).
35. *Op. cit.*, pp. 256.
36. *Purg.* XXXII, 103.

theological wisdom; Bonaventure (with St. Anselm and perhaps Hugh of St. Victor) another; Dionysius and perhaps Richard another, Bede and Chrysostom yet another; and Gratian stands for legal wisdom and Solomon for regal; and Nathan and Abbot Joachim for two stages in prophecy; and Peter of Spain the logician and Donatus the grammarian for two disciplines that sovereign wisdom makes use of; and Boethius represents philosophy wedded to rhetoric,[37] while Siger — to return to him at last — stands for philosophy pure and simple; the mind's activity as it speculates on ultimate causes by the light of reason alone, and employing the properly human procedure of logical reasoning (hence the verb 'sillogizzò' in verse 138). [38] The choice of Siger for this part in Dante's heavenly play was a stroke of genius; for what Siger stood for, what he consciously voiced in the Paris of his time, was the possibility that reason might reach conclusions that were *not* those of theology. And Dante's choice, as Siger's eulogist, of his great adversary shows the same characteristic genius and audacity; whilst in the eulogy itself appears something of that delight in the enigmatic which is one of the many facets of this poet's style.

37. *Conv.* II, xii, 2; xv, 1.
38. On the syllogistic mode of thought as proper to man in the scale of being see St. Thomas, *Summa theol.* 1a. 58, 3 and 4. On Dante's conception of philosophy in general, see Gilson, *Dante et la philosophie, passim.* I may perhaps refer also to my lecture 'Religion and Philosophy in Dante,' in *The Mind of Dante*, ed. U. Limentani (Cambridge: University Press, 1965), pp. 47-78.

9

THE SON'S EAGLE: PARADISO XIX

C anto XIX of the *Paradiso* comes in the long middle section between Dante's ascent into the Sun with Beatrice in canto X and their rising to the Fixed Stars in canto XXII. Between these points run the thirteen cantos concerned with the spheres of the Sun, Mars, Jupiter, and Saturn, all lying beyond the earth's shadow which terminates in the heaven of Venus, the planet immediately below the sun. With canto XIX, and through the following one, we are the sixth heaven, that of Jupiter.

The first thing to note about this heaven is a feature it shares with the other three of this region of Paradise. In each of these heavens the action involves one dominant symbolic figure: in the Sun the rings of revolving lights, in Mars the white Cross on the fiery ground of the planet, in Jupiter a golden eagle, in Saturn a heavenly ladder. It is a spectacular series of tableaux. Except for the ladder in Saturn, these figures are themselves composed of the blessed souls whom Dante sees. Here in Jupiter it is the lovers of justice on earth who themselves form the body, wings and head of an immense eagle. The actual formation of the image is given particular emphasis, and to brilliant effect, in canto XIV as regards the Cross and in canto XVIII as regards the Eagle; but in each case the for- mation of the figure is complete before the next canto begins. Thus when our canto opens the Eagle is already before us fully formed:

> Parea dinanzi a me con l'ali aperte
> la bella image . . .

('Before me, with outstretched wings, was the fair image'.)

However, if this canto is so far continuous with the previous one, it soon introduces a theme for which, it may seem, nothing has prepared us in canto XVIII, or indeed in the rest of the *Paradiso* so far; indeed nothing since the disappearance of Virgil from the poem

near the end of the *Purgatorio*. For though Virgil is not named here
(and only once elsewhere in the *Paradiso*, at XVII, 19) it is he who
is inevitably brought to mind by the theme which occupies the bulk
of this canto (vv. 22-111) and the whole of canto XX, thus
dominating the Jupiter heaven: the theme or problem of the salvation of the virtuous non-Christians.

Why does this matter arise just here? In particular, what has it to
do with the symbolic Eagle of this heaven? For this is surely a
political symbol, whereas the new theme is purely theological. The
symbol, originally pagan, still speaks, one would suppose, of a purely human and temporal order, the Empire, while the new theme concerns man's access to a supernatural order, with man's transcending
time and all the limits of humanity. Nor has the *Paradiso* up to this
point, apparently, failed to stress the particular contrast. In canto
VI the discourse of Justinian traced the history of Rome from the
Republic to the Empire of Augustus and thence to the Christian Empire, all in terms of the flight of the Roman eagle; and though the
bird was declared sacred – 'God's bird',[1] 'il sacrosanto segno', its
flight was not heavenwards, it kept to the world of time. And on its
actual appearance in canto XVIII (no longer as a metaphor but as a
heavenly reality) it still seemed to bear the same significance. The
description of its formation was in effect an imperialist manifesto.
The great bird was formed out of an 'M', the last letter of the last
word of that sentence from the Vulgate book of Wisdom which the
souls in Jupiter literally spelled out on the planet's face: 'Diligite
justitiam qui judicatis terram.' For a genuine love of justice, Dante
believed, would draw all lesser rulers together under the universal
sway of the Emperor, since he, of all human authorities, was the one
most directly related to the essence of men, to the 'perseitas
hominum',[2] and so to the human race as a whole. Through the

1. *Par.* VI, 4: 'l'uccel di Dio'; cf. *Aeneid* I, 394: 'Jovis ales.'
2. 'Cupiditas . . . perseitate hominum spreta, querit alia; karitas vero, spretis aliis omnibus,
querit Deum et hominem, et per consequens bonum hominis,' *Mon.* I, xi, 14. 'Perseitas' has
no 'entry' in the *Enciclopedia Dantesca*. Nardi allowed that 'perseitas hominum' could mean
man considered as a substance (not an 'accident') but maintained that in this context it
should be taken 'in senso etico e non in quello metafisico,' and thought it equivalent to the
bonum hominis assoluto e per sé, cioè Dio' (*Nel mondo di Dante* [Roma: 'Storia e
Letteratura,' 1944], pp. 96-99). But in fact the immediate context shows that Dante is
distinguishing the 'perseitas' from the 'bonum' of man. Cupidity and charity are set in exact
contrast: what cupidity spurns, charity seeks, and *vice versa*. Charity seeks God and man,
and *consequently* the good of man; therefore, by implication, cupidity spurns the good of
man *in consequence of* its spurning his 'perseitas'; which is therefore not identical with his

celebration of justice in the latter half of canto XVIII – and right down to the bitter closing lines against the reigning pope – are clearly discernible, in fact, themes and arguments of Book I of the *Monarchia*.

This last point will be shown in more detail presently; for the moment, I limit myself to noting the surely obvious fact that the Eagle in Jupiter, whatever else it may *also* mean, is still the military ensign and imperial Roman symbol of canto VI. Yet it cannot be simply that same ensign and symbol over again – a mere reminder of earthly conquest and dominion however sacred. As poised and painted here in heaven, it is the form actually taken by the blessed themselves: it is not an image invented to suggest, as a metaphor or simile, a certain experience; it is presented *as the experience itself*, as precisely the object Dante saw here, a particular manifestation of the eternal life; the manifestation appropriate to those of the blessed who were distinguished on earth by their intense love of justice. Hence the reality which it immediately represents must itself be heavenly, eternal. What then is this reality?

The question has already been answered, implicitly, in canto XVIII; where Dante, on ascending into Jupiter, greeted the Eagle's appearance there as evidence that 'nostra giustizia,' all the justice we may realise here on earth, is an 'effect' of the heaven this planet adorns.[3] But not, of course, an effect of this heaven considered as merely physical, but rather, like all the spheres in Dante's cosmos, as a medium for transmitting angelic 'influences' which themselves have their ultimate source in God. But can we be more specific as to the angelic order that operates in and through Dante's Jupiter heaven? I think we can if we take our cue from a passage in the *Convivio* where Dante relates the various angelic orders and hierarchies to the one God; and which I once had occasion to use, in a similar connection, in a study of the solar heaven. 'The contemplation of the

---

'bonum.' What then is it? I see nothing to prevent us taking it as denoting *man considered in his essential nature*; cf. St. Thomas, *Contra Gentiles* II, 41, 'Per se autem dicimus tale quod per essentiam suam tale est'; or again, 'per se enim dicimus secundum quod ipsum,' *ibid.*, II, 55. But the context also shows that the human essence which 'perseitas' denotes involves a close relationship to God; if charity seeks 'God and man, and so the good of man,' then that in man which its contrary, cupidity, does *not* seek must involve a relation corresponding to the conjunctive phrase 'God and man.' This point is well brought out, though he argues it rather differently, by G. Vinay in his edition of the *Monarchia* (Firenze: Sansoni, 1950, p. 64).

3. *Par.* XVIII, 115-117.

Trinity,' I there wrote, 'is expressed by Dante in terms of the traditional division of the angels into nine Orders composing three Hierarchies. The highest Hierarchy contemplates especially the Father, the middle one the Son, the lowest . . . the Holy Spirit.' [4] Thus when Dante arrived in the fourth heaven, that of the Sun, he entered the special province of the Hierarchy which stands in special relationship to God the Son, the Word or Logos; the province that includes also the next two heavens, those of Mars and Jupiter. Now each of the divine Persons is contemplated by his special Hierarchy under three aspects corresponding to the three Orders comprised in it; he is viewed as he is *simpliciter*, and then in relation to each of the other two Persons. Hence, of this middle Hierarchy whose special interest, so to say, is God the Son, the first and highest Order contemplates the Son or Logos as he is in himself; and it is precisely this Order that moves the Jupiter heaven; while the second and third Orders here, moving respectively Mars and the Sun, contemplate the Logos in relation, respectively, to the Father and to the Spirit.

Whether or not this pattern of relations between the Trinity and the Orders of angels governs the *Paradiso* as a whole, certainly it illuminates the heavens of the Sun, Mars, and Jupiter. In the three Jupiter cantos, on my reading of them, Dante's thought is directed towards the Second Person, the Logos of St. John's Prologue, that mysterious Word in which alone is expressed the fulness of the Godhead. Thus in XVIII, 109-111, where the gradually forming Eagle is likened to a picture in process of being painted, the painter being God himself, the simile recalls the special association in Christian theology of God the Son with art and beauty as well as with wisdom. [5] Again, a few verses on (118-23) where Dante prays to the Mind ('mente') whence derives the 'moto e virtute' of the Jupiter sphere, he is not addressing the Godhead in general, still less an angel, as some have supposed, but precisely God the Son; this 'mente' being immediately identified with Jesus driving the buyers and sellers out of the Temple. And, to come to Canto XIX, and to a passage on which more will be said presently, the great assertion of

4. 'The Celebration of Order: *Paradiso* X'; see ch. 8 of this book.
5. St. Augustine calls God the Son, 'ars quaedam Dei,' *De Trinitate* VI, 10 (PL. XLII, 931); cf. Aquinas, *Summa theol.* la. 39, 8: 'species autem sive pulchritudo habet similitudinem cum propriis Filii.'

God's transcendence in verses 40-51, all hinges on the transcendence of God's 'verbo,' the Word, with respect to the created universe.

It can hardly be a coincidence that these repeated allusions to the Logos — divine and incarnate — should occur just at the point where the problem of the *universality* of Christian salvation is raised for the first time in the *Paradiso*. To be sure, canto VII had explained how, through the death of the God-Man, human salvation was made possible; and explained this as a simultaneous triumph of divine mercy and justice. But it had left untouched, it did not even raise the question as to the effective realisation of that possibility *in terms of mankind as a whole* — of the actual availability to all men of the benefit of that marvellous death which was, in principle, *for* all men. The discourse of canto VII, spoken in the heaven of Mercury, ended with the canto's ending; and with the opening of canto VIII Dante was already in the next heaven, Venus, where, if one may so put it, there was much to distract him. And similarly, through the heavens of the Sun and Mars, the problem left unexplored in the discourse of canto VII still remained dormant, only to be roused to life in the pilgrim's mind by the sight of the Eagle of Justice in Jupiter, which is also the 'sign' of the Empire, and therefore, for Dante, of all mankind: a perfectly sufficient prologue to the new theme; the unfolding of which through cantos XIX-XX may also, however, be read as a resumption of the discourse begun in canto VII. In any case, it springs dialectically out of the manifestation to Dante in canto XVIII — a manifestation that is in effect a *challenge* — of, simultaneously, a sign of God's justice *and* a sign of the unity of the human race. And both 'signs' are connected with the Logos, as I shall now show in more detail.

As to God's justice, let me repeat that this is what Dante took the Eagle to be a sign of, as soon as the great bird appeared to him in Jupiter, declaring that all justice on earth is somehow the 'effect' of that heaven (XVIII, 115-117). Thereupon he addresses a prayer to God the Son, begging him — as I interpret verses 118-123 — to direct now against the Roman Curia the same just anger that he had once displayed against the Temple-desecrators; that Curia being the place whence issues the smoke, 'il fummo,' which 'clouds thy ray' (v. 120). Now this last image plainly recalls *Monarchia* I, xi, where the 'fulgor' of justice is said to be besmirched or dimmed only by 'cupiditas;'⁶ the 'fulgor' of justice there becoming the 'raggio' – the ray from the Logos – here. And from this it is but a step to the teaching on justice in chapters ii and v of *Monarchia* II, which may be summed up in two points. First, 'ius' itself, conceived as a right relationship between man and man, is taken back to the mind of God as its ultimate ground; taken back, that is, to the divine idea or 'art' whence the universe proceeds. And secondly, as the natural world reflects that divine 'art', so too, in its own way, should the world of man; and this by the steady pursuit of that 'common good' of human society which is at once the aim of justice ('finis iuris') and the realization on earth of God's will for man considered in his temporal existence.⁷

These points established, we can return to Dante's appeal, in canto XIX, to God's justice on behalf of the non-Christian part of mankind. It must be stressed that this was a Christian appeal, in the sense that it presupposed belief in the Incarnation – that the divine Source of all justice had himself appeared on earth, that the 'ars Dei' (as Augustine called the Logos) had taken human nature, the Word had become flesh. And among the attributes of the Incarnate Word acknowledged by Christian tradition, justice was not the least. He was 'the sun of justice' in Malachi who would arise 'with healing on his wings'; he was 'the Just one' of Acts 7:52; above all he was the Johannine 'Son' to whom 'the Father had given all judgement' (John 5:22) – that is, the judgement at the end of time which is the underlying subject of our canto. Dante then, in addressing his appeal to the Eagle for justice to the pagans, is appealing, implicitly, to Jesus Christ; which means, in historical terms, that he, a western

6. 'Quantum ... ad habítum, justitiam contrarietatem habet quandoque in velle; nam ubi voluntas ab omni cupidiatate sincera non est, etsi assit iustitia, non tamen omnino inest in fulgore sue puritatis', *Mon.* I, xi, 6; cf. *Par.* XVIII, 118-120: 'Per ch'io prego la mente in che s'inizia/tuo moto e tua virtute che rimiri/ond' esce *il fumo che 'I tuo raggio vizia ...*'
7. The definition of 'ius' as 'realis et personalis hominis ad hominem proportio' comes in *Mon.* II, v, 1; its reduction to the mind of God (conceived as the original Artist who has designed the world according to the model found in himself, in his own 'natura') is expounded in *Mon.* II, ii, 2-6: 'quemadmodum ars in triplici gradu invenitur, in mente scilicet artificis, in organo et in materia formata per artem, sic et naturam in triplici gradu possumus intveri. *Est enim natura in mente primi motoris, qui Deus est*; deinde in celo tanquam in organo quo mediante similitudo bonitatis ecterne in fluitantem materiam explicatur.... Ex hiis iam liquet *quod ius, cum sit bonum, per prius in mente Dei est.* ... Et iterum ex hoc sequitur *quod ius in rebus nichil est aliud quam similitudo divine voluntatis*; unde fit quod quicquid divine voluntati non consonat, ipsum ius esse non possit.... Hoc ergo supponatur, quod illud quod Deus in hominum sotietate vult, illud pro vero atque sincero iure habendum sit.'

medieval Catholic, is appealing from a formulation of Christian belief — as touching the conditions of salvation — as he had received it through the Church, and as he thought he understood it, to the ultimate source and ground of that belief.

Yet it would be hopelessly wrong to call this appeal 'protestant'. A far better epithet is 'humanist;' for what comes to utterance here (apart from Christian faith) is all in Dante that marks him as a child of Greece and Rome, so far as a man of his time could be. It is a certain idea, drawn mainly from Aristotle, of the human as such, of man as a distinct species with its own intrinsic structure and proper capacities and end; this abstraction being given form and substance by the poet's long brooding over the *Aeneid*, by his cult of Rome as the secular City of God, as both centre and symbol of 'humana civilitas,' with a history no less providential than that of Israel. All this is involved in Dante's appeal to the Eagle, because it all represented an order of things which, however nobly human, was by theological definition (or so it seemed) purely 'natural' and therefore outside the Christian realm of Grace. And this distinction between the realms of Nature and of Grace once drawn, the rest followed logically. Transferred into the other world, that human order, being a thing of time and history, seemed to lose its *raison-d'être*: it must be either damned or, if still honoured, be left in Limbo. But what sort of solution to this *impasse* was the Dantean Limbo for adults, that hybrid abstraction half-scholastic and half-classicist, with no warrant in the New Testament (or even in theology)? Certainly it left even its inventor unsatisfied. Hence the appeal to the Eagle here.

But there is one aspect of Dante's humanism which comes out particularly clearly in the opening tercets of canto XIX, which are the immediate prologue to the actual voicing of his distress in verses 22 and following. I mean the idea, basic in the *Monarchia*, of the unity of the human race. In that treatise the Empire is in principle co-terminous with mankind, for its proper function is nothing less than to create a 'humana universitas', a 'tota humana civilitas,' a 'universalis civilitas humani generis.' [8] Now the first idea expressed, and very emphatically, in our canto is that of the unity, the co-inherence of the souls composing the Eagle: they speak as one

8. *Mon.* I, ii, 8; iii, 1 and 4.

person, saying 'I' and 'my' though their 'concetto' is plural ('we' and 'our'). This in fact is the only 'cielo' in Dante's Paradise where the blessed speak only in chorus. Now it cannot be supposed that this stress on unity is not an intended reminder of the universality of the Empire, as expounded in the *Monarchia*; unless we supposed (which would be absurd) that the Eagle itself had no imperial significance. On the other hand, if this were *all* Dante intended to convey by his making these souls speak in chorus, it would be hard not to agree with the critics who have found verses 7-9 excessive and frigid. A more subtle theological explanation has recently been proposed by Silvio Pasquazi who takes the Eagle here as a symbol, not primarily of the secular Empire, but of the unity of the human race considered as the recipient of the Word incarnate, this unity being embodied in Mary, the Mother of the Word, who on this view would have been represented by the 'M' out of which the Eagle was formed (XVIII, 97-114).[9] I find this proposal, though attractive, a little far-fetched. But Pasquazi is certainly right in looking to theology for an answer. The unity in the heavenly Eagle that astounds Dante here cannot be just a symbol of the racial unity stressed in the *Monarchia*; for the unifying principles are different. There, in the *Monarchia*, it was human nature; here in the *Paradiso*, it is grace — grace indeed at its apex, as the phrase 'nel dolce *frui*' (v. 2) insinuates. *Frui* was almost a technical term in theology for the heavenly bliss in the possession of God: it is their shared joy in *that* which unifies these souls.[10] Hence the Eagle-figure they compose is *a heavenly* symbol; and Dante's phrase, far from being the banality one critic takes it for,[11]

9. S. Pasquazi's richly suggestive essay, 'L'Aquila nel cielo di Giove,' came out in *Giornale italiano di filologia*, N.S. II, Vol. XXIII, No. 3 (1971); reprinted in *All' eterno dal tempo* (Firenze: Le Monnier, 1972), pp. 493-517. Possible connections between Mary and the Eagle-figure might be explored in patristic and medieval exegesis of Revelations 12; see E.-B. Allo, *L'Apocalypse* (Paris: J. Gabalda, 1921), Excursus xxvi, pp. 167-179. But a more natural connection is between Dante's eagle in Jupiter and the traditional symbol for St. John the Evangelist (cf. *Par*. XXVI, 53).
10. 'Frui est enim amore inherere alicui rei propter se ipsam'. St. Augustine, *De doctrine christiana*, I, 8. 'Res igitur quibus fruendum est, pater et filius et spiritus sanctus', *ibid*. 1, 10 (Corpus Script. Eccl. Lat., Vienna, 1963, p. 10). Cf. St. Thomas, *Summa theol*. 1a2ae. 11. 3.
11. S. A. Chimenz in his lecture on this canto reprinted in *Letture dantesche*, a cura di G. Getto (Firenze: Sansoni, 1964), pp. 1735-1759: 'l'espressione "lieto nel dolce frui" (cioè nella fruizione, nel godimento di Dio) è forse la piú stentata e dura fra tante che ripetono . . . nella terza cantica, questo stesso concetto' (p. 1738). The last clause of this sentence is surely revealing. And since Chimenz's lecture still seems to enjoy some authority — it is frequently cited — I think it worth remarking that it has nothing of interest to offer us in the matter of relating Canto XIX to Canto XVIII, the problem with which I am here

is very pregnant indeed; a signal that he is now passing, for the moment, beyond politics.

And yet the Eagle is still the eagle-emblem of Rome, nay of pagan Rome; see verses 16-18, and above all verses 101-102! And this it can only be if that emblem already signified, even on earth, a heavenly justice – the ultimate ground and meaning of which, as we have seen, is Jesus Christ, God the Son. Well then, as the eagle's meaning on earth was justice for all who share in human nature, for the entire human race, so, surely, it should be here in heaven. And yet . . . how could Dante at this point *not* remember his master in humanity, the 'very dear father' who had left him when Beatrice appeared on the summit of Purgatory; and left him, not to remain in that Earthly Paradise which in the *Monarchia* is a figure of the 'civilitas' that would come with the Empire of which he, Virgil, was poet and prophet, but to return to the twilight world of Limbo? How could Dante not remember all the others who shared Virgil's exile there, though their lives, like his, did honour to human nature? It is then singularly appropriate that the voicing of Dante's distress should begin just here. There is also, be it said in passing, a certain appropriateness in the fact that Beatrice is quite out of the picture here, and will remain so until the ascent into Saturn in canto XXI.

The distress itself is not distinctly stated until verses 70-78. Its first utterance is only the string of metaphors between verses 18 and 30 expressing an obscure need, an aching 'hunger' which only some new answer from 'la divina giustizia' can relieve (28-30). This answer, when it begins, is prefaced by the brilliant simile of the eager exulting falcon, which in its joyousness is already a hint of relief to come (34-39).[12]. Only note a significant alteration of the noun in the two parallel phrases, 'la divina guistizia' at verse 29 and 'la divina grazia' at verse 38: it is God's *grace* that the Eagle will declare. But the declaration itself is reserved for canto XX. Meanwhile, XIX, 40-118 divides into a weighty 'prolegomena' to canto XX (vv. 40-90) and a long digression (91-148) bearing more on the sins of contemporary Christian rulers than on the fate

---

largely concerned. Chimenz simply assumes a thematic discontinuity between the two cantos – that the theological theme of Canto XIX is abruptly introduced without the reader's being in any way prepared for it. He misses entirely the theological undertones of Canto XVIII.

12. Cf. Ovid, *Metam.* VIII. 237-8: '. . . prospexit ab elice perdix/et plausit pennis testataque gaudia cantu est'.

of the pagans in the after-life. My main concern is with the former passage, verses 40-90, in my view one of the greatest in the *Paradiso*. But it is a difficult one and I am left unsatisfied, more or less, by most of the commentaries. I shall first summarize what I take to be its gist, and then consider more closely certain lines and phrases.

The whole of this crucial passage may be reduced, as follows, to two complementary assertions linked by a transition section: (a) verses 40-66, an assertion that since God infinitely transcends his creation, the divine Mind must infinitely transcend all finite understanding; (b) verses 67-84, a transition passage stating Dante's problem in the form of a questioning of God's justice — a questioning which, on the basis of assertion (a), the Eagle declares to be presumptuous; (c) verses 85-90, an assertion that God is absolute goodness and is therefore the entire cause and measure of all that is or may be thought to be good or just. And the two assertions are complementary, being respectively a negative and a positive statement about God's accessibility to the human mind — that is, about our ability to know him. True, the chief emphasis here is on the negative aspect: the stress on God's transcendence, on his *not* being contained by the universe or by any mind that looks from within the universe, is greater than the stress on God's immanence, on his presence *in* the universe and *in* created minds. In this sense verses 40-66 outweigh vv. 85-90. Nevertheless both aspects are present in the discourse as a whole, and this is important and is usually overlooked. Verses 40-60 are the greatest single assertion in the *Divine Comedy* of God's transcendence, but they should be combined with other statements in the poem affirming his immanence, [13] which affirmation as I say, is not lacking even here; indeed it *has* to be present as one term of the contrast which the poet is here trying to express. In fine, Dante is saying, *not* that God's ways are wholly beyond our discerning, but rather that our discernment of them is extremely limited, though real as far as it goes. Out in the mid-sea, he says (vv. 58-63), you cannot see through the water to the bottom, but from the shore you can. 'A whispered echo,' as Bildad says, in the book of Job, 'is all we hear of him, and who can comprehend the thunder of his greatness?' [14] But even a whisper is something.

13. For example: *Par.* I, 1-3; V, 7-12; X, 1-12; XIII, 52-66 . . .
14. Job 26:14. I suspect that this text was very dear to St. Thomas: see the 'Proemium' to

But how, in any case, does this whisper reach us? Or, keeping to Dante's metaphor here, if at least from the shore the bed of the sea is discernible, by what light is it discerned? Obviously by the same light that does *not* suffice to penetrate the deeper waters out 'in pelago' — the light of natural reason, the 'vostra veduta' of verse 52. This is the only light from the human side that is in question throughout all this passage, apart from a passing reference to Christian faith at verses 82-4. Except in this one tercet there is nothing here — whatever the commentators may say and whatever may be the case in canto XX — there is nothing here about 'grace,' about any *supernatural* assistance given to reason. The discourse is not, strictly speaking, theological, but metaphysical. What the Eagle says, in short, is first that God, as *not* contained by the universe, transcends every created intellect — this in verses 40-63 — and secondly that God, as filling the universe, nevertheless shines in and through the human intellect which is 'one of the rays of the Mind/of which all things are full' (53-54) and which in consequence can see *something* of God, its 'principio,' its Source (56). In God's effects, which is what all things are, and, in itself, our intellect sees a *sign* of God;[15] but how slight and small a sign in respect of the reality (58-63)! And here Dante gets close to the approach to God by negation, 'per viam remotionis,' as worked out by St. Thomas and others. We know God inasmuch as *we know that we do not know him.* As Aquinas says in the *Contra Gentiles*: 'In considering the divine Being we have to use the method of negation (*est . . . via remotionis utendum*). For that Being transcends . . . every form that our intellect is capable of apprehending, so that we cannot apprehend it by knowing what it is, but we obtain a kind of knowledge of it by knowing what it is not.'[16]

The transcendence of God is of course a biblical theme, as verses 40-41 remind us with their echoes of Job 38 and Proverbs 8. And God in the Bible transcends all things precisely as their creator. This

---

Book IV of the *Contra Gentiles*; see also his *Expositio super Job ad litteram*, ed. Leonina, Opera omnia, XXVI, Roma (S. Sabina) 1965, c. 26, lect. 1 *in fine*.

15. On the idea that God is the interior source of human intelligence, see Aquinas, *Summa theol.* 1a. 16, 5, on the identity of God and Truth: 'nam esse suum est ipsum intelligere; et suum intelligere est mensura et causa omnis alterius esse et . . . alterius intellectus.' And again, at 1a, 84, 5: 'ipsum lumen intellectuale quod est in nobis nihil est aliud quam quaedam participata similitudo luminis increati, in quo continentur rationes aeternae.'

16. *Contra Gentiles* I, 14. Cf. *ibid.* I, 11: 'sed quia hoc ipsum quod Deus est mente concipere non possumus, remanet ignotum quoad nos.'

is the axiom presupposed here. All the rest follows as a chain of negative syllogisms, a sorites, with the logical movement governing the syntax itself: 'Colui che volse ... *non potè* ... *che* ... *non* ... *E ciò fa certo che* ... *e quinci* apparr che ... *Dunque* vostra veduta ... *Però* ne la giustizia.' The conclusion of the first syllogism, that God cannot but transcend his creation (40-45), becomes the premiss to a second one on the fall of Lucifer (46-48), and this in turn, through an *a fortiori*, is premiss to a third conclusion, that all finite natures are utterly inadequate 'receivers' of the absolute Good which, having no measure but itself, is simply limitless (49-51); whence it follows — fourth conclusion — that our intellect ('vostra veduta') cannot fail to see that the reality of God must far exceed whatever we may apprehend of it (52-57); which conclusion must hold too of our understanding of his justice (58-63). This chain of reasoning, is then rounded off by the exceedingly dense tercet. 'Lume non è,' etc., verses 64-66, which both leads into the second stage of the discourse, the expression of Dante's doubt (67-78), and anticipates the third stage, the assertion that God is the source and the measure of all goodness (86-90); with the implication that if we judge God to be just or unjust, the criterion itself that we use must derive from him, for 'Cotanto è giusto quanto a lei consuona.' These last five verses before the pause at verse 90 and the simile of the mother stork that follows, may be difficult but are not, I would say, really obscure. More troublesome is the tercet, verses 64-66; but before I come to that I must pause on two earlier places in the discourse where my interpretations differ from those commonly found in the commentaries.

The first of these is the mention of the fall of Lucifer at verses 46-48, and the question is whether 'E ciò fa certo' introduces a proof of, or an inference from the doctrine contained in the previous six verses, 40-45. Does the phrase mean, 'and this is shown by,' or 'and *from* this it follows that...'? Against Sapegno and others I prefer the latter sense, chiefly because it makes the whole tercet gravitate towards 'cadde acerbo', as its conclusion, thus giving all possible force to this phrase; whereas on the other interpretation 'cadde acerbo' remains in the air, an unsupported assertion, and the emphasis hovers uneasily between it and the 'ciò' of verse 46.[17]

17. See *La Divina Commedia*, a cura di N. Sapegno (Firenze: 'La Nuova Itali,' 1957), Vol. III, p. 237. The same interpretation in (for example) the commentaries of M. Porena

The other passage is verses 52-57, 'Dunque vostra veduta,' etc.
Here the issue has been simplified by the recent critical text which
happily upholds the 'non' before 'discerna' in verse 56, which
Sapegno and (for a time) Chimenz had preferred to drop. The question then becomes: what is the subject of 'non discerna'? Is it God –
'suo principio' (56) – or 'vostra veduta' (52)? Is the gist of these
two tercets, 'Man's mind is not so powerful that God's is not much
more so – that God does not see ('non discerna') much farther than
we do'? Or is this the meaning: 'Your mind is not so powerful as *not*
to see ('che *non* discerna') that the divine principle whence it derives
('suo principio') greatly exceeds all that your mind can apprehend of
it ('che l'è parvente,' with 'essere' understood in vv. 56-7)'? Taken
in this latter sense the statement, it seems to me, has a nervous force
which on the other interpretation it entirely lacks. For is it not
rather trite to say, 'Whatever man may see, God sees far more'?
Whereas it is by no means trite to say, 'Whatever you may see of
God, you must see that this is vastly exceeded by what you do not
see of him.' Therefore I decidedly prefer the latter sense and am
delighted to find it upheld, not only by Benvenuto da Imola and
recently by C. S. Singleton, but also by the high authority of
Michele Barbi.[18]

But I must pass on to the perhaps more difficult tercet, verses
64-66, 'Lume non è. . . .' This is a statement in two parts, divided

---

(Bologna: Zanichelli, 1950, Vol. III, p. 180) and A. Pézard (*Oeuvres complètes de Dante*
[Paris: Gallimard, 1965], p. 1540) and C. H. Grandgent, in the revised ed. of C. S.
Singleton (*La Divina Commedia . . .*) Cambridge Mass.; Harvard University Press, 1972,
p. 796, and in C. S. Singleton's translation of the *Paradiso,* Bollingen Series I XXX
(Princeton, New Jersey: Princeton University Press, 1975), p. 211. On the other hand,
Fr. da Buti seems to understand the tercet as I do. " 'E ciò fa certo' cioè questo, che è det-
to, fa certo e pruova questo che dirò ora, cioè che 'il primo superbo . . .'" (*Commento*, ed,
Giannum [Pisa: Nistri, 1862], Vol. III, p. 343); and similarly, if I understand him aright,
Benvenuto da Imola. ' "E ciò fa certo". Hic probat dictum suum *exemplo* prime
creature . . .' (my italics), *Commentum*, ed. J. P. Laicata (Firenze: Barbèra, 1887), Vol. V.
p. 238.
18. See N. Sapegno, *op. cit.*, p. 237. S. A. Chimenz was for the omission of this 'non' from
v. 56 in his commentary on our canto given in Rome in 1956 and reprinted in *Letture
dantesche*, a cura di G. Getto (Firenze: Sansoni, 1964), pp. 1735-1759, but in his commentary on the whole *Commedia* (Torino: UTET, 1966 – see Vol. III, pp. 176-177) he
accepted the 'non,' with the proviso that it is pleonastic, 'come rafforzativo della con-
clusione negativa del ragionamento.' It is, of course, accepted by G. Petrocchi: *La
Commedia secondo l'antica* vulgata (Milano: Mondadori, 1966-67), Vol. IV, p. 315. As
for the sense of vv. 52-57 – taking it as agreed that '*vostra* veduta' is right in v. 52 (see
Petrocchi, *op. cit.*, p. 314) – basically three interpretations are conceivable – (1) Taking
'principio' as the *object* of 'discerna' (with or without the 'non') one may with Chimenz (see

his Turin commentary cited above, Vol. III, p. 177) understand Dante as saying that
'l'uomo può conoscere della mente divina solo quello che vede (che gli è "parvente", v. 57),
o poco più, e gli resta occulto quel che è nel profondo della mente di Dio.' In other words,
man can know of God only what he can know – or a little more! And it was, perhaps, to
avoid this feeble tautology that Sapegno (op. cit., p. 237) specified that the human limita-
tion in question was that imposed by *sense* knowledge, 'dai termini che le [i.e., to man's in-
telligence] son porti dalla conoscenza sensibile.' This solution has three weaknesses: (a) the
questionable identification of 'parvente' with 'known by or through sensation,' (b) the
vagueness in which it leaves the phrase 'molto di là,' and (c) that, like solution (2), as we
shall see, it leaves vv. 52-57 only loosely connected with vv. 40-51. – (2) Taking 'princi-
cipio' as *subject* of 'discerna,' one might paraphrase thus: the human mind is not so powerful
but that God, its Origin, sees very much further than it does; see, for example, Fr. da Buti
(*Commento, ed. cit.*, Vol. III, p. 344), M. Porena (*op. cit.*, Vol. III, p. 180), A. Pézard (*op.
cit.*, p. 1542). As I have said, I find this position rather trite, but I feel too that its accep-
tance somewhat weakens the logical cohesion of the whole discourse from vv. 40 to 57,
the cohesion expressed in the rhythmically emphatic 'dunque' introducing the conclusion to
be drawn from the premiss given in vv. 40-51. For this premiss affirmed God's
transcendence not as *knowing* more than his creatures, but as possessing an infinitely
greater, an immeasureably richer (vv. 50-51) *being*. Appropriately therefore the conclusion
affirms this being to be far beyond – 'molto di là da' – our vision's range. – (3) Taking
'vostra veduta' as subject of 'non discerna' but reading vv. 56-57 as *oratio obliqua*, we get,
I am sure, the right solution, as lucidly spelled out by M. Barbi: 'non può la nostra [sic]
veduta esser di sua natura tanto possente, che non debba riconoscere esser il suo principio
molto di là da quello che le apparisce, ossia che non debba riconoscere che la mente divina
le resta in gran parte nascosta al di là dei limiti a cui ella può giungere con le sue forze
naturali' (*Problemi di critica dantesca*, la serie [Firenze: Sansoni, 1934], p. 290). This was
Benvenuto da Imola's interpretation (*Comentum, ed. cit.*, Vol. V, p. 239) and N. Tommaseo's (*La Commedia* ... con ragionamenti e note [Milano: G. Rejna, 1854], p. 669)
and G. Vandelli's (in his revision of the Scartazzini edition of the *Commedia* [Milano:
Hoepli, 6a ed., 1911], p. 833), and is followed in the translations of J. D. Sinclair (Vol.
III. *Paradiso* [London: The Bodley Head, 1948], p. 273) and C. S. Singleton (*Paradiso*,
Bollingen Series, LXXX [Princeton, New Jersey, Princeton University Press, 1975], p.
213).

For me the chief merit of this reading of vv. 52-57 is that, more than the others, it tallies
with my general experience of Dante's style in the *Paradiso*; and this in respect, especially,
of intellectual energy (a) and syntactical and verbal symmetry (b). – (a) Whereas in
solutions (1) and (2) the two factors in question, man's intellect and God's being and/or
mind, are merely compared as lesser to greater, in solution (3) this comparison is achieved
through a certain positive exaltation of the lesser factor; Dante would be affirming, implicitly, our power to *see* that God infinitely transcends us. Thus the contrast is sharpened
to the point of paradox – the power of man's mind being at once and by the same token
affirmed and denied, with respect to the object which is God; the affirmation answering to
vv. 52-54, the negation to vv. 40-51. Moreover this reading would imply the presence in
this passage, along with Dante's sense of God's transcendence, of his conviction, expressed,
e.g. in *Par.* XXIV, 130-134, that God's existence at least can be proved by natural reason.
And that for philosophers of that time there need have been no incompatibility between
this positive theodicy and a deep sense of God's mysteriousness, is proved, to go no further
afield, by the example of Aquinas (compare *Contra Gentiles* I, 13 and 14; 15-29 and 30).
For these reasons I find that solution (3) gives a force and density to Dante's utterance
here such as (1) and (2) are very far from implying. – (b) Moreover it sets the double
negative vv. 55-57 in exact symmetrical correspondence with that contained in vv. 43-45:
'non pò ... non discerna' answering to 'non poté ... non rimanesse', and in such wise that
each pair of negatives has a common subject: God in vv. 43-45, man in vv. 55-57. But
this symmetry, which seems in its orderliness so characteristic, would be destroyed by solution (2), as the reader can judge for himself; and only maintained by solution (1) at the cost
of making the last 'non' of the series pleonastic.

by the semi-colon after 'mai' and opposing light to darkness, that is,
true knowledge to error. Since, as we have seen (vv. 52-54), our intellect is nothing but a 'ray' from God's mind, all the knowledge of
truth it may possess or acquire derives in the last resort from the
luminous 'clarity' of the Logos. As for error, 'tenèbra,' this comes
from the side of the body, 'la carne,' but in one or other of two distinct ways, of which one is morally neutral and the other not. We
may, that is to say, be merely deceived by sense appearances as such
– and this is 'l'ombra de la carne' – or, what is far worse, we may be
deflected into false judgements by the bias of passion – and this is 'il
veleno [de la carne].' This distinction is amply supported by other
texts in Dante.[19] There is no need at all to bring in the concept of
Grace, as Sapegno and Pasquazi and others do.[20] The whole tercet
follows on from the previous statement on the limits of our natural
knowledge of God; to which however it adds two points; first, it
makes explicit that all our perception of truth derives from the
divine Mind; secondly, it stresses our liability to error and that this
comes from our side. It is this latter point that immediately in-

19. References to deception by sense appearances as such: *Inf.* XXXI, 22-27; *Purg.* X,
112-114; XXIX, 47. By the bias of passion: *Purg.* XVI, 92: XIX, 10-24; *Par.* I, 135;
XIII, 118-120.
20. N. Sapegno, *op. cit.*, p. 238, citing da Buti: 'Senza la grazia illuminante d'Iddio noi
siamo ciechi, o per lo dimonio che ci accieca, o per la concupiescenza della carne che n'of-
fusca o per piacere del mondo che ci corrompe.' The same interpretation is given, though
less assertively, by Benvenuto da Imola, *ed. cit.*, V, pp. 240-241; and among modern
scholars by C. S. Singleton in his revision (1972) of C. H. Grandgent's commentary, *op.
cit.*, p. 797, by E. Mazzali in *Lectura Dantis Scaligera*, Vol. III, *Paradiso* (Firenze: Le
Monnier, 1968), p. 674, and by S. Pasquazi in *Nuove letture dantesche* (Firenze: Le Monnier, Vol. VI, 1973), p. 274. Pasquazi's is an extreme statement of the view that 'Lume
non è,' etc., refers to 'grazia illuminante' and of its logical consequence, that in the rest of
the tercet, 'anzi è tenebra/od ombra de la carne o suo veleno,' Dante makes his Eagle assert
that such knowledge of God as man can have by nature ('la conoscenza naturale umana') is
mere 'darkness.' This extraordinary conclusion evidently arises (a) from Pasquazi's
overlooking the connection between the 'lume' of v. 64 and the 'raggi' of vv. 53-54, and
(b) from his not distinguishing the two causes of human error clearly distinguished by the
poet in v. 66: 'od . . . o'. This distinction was understood by Porena (*op. cit.*, p. 180) as
also by Tommaseo whose note here makes the point succinctly: 'd'ignoranza o perversità
carnale' (*op. cit.*, p. 670). To sum up, I hold that the Eagle is *not* dismissing as 'darkness' all
knowledge, even of God, acquired by the natural light of human reason; rather, that it is
declaring (a) reason's limitations, as having to start from sensation (cf. *Par.* IV, 40-42),
and (b) its liability to be biased by the passions. Furthermore, I take vv. 64-66 as a
preparation for the great declaration in vv. 86-90 that all morality finds its source and absolute basis in God's nature – the point well expressed by P. H. Wicksteed: 'Our very demand for justice is but a ray of light from God Himself. It is some imperfect apprehension
. . . of justice, outflowing from the inmost being of God, that makes us demand justice in
the universe' (quoted by J. D. Sinclair commenting on his translation of *Par.* XIX, *op. cit.*,
p. 283).

troduces the Eagle's statement of Dante's protest at the exclusion of
the good pagans from salvation: and the same point is echoed implicitly twenty verses later (85) by the exclamation, 'Oh earthly
animals! Oh dull minds!'

I am now near the end of this paper and the reader may think it
strange that I have left no space for a really close discussion of what
is surely (he may say) the main dramatic and thematic point of
Paradiso XIX, Dante's question about the pagans. Well, in notes
21-26, subjoined to this essay, I refer to such books and articles as
seem to me most usefully relevant to such a discussion. For the rest,
I have two reasons for not, at present, going more deeply into this
matter. The first is that Dante's question here ought to be studied in
the light of his own reply to it (given of course through the Eagle) in
canto XX: the question and the answer should be treated together,
and this is a paper only on the canto of the question. On the other
hand — and here is my second reason — the division of the cantos
does correspond to a division into two main parts of the entire discourse of the Eagle in the Jupiter heaven in that, whereas in canto
XIX Dante's question does not, on the whole, seem to be allowed,
in canto XX it rather suddenly becomes admissible. True, the
reader is being prepared for this change before the end of canto
XIX, in the sketch of the Last Judgement (vv. 106-114) which is
all to the disfavour of the Christians — the Christian rulers — in the
condemnation of whom the pagan Ethiop and the Persians are
shown as heartily concurring. Still, the general tone and stress of the
Eagle's speeches in our canto is surely unfavourable to Dante's question; the plea to God to make his justice intelligible is met, in the
main, by an assertion of its inscrutability. And it is chiefly this assertion that I have tried to analyse.

I cannot however leave Dante's question altogether without comment. He asks, why should the virtuous non-Christian who has
never heard the Christian message be condemned for his unbelief
(vv. 70-78)? Now 'condemned' here ('ov' è questa giustizia che'l
condanna?') must mean 'relegated to Limbo,' for we are being asked
to image a man who has committed no sin ('sanza peccato in vita o
in sermoni,' v. 75). It follows that the man's unbelief itself was no
sin — indeed the supposition of innocent unbelief is the very nerve of
Dante's protest. But by this time theological tradition was equally
firm on the point that unbelief in this purely negative sense would be

no sin; that is to say, the non-assent to the Gospel of those to whose minds it had not in *any* way, explicitly or implicitly, been presented.[21] . *Fides ex auditu*, 'faith comes from hearing,' as the theologians said, citing Romans 10:17; and a message unheard could not be culpably rejected, as St. Bernard remarked long before Dante, and just as vigorously.[22] To speak, as Porena does,[23] of Dante's question as 'daringly rationalistic' and 'almost impious' only argues a great ignorance of medieval theology; even if one grants, as I think one may, that in general the medieval theologians did not very greatly concern themselves about the ultimate fate of the Muslims and pagans. The New Testament doctrine that God wills the salvation of all men has been only very gradually developed in the Church; though repeated by Church Councils since the fifth century, it never in fact received much emphasis, at the official level, until the Papacy's reaction against Jansenist narrowness in the seventeenth century.[24] Still, the problem was certainly not ignored

21. The solution of this question presupposed the analysis of ignorance as a factor in human activity considered ethically; with a view, that is, to determine how far ignorance might excuse a sin, or extenuate its guilt, or even perhaps itself be imputable as sin. For an exhaustive account of theological thought on this point through the twelfth and thirteenth centuries, see O. Lottin, *Psychologie et morale aux XIIe et XIIIe siècles* (Louvain: Abbaye de Mont César, 1942-1960, Tome III, 2a Partie, I), pp. 18-96; and with special reference to the 'ignorance' of the pagans, L. Capéran, *Le problème du salut des infidèles* (Toulouse: Grand Séminaire, 1934), pp. 41-43, 184-201. Of these works Lottin's is the more detailed in documentation, but together they form an indispensable introduction to the theological background of Dante's question in *Par.* XIX. Cf. also *Dictionnaire de théologie catholique* (Paris: Letouzey, Vol. VII, 1927), col. 1727, 1845-1865. St. Thomas treats succinctly of 'purely negative unbelief in *Summa theol.* 2a2ae, 10, 1 ('ignorantia secundum negationem puram, sicut in illis qui nihil audierunt de fide, non habet rationem peccati, sed magis poenae'); cf. *ibid.*, 34, 2 ad 2: 'ipsa infidelitas non habet rationem culpae, nisi inquantum est voluntaria.'

22. In a famous letter to Hugh of St. Victor about baptism St. Bernard touches on the case of those who die unbaptized in lands where the Gospel has not been preached: 'Quid ergo? Necdum lex promulgatur et iam praevaricantes tenentur? *Et quomodo*, inquit [St. Paul, Romans, 10: 14-15] *credent in eum quem non audierunt? Quomodo vero audient sine praedicante? Quomodo ... praedicabunt nisi mittantur?* Necdum iniuncta, necdum vulgata, necdum audita praedicatio est, et ... tam durum est Dominus ut necdum sata iam metere velit, et non sparsa colligere? Absit, ... Qui unus est Magister in caelo et terra et, qui magister tantum in Israel erat, familiari privatoque colloquio tradebat quod traderet, docebat quod doceret, non quod exigeret et ab absentibus.' *S. Bernardi Opera*, ed. J. Leclercq and H. Rochais (Rome: Editiones Cistercienses, Vol. VII, 1974), pp. 185-186. The reference at the end of the text is, of course, to John, 3: 1-15.

23. 'Parole non soli libere ma quasi empie, che ci mostrano un Dante audacemente razionalista,' M. Porena, *op. cit.*, p. 181.

24. The very gradual development of Catholic teaching on this matter may be followed chronologically in Denzinger-Schönmetzer, *Enchiridion Symbolorum*, ed. 32 (Freiburg im Br., Herder, 1963): nos. 333, 340, 623-624, 780, 1362, 1522-1523, 2005, 2304-2306, 2429, 3014. See also P. Tihon in *Dictionnaire de Spiritualité* (Paris:

by thirteenth-century theologians. How could it have been? Their basic principles were (a) that God willed all men to be saved, and (b) that this salvation necessarily entailed faith in Christ; and how could both these propositions be true when it was obvious even to them that men had lived and died before the preaching of the Gospel, and that many now lived and died without hearing that preaching? Their answer was to distinguish between explicit and implicit faith, and to find the concept of implicit Christian faith confirmed by such texts as Hebrews 11:6: 'Whoever comes to God must believe that he is, and is the rewarder of those who seek him.' For St. Thomas this text included all that a pagan need believe in order to be saved; for to believe in God as rewarder – or more simply, to believe in Providence – is implicitly to believe in Christ. Nor was he by any means the only theologian of his time to suggest this kind of hidden contact between the pagan soul and God's fatherly love.[25]

But to return to Dante, the odd thing is that he seems to know nothing of all this; for does not his question here assume (especially in view of the answer it receives in Canto XX) that there is no alternative to *explicit* faith? This, and not any 'audacity,' is what I find surprising in the question. Nor would Aquinas or Bonaventure, I think, have admitted it in precisely the terms in which Dante puts it; because, *prima facie* at least, these terms involve two assumptions which the main Catholic tradition was at least strongly inclined to

---

Beauchesne, fasc. 41, 1966), art. 'Grâce', col. 729-731. Tihon brings out the significance in this development of the Church's reaction to Jansenist narrowness in the seventeenth century, and the importance of Vatican Council II's having at last proclaimed 'sans réticence la solidarité spirituelle des baptisés avec chacun des hommes,' especially in the Dogmatic Constitution *Lumen Gentium* and in the Declaration on non-Christian religions. The basic problem may be formulated thus: how far and in what sense does Catholicism admit the possibility of an *implicit* faith in Christ? For a good general introduction to the matter, see *Sacramentum Mundi, An Encyclopedia of Theology*, ed. K. Rahner *et. al.* (New York: Herder and Herder, Vol. V, 1970) pp. 405-438; also L. Capéran, *Le probléme . . .* , *op. cit., passim*; Y. Congar, *La foi et la théologie* (Paris: Desclée, 1962), pp. 3-40, 72-120.
25. See the works cited in n. 24 above. Capéran deals with medieval theology from the early twelfth century down to Aquinas in ch. 6 of his book, *op. cit.*, pp. 170-201. I do not know of any really recommendable study of St. Thomas's teaching on implicit faith. References to his use of the term 'fides implicita' are in *A Lexicon of St. Thomas Acquinas*, by R. J. Deferrari and M. I. Barry (Washington, D.C.: Catholic University of America Press, 1948-53), p. 420. The following *loci* are particularly important: *Expositio super Epist. Pauli Apostoli ad Hebraeos*, XI, lect. 2; *De veritate* XIV, 11, *corpus art.* and ad 1, 2, 5: *Contra Gentiles* III, c. 159; *Summa theol.* 1a2ae. 89, 6; 106, 1 ad 3; 2a2ae. 2, 7 ad 3; 4, 1; 10, 1. I try to go more deeply into this subject in the last essay contained in his book, 'The Two Dantes', *passim*.

reject: (a) that there is *any* adult human being to whom God does not make faith, and consequently grace, available in some way; and (b) that a man can go through life entirely untouched by grace and yet never sin. But here we touch on the strangest of Dante's theological oddities, his Limbo for adults, which is a subject beyond the scope of this paper.[26]

Our canto ends with the diatribe against the secular rulers of Europe, in symmetry with the assault on the pope at the end of Canto XVIII. The transition from the theological theme of the salvation of the pagans to this concluding political *serventese* is effected by the passage about the Last Judgement (vv. 103-114) where the Christian rulers will be put to shame before the pagans (and Muslims?) represented by Ethiops, Persians, and implicitly by those Romans whom the world so justly has revered (vv. 101-102). Then the vision of judgement turns into the series of prophecies of obloquy which make up the diatribe itself (v. 115 to the end). After one tercet on the Emperor, it is the turn of Philip IV of France – the mention of whose death, by the way, at verse 120 dates this canto after November 1314 – and then, in their turn, of the lesser kings and princes. The piece is not poetically very remarkable. The main poetic and intellectual force of *Paradiso* XIX is concentrated in the central passage about God as utterly transcending the created world and yet, at the same time, as being the source and ground of all our human awareness of truth and justice.

26. This important and fascinating topic has been unduly neglected by Dante scholars; but see F. Mazzoni's excellent study of *Inferno* IV in *Studi Danteschi*, XLII (1965), 29-206.

10

THE TWO DANTES (I)

Limbo and Implicit Faith

Dante was attached, simultaneously, to Christianity and to paganism.[1] This was not a half-way position, nor a wavering between two conceptions of life according to mood or circumstance. The attachment to paganism was more like that which a man may feel to his youth, except that paganism was a stage in the history of Dante's race, not of himself individually. Yet there is a sense in which the pagan 'object' of his attachment was not something past and done with, existing only in history or legend or works of art; rather it was a permanent part of himself, an *alter ego*; it was that second self which his imagination took into the Other World in the form of Virgil and which, once it had assumed this form, was allowed to take charge of, to guide and govern the Christian protagonist of the resulting poem. Because the hero of the *Divine Comedy* is a Christian the poem is Christian, but through two-thirds of it the hero is guided by a pagan. And even 'guided' is too weak a term; Virgil in the poem is the hero's 'leader', 'master', 'teacher', 'lord'. Above all he is Dante's 'father' — 'my sweet father', 'sweet and dear father', 'my more than father'. Seldom in literature has the filial sentiment, blending reverence and affection, been so finely expressed as in this relationship which carries the central narrative line through so much of the great poem. And it is of its essence that the father here is a pagan, the son a Christian; simultaneously so close and so separated.

I shall not, in this essay, linger on the details of the relationship as it unfolds through the *Inferno* and the *Purgatorio*. This has often been done and in any case my present aim is different. What I wish to do is to take this spiritual distance between the two poet-per-

---

1. I know that Dante calls paganism 'a stench' and its gods 'false and lying' (respectively, *Paradiso* XX, 125 and *Inferno* I, 72). The present essay tries to reach a correct understanding of such statements.

sonages within the same poem as a starting point for some reflections on Dante's concept of human nature, and particularly on
human nature as a limit which had to be crossed — transcended and
left behind — in the hero's quest for God.

Let us start from the arresting phrase with which the *Comedy*
opens: 'Nel mezzo del cammin di nostra vita', 'half way through the
journey of our life'. Nothing could be simpler; we all know, and are
assumed to know, what 'our life' means; and the path-metaphor
comes so naturally that the reader may scarcely avert to it. Yet a
whole culture speaks through this line, and one nourished, in the
first place, on the Bible. Dante's contemporaries were doubtless
better prepared (if not by actual reading, by church-going) to catch
the frequent biblical echoes in his verse, and so to recall here the
Vulgate rendering of Isaiah 38, 10: *Ego dixi: in dimidio dierum
meorum vadam ad portas inferi*, 'I said: in the mid-point of my days I
will go to the gates of hell'. The announcement of the general theme
of the *Inferno* could hardly be plainer, once you have noticed it.

But if we stop to think, complications arise. For it is clear that the
time-reference, 'nel mezzo', completing the spatial metaphor of 'cammin,' correlates with the beginning and the end of human life,
between which it marks the mid-point, and therefore with birth and
death; so that the metaphor might be taken as implying that 'our
life' simply ends with death, at least for the individual. Yet that is
clearly not what Dante believed; his whole message runs in the contrary direction, he has a special and conspicuous place in his Hell for
those who hold that 'the soul dies with the body'.[2] Hence, read in
this way, the initial metaphor of the Poem would seem to be
nothing but good rhetoric, a device for gathering an audience as
wide as humanity itself; the poet's subject being the humanly universal one, 'nostra vita'.

Nevertheless, I suggest that even from a doctrinal point of view
there may be more in this line than meets the eye. Certainly Dante
held, with most (not all) educated men of his time, that the human
soul was by nature immortal, and even that reason could
demonstrate this, or at least show it as probable. But there are hints
in his prose writings, the *Convivio* and the *Monarchia* (particularly
towards the end of this work) to limit the reference of the adjective

2. *Inferno* X, 15.

in the phrase 'human life'. After death the soul would live on 'in a *more than human nature*' —[3] that is, as possessing immortality through its share in the 'divine' principle of mind or intellect; it being assumed nevertheless that this principle is intrinsic to the soul's nature — not a supernatural gift, not a 'grace' — although unable to realise its full potential so long as the soul is joined to a mortal body. Thus the life of man would divide into two stages, one properly human, in time and before death, the other 'divine', after death.

The *Convivio* is a kind of introduction to philosophy for laymen, written between 1304 and 1308, and in Italian, not Latin —[4] a deliberate innovation made, of course, with that audience in mind. Dante planned it as a commentary on fourteen of his own poems, but left it unfinished; all we have is an introductory book (I) and commentaries on three poems (II-IV). It is a unique revelation of his mind in middle age — he was over forty when he discontinued it — yet it hardly strikes one as the work of a man who had fully found himself either as thinker or as writer. That, I feel, would be one's impression of the *Convivio* even if we did not have the *Comedy* with which to compare it. Transitional and open-ended, the *Convivio* — like the *De vulgari eloquentia*, written within the same period and also left unfinished — is the work of a man taking stock of past experiences rather than attempting to express, once for all, a total vision (which is the point of view of the *Comedy*). It grew in fact out of a pause in Dante's life, a moment of relative inactivity both poetical and political. His political career had been cut short by his exile from Florence and its immediate aftermath (1302-'4) and his political hopes would only revive with the Italian campaign of

3. 'in natura più che umana', *Conv.* II, viii, 6: similarly, at III, ii, 14 the rational soul 'participa de la *divina* natura'; again, of the five 'natures' which compose the human being, it is the 'ultima', the rational, that is 'vera umana, *o meglio dicendo, angelica*', III, iii, 11. Yet, for all this tendency to assimilate the rational power in man to a nature that would, strictly speaking, be superhuman, Dante, even in the *Convivio*, insists that man is a unity, 'una sola sustanza', III, iii, 5, and cf. viii, 1. Even here he doesn't contradict the Thomist — and Catholic — thesis that man has only one *anima* (*Summa theol.* 1a. 76. 3) and in *Purgatorio* IV, 1-6 he will affirm this explicitly. The 'super-humanity' of the intellect consists, for him, in its kind of activity and imperishibility, not in its 'essence'. Hence the final formulation in *Mon.* III, xv, 5: 'Si ergo homo medium quoddam est corruptibilium et incorruptibilium, cum omne medium sapiat naturam extremorum, *necesse est hominem sapere utranque naturam*'. This comes rather close, however, to a dualistic theory of man; and cf. I, xii, 6.

4. By 1308 D. and perhaps not yet begun the *Comedy*, and certainly not got far with it. The *Monarchia* was written later; indeed, perhaps later than the first five cantos of *Paradiso*: see the edition by P. G. Ricci, Milan, 1965, p. 158.

Henry VII (1310-13). His output of lyric poetry was ending and the great reassertion of his artistic powers, which would issue in the *Divine Comedy*, was yet to come. So the *Convivio* gathers up and works forward from the results of those philosophical studies in which, he tells us, he had found relief after the death of Beatrice as far back as 1290.[5] Understandably the resulting complex of ideas and themes is loose-knit, imperfectly unified. The splendid defence of the Italian language in Book I is followed by what amounts to an apology for philosophy conceived as man's effort to participate consciously in a life whose full scope and perfection, however, is beyond human powers, being in essence 'divine' (Books II-III). By contrast, but also in consequence, Book IV is marked by an abrupt return to the human and humanly intelligible and controllable world, to ethics and politics. But all through the *Convivio* we find a certain indifference to theological considerations; one of its more striking differences from the *Comedy*. Certainly the writer is a Catholic Christian, but he is evidently far more concerned to draw out certain cherished philosophical insights than to anticipate possible objections from the side of the theologians (some of whom were no mean philosophers).

Thus we see Dante in the *Convivio* coming out with ideas about the perfectibility of man in this life, and of the soul in the next, without its apparently crossing his mind that he was begging the question (from the standpoint of orthodox Christianity) as to whether man *could* reach perfection, here or hereafter, unassisted by divine grace. In the *Convivio* the Christian doctrine of grace – and so of man's *de facto* inherent sinfulness and natural incapacity to bring himself, by his own effort, to union with God – is virtually ignored.

This was the effect (so far as it may be explained abstractly) of two lines of intellectual influence, the one Neoplatonist, the other Aristotelian. On the one hand Dante is inclined to identify intellect as such with a participation in the 'divine'.[6] On the other hand, as an enthusiastic Aristotelian he was enchanted by the idea he saw set out in the *Nicomachean Ethics* of an effective direction of the moral

5. *Conv.* II, xii.
6. See note 3 above, to which another pregnant text may be added: 'onde si puote ... vedere che è mente: che è quella fine e preziosissima parte de l'anima che è *deitade*', *Conv.* III, ii, 19.

life by philosophical reason. Could men only be induced to listen to
philosophy, there was nothing to prevent them achieving the virtue
and happiness consonant with their nature, 'the human good' —[7]
and this here and now, on earth, by the right use of reason and free
will. Such ideas were much in Dante's mind and heart during the
first decade of the fourteenth century, before the crisis which
brought on the writing or the resumption of the *Comedy*. And with
them went what I have elsewhere described as 'a tendency to regard
human life, properly speaking, as . . . directed to ends attainable on
earth, and to relegate to a life after death the whole possibility and
process of man's divinization' —[8] this latter being the eventual
perfection of the divine principle in us, the intellect, which Aristotle
had discerned, though at the same time he had declared that the life
of intellect in its fulness transcends the merely *human* life of 'our
composite nature' (soul-and-body) — 'it would be too high for man;
for it is not in so far as he is *man* that he would live so, but in so far
as he has something divine in him'.[9] Pondering on these and other
texts of the Philosopher, and seemingly unaware of their potentially
non-Christian implications, Dante came near to conceiving of both
earthly and heavenly happiness (but especially the former) as accessible to man simply through the nature he possessed; the former,
through his nature as human (reason immanent in a mortal body),
the latter through his nature as sharing in 'divinity' (reason as
transcending the body).

The *Comedy* is quite another matter. To pass from the *Convivio* to
the Poem is to be aware, almost at once, of two decisive differences.
The first is a shift of the focus of interest from life within time to its
end-result after death (with which we may connect, with special
regard to the *Monarchia*, a shift of focus from man as social to man
as individual, the permanent standpoint in the *Comedy* being that of
an individual consciousness, of the voyaging 'I' who seeks fulfilment
in a final wholly personal vision). And secondly, in the *Comedy* the
soul's journey to its last end is represented, with the utmost clarity
and in a variety of ways, as a thing altogether impossible without
supernatural assistance both intellectual and moral. Any idea of a
'flight of the alone to the Alone'[10] such as the *Convivio* might, here

7. *N. Ethics* I, 13; 1102a 14.
8. *The Mind of Dante*, ed. U. Limentani, Cambridge, 1965, p. 67.
9. *N. Ethics* X, 7; 1177b 26-30.
10. Plotinus, *Enneads* VI, 9, 11.

and there, encourage is now implicitly ruled out. The entire action of the poem hinges on the protagonist's submission to the rule and guidance of Virgil and Beatrice, themselves the instruments, ultimately, of God.

The differences then consist in a new concentration, as regards the aim of life, on a personal union with God beyond and outside time; and as regards the way to that end, on the need for accepting divinely appointed guides. However, in this essay I am mainly concerned with a deep strain in Dante — in the way he visualises the situation of man on earth — which, as it seems to me, never wholly conformed to the new pattern imposed by that shift towards other-worldliness and the surrender of autonomy. And to identify that strain, as I call it, to hear the voice of the 'other Dante', I shall go chiefly to the last and most closely reasoned of the four Books of the *Convivio*, which sketches a humanist ethic for life in time, based on man's inherent 'nobility' and capacity for a 'virtue' that is self-achieved. And my working hypothesis is that this *Convivio* ethic offers a clue for the understanding of what is most distinctive (and strange) about Dante's Limbo — its adult inhabitants.

From the point of view I am adopting, the *Monarchia* belongs with *Convivio* IV, though I am aware of the chronological difficulty involved in thus contrasting the two prose treatises with the poem; for the manuscript evidence rather favours dating the Latin work to the last years of Dante's life, after the bulk of the *Comedy* had been written.[11] But the *Monarchia* is marked by a confidence in man's ability to organise his life on earth, for purely human and temporal ends, very similar to what we find in *Convivio* IV; it only spells out what Dante thought this meant in political terms. The care for man's temporal happiness, removed from the Church, is made the exclusive charge of the civil power; and this on the basis of a distinction, rigorously drawn, between the *two* 'final ends' (*duo ultima*) of human life, one in time, the other in eternity. For the peculiarity of man is that he is composed of two 'natures', a mortal and an immortal; hence he alone among created beings has been designed for two distinct fulfilments, on earth as a man, in heaven as a 'god'.[12] The thesis is paradoxical, but it grows naturally (as we shall see in more detail later) out of ideas already adumbrated in the *Convivio*.

11. See note 4 above.
12. *Mon.* III, xv, 3-7; cf. I, xii, 6.

In this sense the two works are continuous. But neither, in *this* respect, is continuous with the *Comedy* considered as an 'action', a story; for the poem's story concludes, not with the protagonist's achieving moral virtue (though this too is implied), nor with his reaching an earthly Promised Land, but with his being lifted to a direct vision of God. If the poem has any continuity, on this score, with the two prose works, it should be looked for chiefly in the *motive* of the hero's journey towards that vision; inasmuch as the journey is undertaken, not for the hero's personal perfection only, but also for the betterment, moral and political, of human society on earth – 'in pro del mondo che mal vive'.[13]

In any case the chief novelty of the *Comedy*, from my present point of view, is its stress on the soul's need for help and guidance, through life and death, from higher powers. In this respect it has no precedent in Dante's minor works, unless we count the glimpse at the end of the *Vita Nuova* of the poet's 'pilgrim spirit' being drawn heavenwards by a 'new understanding' given it by Love (the direct object of which, however, was Beatrice, not God):

> Oltre la spera che più larga gira
> passa 'l sospiro ch'esce del mio core:
> intelligenza nova, che l'Amore
> piangendo mette in lui, pur su lo tira.[14]

But that brief vision was anyhow soon obscured by other interests,[15] without which indeed the 'poema sacro/al quale ha posto mano e cielo e terra' would have lacked much of its 'terra'.[16] On the other hand, the *Convivio* and the *Monarchia* lack much of the heavenly – and the purgatorial – component; the former has little about the soul as immortal, the latter almost nothing. And what little the *Convivio* does have is drawn chiefly from non-Christian sources, from the Greek and Arabic philosophers available to Dante (though made so, in fact, largely by Christian scholars like Albert

---

13. *Purg.* XXXII, 103: 'for the good of the world, which lives badly'.
14. *Vita Nuova*, XLI: 'Beyond the sphere that circles widest passes the sigh that issues from my heart: a new understanding, which sorrowful love gives to it, draws it ever upwards'.
15. See *Conv.* II, vi-xii for the supplanting of Beatrice by Lady Philosophy in D's mind and heart.
16. *Par.* XXV, 1-2: 'the sacred poem to which both earth and heaven have set their hand'.

the Great and Aquinas). What he relevantly found — or thought he found — in these sources may be summed up in three propositions: (a) the soul is immortal in virtue of its intellectual 'part'; (b) precisely as intellectual the soul cannot be satisfied by the knowledge it acquires through the bodily senses; (c) consequently death, when we cease to be 'bound and imprisoned by our bodily organs', is precisely the condition of our attaining the full knowledge we naturally crave for.[17] An inborn craving for knowledge: a condition, the body, holding it back from satisfaction: then a release from that hindrance. Thus in the *Convivio* the brief allusions to a *post mortem* life for the mind come near to representing the mind as *self-propelled* towards God — propelled simply by its inborn capacity for some kind of union with the supreme object of intelligence, 'lo sommo intelligibile'. In the *Paradiso* this theme will reappear and be splendidly developed —[18] but always within the framework of submission to guidance and divine grace; it being presupposed that Dante's soul could not have begun to move towards God if God had not come to meet it through his appointed instruments — the Roman poet, the Florentine girl, the canonised mystic Bernard of Clairvaux.

This question of the continuity of the *Comedy* with the minor works was a good deal debated by Dante scholars in the 1940s and '50s. As I had occasion to write some years ago and feel able to repeat today, 'after Nardi's and Gilson's work in the 1930s it had become evident that Dante could no longer be called a Thomist without very considerable qualifications; and in particular that the *Convivio* and the *Monarchia* show clear traces of a certain dualism — in assertions, more or less explicit, of the independence of philosophy from theology and of the civil power from the Church, and of the twofold 'final end' of man. . . . The question then arose whether this dualism persisted into the *Comedy*, and if so precisely to what effect; the result being . . . to concentrate attention on the contrasted symbols of Virgil and Beatrice, and more generally to raise the issue of the 'humanism' or otherwise of the *Comedy*'.[19] This was written when I was still inclined to date the *Monarchia* before the *Comedy*: yet I would still maintain that there is a fundamental

17. For point (a) see *Conv.* II, viii, 7-12, IV, xxii, 13-18; for (b) see III, xv, 6-10, IV, xiii, 6-9; for (c) II, iv, 17.
18. For example in IV, 115-32; XXXIII, 46-8.
19. 'Dante Studies in England', 1921-64, *Italian Studies*, XX, 1965, p. 7.

difference — such as I have tried to indicate above — between the
Comedy and the two other works taken together. This seems to me
clear even supposing that the *Monarchia* belongs to the last decade
of the poet's life and that *doctrinally* there is agreement between it
and the *Comedy* where both works touch on the same themes.

In the *Comedy* for the first time in Dante's writings, God is *active*
in man's regard — or better, perhaps, in Dante's. In the *Convivio*
God is the remote goal of human desire; in the *Monarchia*, chiefly
the ultimate ground of civil and ecclesiastical authority; but in the
Comedy he is the goal of human (that is, Dante's) striving here and
now, and he actively operates here and now to make both the striving and its successful outcome possible. It is this that marks the
Comedy all through with a new humility, a new sense of personal in-
sufficiency and unworthiness, a new and continual recourse to supernatural assistance — signified, of course, no less by Virgil (as *Inferno*
II makes clear) than by the Christian agents in the hero's salvation:
Mary, Lucia, Beatrice, Statius, St Bernard. And it is this factor that
compels one to read the *Comedy* as the effect of a personal crisis, a
'conversion'. Some such crisis is fairly visible already in the first two
cantos of *Inferno* and it becomes dazzlingly evident by the end of the
Purgatorio; evident, that is, as a fact, for its nature is disputed. What
had Dante been converted from? Carnal or spiritual sin, or both?
Certainly, hints at carnal sin are dropped *en route*, especially in the
Purgatorio where Dante meets his old friend Forese among the penitent gluttons, and in the reproaches of Beatrice.[20] But all that is less
to my purpose than the implicit confession, at the end of the
Purgatorio, of an intellectual aberration, of a misuse or misdirection
of the mind. Dante has just witnessed, under the Tree in the Earthly
Paradise, a symbolic action representing the degeneration of the
Christian world. This ended, Beatrice explains that what he has seen
enacted is a crime against God himself, a 'blasphemy by deed'
('bestemmia di fatto'); the clue to which lies in the meaning of the
sacred Tree, now twice violated; by Adam first and now by the
degenerate Church. But she speaks in riddles and the poet is baffled;
whereupon Beatrice declares that this present obtuseness of his
should bring home to him the total inadequacy, in spiritual matters,
of 'that school' which he had followed.[21] Thus at this crucial

20. *Purg.* XXIII, 115-23; XXXI, 43-63.

moment in the action of the poem, the present Dante, its protagonist, dissociates himself intellectually from a former Dante.

Nowhere else in the *Comedy* does he make it so plain that his crisis had been mental as well as moral. Yet the 'school' is left un-named and its teachings undefined, except negatively: it was a teaching that gives no insight into spiritual matters and the path it follows is remote from the 'via divina', the 'way of God'. Note that Beatrice speaks in the past tense of Dante's association with 'that school'; so that what now blocks his understanding of her words are its *after*-effects; of which he himself, however, is unconscious, and not through natural lapse of memory but because, as Beatrice goes on to point out, he has drunk of the water of Lethe (lines 94-6). Now the effect of Lethe, we have been told, is to remove the memory of sin; [22] therefore Dante's following that school had involved a moral fault on his part – presumably intellectual pride. But the main stress in all this passage falls on the opposition between, the one hand, a certain school of thought or way of think-ing and, on the other, Beatrice's 'word' (line 87) and 'the divine way' (88-90) – these last being clearly two aspects of a single super-natural order, the will of God with respect to mankind (symbolised in the Tree) and as manifested through Revelation and the Christian message. To this message Dante has in part rendered himself insen-sitive by adopting certain intellectual principles and procedures, the general nature of which is sufficiently indicated by their stated op-position to the supernatural order with its mysteries: let us call it, loosely but with enough precision for the present, a rationalism con-tent to stay within the limits of human knowledge and regarding

21. *Purg.* XXXIII, 82-90. The first speaker is Dante, the second Beatrice:

> 'Ma perché tanto sovra mia veduta
>   vostra parola diṣiata vola,
>   che più la perde quanto più s'aiuta?'
> 'Perché conoschi', disse, '*quella scuola*
>   *c'hai seguitata*, e veggi sua *dottrina*
>   come può seguitar la mia parola;
> e veggi *vostra via* da la *divina*
>   distar cotanto, quanto si discorda
>   da terra il ciel che più alto festina'.

'But why do your desired words soar so far beyond my sight, that the more it strains the more it loses them?' 'So that you may know', she said, 'that school which you have follow-ed, and see how its teaching can follow my word, and see that your way is as far from the divine way as the heaven that highest spins is from the earth.'

22. *Purg.* XXVIII, 128.

with a certain detachment the Christian mysteries formulated by theology. Something of this kind, we can be sure, is being confessed by the poet, and confessed as an error, both intellectual and moral, now utterly repudiated. Later on, once the ascent into Paradise has begun, Dante will, from time to time, be bewildered by the novel experiences; but never entirely baffled by the comments and explanations he will receive from Beatrice. Only now, just prior to the ascent, does he declare himself entirely baffled; only now does he expressly mark a difference between his past self as a 'philosopher' and his present self as a neophyte in the school of Christian wisdom symbolised by Beatrice.

Nevertheless, all this being said, there remains, I think, more than a grain of truth in Gilson's remark that 'un petit coin de Dante' escaped immersion in Lethe – [23] meaning that something of Dante's 'former self', as I have called it, persisted into the Comedy, marking it with a certain intractable eccentricity from the standpoint of Catholic tradition. This is not to call him a heretic; everyone familiar with his writings – the Convivio, the Monarchia, the Letters as well as the Comedy – knows that he would have rejected that charge indignantly. But it is a doctrinal point that I want to make; one that has nothing to do, as such, with the unlimited freedom Dante allows himself as a moral critic of the popes and the Roman Curia; which in any case does not seem to have shocked his Catholic contemporaries. Nor indeed do they seem to have been so much struck as we might expect them to have been by such theological oddities in the Comedy as I shall attempt to point out. Oddity, of course, is relative to a norm; and the norm in this case is the Catholic doctrinal tradition, not only as it then existed, but as it has developed since; and in the light of which (whether we are Catholics or not) we ought to be able to observe Dante historically, noting 'period' features in the doctrinal aspect of his work of which he himself could not be aware. If Dante is, in some respects and in relation to Catholic tradition (in the sense indicated), theologically eccentric, we may in part explain this in terms of his time-context and his culture – assuming that a given cultural situation underlay, even if it didn't determine, his choice of formulas and symbols.

23. Dante et la philosophie, Paris, 1939, p. 100.

The world reflected and reflected upon in the *Comedy* was a society in crisis; the long decline of the medieval world had begun. Dante's judgement on this world was coloured by his conservatism; by his aversion in particular to the powerful French monarchy and to the rising middle class of merchants and bankers. Nevertheless, he is a marvellous witness to the political, religious and intellectual life of his time. My concern is mainly with the intellectual aspect. Now intellectually Dante was a child of the thirteenth century, and the principal intellectual event of that epoch had been the emergence, in the Christian schools themselves, of something like a serious rival to theology. For the first time for many centuries the Church found herself faced, in Europe itself, by a mental world of wholly non-Christian provenance, the product of Greek and Graeco-Arabic philosophy and science. Perhaps the clearest single testimony to the existence and nature of this new rival to theology is the list of 219 theses condemned by the bishop of Paris in 1277.[24] The list is presented as a summary of 'errors' circulating in the Arts Faculty of the University; and the propositions in question, though not a logically coherent system, do amount to a general view of the world and of man quite incompatible with Christianity. The universe is presented as a down-flow of emanations proceeding eternally and necessarily from the First Being: first the Intelligences, then the heavenly bodies whose motion they cause, then the sublunary world of material forms perpetually coming to be and passing away. Of these last, the *contingentia*, which include the human race, God is only remotely the cause (*causa remotissima*). Hence he does not know them directly and individually; hence providence, as Christians understand it, is a myth. Matter is eternal. Individual men have neither intellects of their own nor free will; they are transient entities enclosed in an order of secondary causes with no direct access to God. Theology is 'based on fables'. Man has nothing to

24. The text is in *Chartularium Universitatis Parisiensis*, ed. Denifle and Chatelain, Paris, 1889-97, vol. 1, no. 4: reprinted and arranged in logical order by P. Mandonnet, *Siger de Brabant et l'avérroïsme latin au XIII siècle*, 2 vols., Louvain, 1908-11 (II, pp. 175-91).N.B. Having just called Dante a 'child of the 13th century', let me add that this description is intended in part to indicate certain *limitations* in his culture with respect to the period in which he was writing the *Comedy* — when certain aspects of his culture were already old-fashioned: see espec. G. Padoan, *Il pio Enea, l'empio Ulisse*, Ravenna, 1977, pp. 7–29.

look forward to after death. 'Happiness is to be had in this life and not in another'.[25]

In a sense all this can be regarded as a conceptualization (in terms of certain identifiable philosophical influences) of the idea of 'Nature' — that is, of a fixed causal system operating between the human world and God. The idea of a 'natural order' was not in itself new; twelfth century Christian thought was familiar with it. But the coherently worked out philosophical expression of this theme, and the distinct formulation of the problems which it posed for theology, this was the work of the century of the new Universities and the new Mendicant Orders, of Albert the Great and Roger Bacon, Aquinas and Bonaventure, of the Latin Averroists, of the young Dante. And of course the dominant intellectual influence was now Aristotelian: by the end of the century the writings of Aristotle and his commentators had become the chief sources of philosophical and scientific culture for all educated Europeans. When Dante called Aristotle 'the master of the human reason' [26] the meaning he intended was rather particular — he was thinking especially of ethics —[27] but the phrase would have been accepted by his readers as valid in a general sense; Aristotle was *the* master in the rational investigation of reality. He was 'the master of those who know';[28] he was 'that glorious philosopher to whom above all others Nature has disclosed her secrets',[29] Nevertheless Aristotle was a pagan, and if all the Universities now offered courses on his philosophy, on his disclosures of Nature's secrets, these things after all represented ways of thinking which might easily, in particular cases, raise objections to the Christian mysteries, or at least make them appear irrelevant to the study of Nature or of man as part of the natural order — the dangers that Petrarch was later to feel so acutely.[30] Dante's attitude was very different from Petrarch's but it

25. These two last propositions are those most relevant to my present inquiry. As R. A. Gauthier has shown in a brilliant study, they (and two or three others in the official list) reflect the influence of the humanist ethic of Aristotle; see 'Trois commentaires "avérroistes" sur l'Ethique à Nicomaque', *Archives d'Histoire Doctrinale et Littéraire du Moyen-Age*, XVI, 1946-8, pp. 187-336.

26. *Conv.* IV, vi, 8.

27. See Gilson, op. cit., pp. 144-51.

28. *Inferno* IV, 131.

29. *Conv.* III, v, 7.

30. See *De sui ipsius et multorum ignorantia* and *Invective contra medicum*, III. Both texts are in *Francesco Petrarca: Prose*, ed. Martellotti and others, Milan-Naples, 1955.

is by no means an idle question to ask whether the influence of Aristotle (or of his Arabic commentators) may not be behind certain oddities (from the Christian point of view) in the *Comedy*.

Three topics especially, in the poem, seem to raise this kind of question: the role of secondary causes in the creation of the universe; the Angels and astral 'influences'; the relation of human nature to divine grace. Here I am concerned with the third of these topics, and especially with its bearing on the Dantean Limbo (*Inferno* IV), and more particularly with the unbaptized adults in Limbo whose major representative in the poem is Virgil. Dante's Limbo was, of course, a variant on a theological tradition – the form a certain doctrine assumed in his imagination. The doctrine itself involves rather complex and far-reaching problems and some of these I shall touch on in this essay, but only so far as I think it necessary for an understanding of the adults in Dante's Limbo. And the interest, for me, of this aspect of his Limbo is that it seems to offer a particularly promising clue to what is distinctive about the way Dante 'thought' his Christianity – in other words, the form which Christian belief took in his mind and imagination; it being assumed that this form was not unaffected by philosophical theory and, as regards his Limbo in particular, by his prolonged and intense study of the *Nicomachean Ethics*. But I owe it to the reader to give, without further delay, a brief outline of what 'Limbo' signifies in the Catholic tradition. And here a little theology is unavoidable.

In traditional Catholic theology, then, Limbo (*limbus*, 'border') is the name given to a place or state of those of the dead who were, or are, neither saved nor damned. The difference in the tenses is required because the tradition is that some disembodied souls were in that neutral state only for a time, whilst others are in it forever.[31] Let us call these two categories A and B. Category A consists of those people – more or less identified with the pious Jews of the Old Testament – who lived before Christ but believed in him as the Saviour who was to come, and so died 'justified' and in the grace of God. However, they could not actually benefit thereby, and pass on to enjoy the vision of God, until Christ himself had died on the Cross. In principle they were, indeed, already redeemed, but by a kind of delayed action which did not take effect until Christ

31. Denzinger-Schönmetzer, *Enchiridion Symbolorum*, ed. 32, 1963; nos. 858, 926, 1306, 2626. *Dict. de théologie catholique*, IX, 1, col. 760-72.

'descended into hell', as the Creed says. Until that moment they in-
habited the 'Limbo of the Fathers', *limbus patrum*.[32] This doctrine
was supported by biblical data — God's special favour towards the
Jews under the Old Law and certain New Testament texts (e.g.
Ephesians 4, 9, I Peter 3, 19). Dante does not distinguish the *limbus patrum* from the rest of Limbo, but his Virgil recalls the depar-
ture of its inhabitants when Christ opened the door for them, victorious after his Passion (*Inferno* IV, 52-63).

Category B, on the other hand, is entirely composed of souls
who, for no personal fault of their own, are altogether outside the
realm of grace and will never enjoy the beatific vision.[33] They
represent a later theological development than the souls in category
A. Their existence is, in fact, an inference from certain principles
which may be distinguished as follows: (1) Owing to the 'Fall' at
the beginning of human history all human beings start life deprived
of grace (this, properly, is 'Original Sin') and so with no prospect of
the face-to-face, 'beatific' vision of God.[34] (2) God has chosen to
restore mankind to its original state of grace, but only through the
'one mediator' Jesus Christ: only by faith (explicit or implicit) in
him and by baptism (whether conferred sacramentally or 'desired')
can man come into the state of grace and so inherit God's
kingdom.[35] (3) But obviously, many human beings die in infancy
without baptism, and before they could make any conscious act of
faith or have any conscious desire for baptism (not to mention that
many who are unbaptized grow up morally infantile or as half-wits,
etc., and thus only doubtfully capable of an option for Christ that
would supply the want of sacramental baptism). (4) On the other
hand such human beings are, by definition, innocent of grave *personal* sin and therefore do not incur the extreme punishment of grave
sin, damnation proper. What then happens to their souls after
death? The answer, first propounded by theologians and then
officially sanctioned by the Church, is to say that they survive
forever in the 'Limbo of the Children', *limbus infantium*. As unbaptized they remain in the deprivation of divine grace which is
'original sin' and they will never see God. But as personally inno-

---

32. Aquinas, *Summa theol.* 3a, 52, 5.
33. See references in note 31; Aquinas, *Summa theol.* 3a. 52, 7.
34. Denzinger-Schönmetzer, op. cit., nos. 780, 1512, 1521 (and pp. 827-8).
35. ibid. nos. 780, 1510-16, 1523 (and pp. 877-8).

cent they suffer no pain. Whether, nevertheless, they are conscious
of lacking the supreme Vision or find themselves perfectly content in
the merely 'natural order' are matters of opinion on which the
Church has not pronounced. The latter view was that of St Thomas
(in his later writings) [36] and it has tended, on the whole, to prevail
in the Church since his time. As for Dante, as he accepted the *limbus
patrum*, so he accepts the *limbus infantium* (*Inferno* IV, 30,
Purgatorio VII, 31); but his general picture of Limbo is marked by
two distinctive features. First, he represents all the Limbo-dwellers
as yearningly conscious of their lack of the supreme Vision; and here
he is with St Bonaventure and against St Thomas.[37] Secondly, and
this is vastly *more* remarkable, his Limbo includes intellectually and
morally full-grown adults, those shades in the Noble Castle (*Inferno*
IV, 67-151) who are the chief subject of this essay.

Let me now offer some personal comments and queries on the
above data. I speak from a moderate knowledge of the history of
Catholic doctrine and subject to correction by better scholars.

First then, it appears to me that while the Church has always
taught (following St Paul in 1 Timothy 2, 4 and Romans 11, 32)
that God wills the salvation of all men, this doctrine did not in fact
receive much emphasis until comparatively recent times.[38]. In
Dante's time, I think it fair to say, Catholic theology by and large
did not much concern itself with the ultimate destiny, in God's
sight, of the pagan world whether before or since the coming of
Christ. Secondly, I would say that, as a consequence of this relative
unconcern about the non-Christian world, medieval theologians by
and large were only rather slightly and marginally interested in the
question how far and in what sense one could speak of *implicit* faith
— in the sense of a faith in Christ co-existing, unconsciously, either
with complete ignorance of him or, as in the case of Jews or

36. cf. *QQ. Disp. de Malo*, V, 3-4.
37. St Bonaventure, *In 2 Sent.*, D. 33 q. 2 Resol. On this point see F. Mazzoni, 'Il canto
IV dell '*Inferno*', *Studi Danteschi* XLII, pp. 75-6.
38. The very gradual explication of this doctrine can be followed chronologically in Denzinger-Schönmetzer, op. cit., nos. 333, 340, 623-4, 780, 1362, 1522-3, 2005, 2304-6,
2429, 3014. The point I have made here is supported by P. Tihon, S.J., in the *Dictionnaire de Spiritualité*, fasc. 41, Paris, 1966, art. 'Grace', col. 729-31. Tihon shows the
significane in this respect of the Church's reaction to Jansenist narrowness towards the end
of the 17th century, and the importance of the 2nd Vatican Council's having at last
proclaimed 'sans réticence la solidarité spirituelle des baptisés avec chacun des hommes', especially in the Dogmatic Constitution *Lumen Gentium* and in the Declaration on non-
Christian religions.

Moslems, with unorthodox views about him.[39] The concept itself of
fides implicita was not lacking (cf. Aquinas, *Summa theologiae*, 2a2ae.
2, 5-8; 10, 4 ad 3) but it was hardly a central preoccupation of
theologians, nor, in particular, do its implications for an assessment
of the spiritual state of the world outside Christendom seem to have
been taken very seriously. These considerations will be presupposed
when I come to examine Dante's approach to the same problem.

Then again, other, though related, questions may be raised by
considering the general moral state of non-Christians — that is, not
simply as non-believers but as sinners; and they are raised very
sharply by Dante's *Inferno*, as we shall see. In this connection we
meet the theological concept (but already pervasive in the New
Testament, especially in St Paul) of 'healing grace', *gratia sanans*, as
a divine help that strengthens the will against evil, 'healing' the
moral infirmities left by Original Sin.[40] And at once the question
arises for the reader of Dante — especially in regard, as we shall see,
to his Limbo —: Is grace in this sense necessary for the entire
avoidance of personal 'mortal sin', that is sin that incurs damnation?
To this question the more usual answer in the Church, since St
Augustine, has been that grace in this sense *is* necessary, and that
was the view taken by Aquinas;[41] but, as we shall see, it can only be
rather doubtfully ascribed to Dante. Finally, one might ask whether,
according to normal Catholic teaching, a person to whom God had
never in fact offered grace — for whom, consequently, it has never
been *possible* to give, in any way, a faith-assent to Christ — may
nevertheless incur damnation through some personal mortal sin
other than, and not implying, the refusal to believe. I raise this ques-

39. On this matter in general see L. Capéran, *Le problème du salut des infidèles*, Toulouse,
1934 (new and revised ed.); *Dictionnaire de théologie catholique*, art. 'Infidèles', VII, 2, col.
1726 ff.; *Sacramentum Mundi:*, 'An Encyclopedia of Theology', ed. K. Rahner, S.J., *et. al*,
5, 1970, pp. 405-38. Even the great Aquinas never sets himself *ex professo* and thoroughly
to explore the implications — theological, anthropological, psychological — of that notion of
a *fides implicita in divinam providentiam* which he allows, in passing, that some pagans may
have had, and which would have sufficed to save them (*Summa theol.* 2a2ae. 2, 7 ad 3; cf.
the other texts referred to in ch. 9, note 25). It is instructive in this respect to study two
Questions in the *Summa* which deal *ex professo* with explicit/implicit faith and with the lack
of faith, 'infidelitas' – respectively 2a2ae. 2, 5-8, and 2a2ae. 10 *passim*. Only in passing (at
2, 7 ad 3 and at 10, 1 and 4) is any interest shown in the situation of the pagan world
vis-à-vis salvific faith.
40. Aquinas, *Summa theol.* 1a 2ae. 109, 2, 4-9.
41. Denzinger-Schönmetzer, *op. cit.*, nos. 223-8, 239, 1521, 1525; *Summa theol.* 1a2ae.
109, 2, 4 and 8; *De veritate* XX, 12 ad 2; *De maelo* V, 2 ad 8.

tion because, as we shall see, the *Inferno* implicitly raises it. Yet surely it is an unreal question, corresponding to no factual situation past,
present or future, once granted the principle mentioned above, that
God really wills the salvation of all. For if that be true, then God
offers a real possibility of faith, and so of grace to all who are sub-
jectively capable of the assent and commitment which faith in the
Gospel would entail. It follows that there never has been a human
being, capable of moral choice and so of personally doing right or
wrong, who was in the situation that the question envisages.[42]

The points made in the last two paragraphs will be presupposed
in my analysis of the way Dante propounds and attempts to solve
the question of the salvation of unbelievers. These points are five.
(1) Already in Dante's time it had long been accepted Catholic
teaching that God wills the salvation of all men – this being regarded, of course, as a gift of God (a 'grace') which only takes effect in
the saved through their faith in Christ. (2) It follows that, if anyone
is in fact damned, he must first have been offered the possibility of
salvation through faith in Christ. (3) Granted these two points, the
question naturally arises about the fate of those who seem to be in-
voluntary believers: may they be saved through some *implicit* faith
in Christ? (4) It appears that this problem was not urgently felt by
theologians up to and including the time when Dante wrote. (5)
The weight of theological opinion at this time was, and for long had
been, that morally adult human beings could not altogether avoid
mortal sin without the help of God's grace.

So much by way of preamble. Now let us look more closely into
some of the problems raised by the adults in Dante's Limbo – souls
of human beings who had died after reaching, apparently, moral
maturity but are now neither saved nor (in the ordinary sense)
damned. Broadly – allowing for further subdivisions and some
remarks in conclusion – my treatment will fall into two parts: in the
first (I, A) I shall ask how far Dante, in the *Comedy*, makes use of
the concept of 'implicit faith'; in the second (II) I shall offer a fairly
detailed analysis of the goodness or 'virtue' that Dante seems to

---

42. Denzinger-Schönmetzer, *op. cit.*, nos. 332, 623-4, 1522, 2005 etc.; also *Dict. de
théologie catholique*, VI, 2, col. 1599, 1636-40, 1656-60. In view of this developed
teaching of the Church on God's universal 'offer' of grace to mankind, it is by now clear
that to think of mortal sin while prescinding from this offer is a mere abstraction – though
Aquinas, influenced by the later Augustine, seems occasionally to think in this way; see
2a2ae. 2, 5 ad 1; 10, 1.

ascribe to his Limbo adults. As a pendant to the former section I shall discuss, briefly, the non-Christian personages in the *Inferno* who are not in Limbo but are represented as well and truly damned in the usual sense (I, B).

I 'IMPLICIT FAITH' IN THE 'COMEDY'

A. *Virgil and the Limbo-Dwellers*. Dante plainly expects us to admire his Limbo adults; through two-thirds of his poem the fine qualities of one of them, Virgil, are kept constantly in view. But they have certain defects which account for their being where they are – not a happy place – and destined to stay there, apparently forever. These defects are, in respect of those who had lived before the coming of Christ, that 'they did not adore God rightly' (*Inferno* IV, 38) – with which flawed worship we may associate, provisionally, Virgil's confession 'I was a rebel against his [God's] law' (ibid. I, 125); and in respect of those who have lived since Christ, that they were not baptized and therefore, it is implied, lacked Christian faith. Such is the total account to the discredit of the Limbo adults that we are given in the first and the fourth cantos of the *Inferno*; [43] nor is anything essential added, on this head, in the rest of the *Comedy*. Now the want of baptism in the post-Christian group is reducible to want of Christian faith, since baptism is mentioned only in function of this faith, to which it is 'the door' (*Inf.* IV, 36); so that in this respect the defect is the same in both groups, the pre- and the post-Christian. And it is this defect that is stressed, in fact, in the rest of the poem; whenever a pagan comes up for commendation it is his want of faith that is the limiting defect. So it is in Virgil's sad words to Sordello: 'Io son Virgilio; e per null'altro rio/lo ciel perdei che per non aver fé'. [44] So it is in the account of the miraculous offering of faith – or more precisely, of the occasion for it – to Trajan and Ripheus in *Paradiso* XX. Meanwhile the more positive faults alluded to at the beginning – Virgil's having been a 'rebel' against God and the other pre-Christian pagans' not having

---

43. I, 125; IV, 33-42.
44. *Purg.* VII, 7-8: 'I am Virgil; and for no other fault have I lost heaven but my lack of faith.'

worshipped rightly, 'debitamente' — these recede into the background.

Nevertheless the hint has been dropped — that double reference at the very start of the *Comedy* to some fatal impiety on the part of the 'good pagans' who lived before Christ. This must keep us from simply assuming (as many critics do) that *mere* absence of faith, unbelief as a purely *negative* fact sufficiently accounts for the exclusion from grace of these Limbo-dwellers. There is a latent *positive* fault which must be brought into relation, in the end, with the more obvious factor of unbelief; and brought by us, for this is a point the poet leaves to the reader's discernment. He does however — and this is important — seem to want us to understand that the impiety and the unbelief are two sides of one and the same spiritual situation of the adults in Limbo. Indeed, these two faults are even represented, in a sense, as interchangeable, inasmuch as Virgil at one moment explains his detention in Limbo as the consequence of his 'rebellion' (*Inferno* I, 124-6) and at another as due simply to his unbelief (*Purgatorio* VII, 7-8). All the same, the two explanations are logically distinct; it is one thing to say 'I rebelled', another to say 'I did not believe'. So the problem remains of discovering how plausibly to correlate these two 'faults'. I shall suggest, before the end of my essay, a solution to this problem. But this difficulty itself is only one of several presented by our general theme, the theory of human nature that underlies the Dantean Limbo.

Leaving in abeyance then, for the time being, further examination of Virgil's 'impiety', let us take our study of his unbelief a few steps further — his unbelief and that of the other Limbo adults whose spiritual situation, in this respect, Virgil undoubtedly represents. And at once two questions arise out of what we have so far observed concerning Virgil. First: Is there any clear reason (apart from those hints at a positive impiety of the 'good pagans' which have been noted) for supposing that Dante does *not* present mere unbelief, in adults, as *ipso facto* a barrier against grace? In other words: Does Dante clearly show us any fault in his pagan adults which would have excluded them from grace, apart from the bare *fact* of their unbelief? And secondly, does it appear in the *Comedy* that the adult Limbo-dwellers ever *could* have been believers, that it had ever been possible for them to be saved by at least implicit faith in Christ?

To the first of these questions it isn't at all easy to give a definite answer. On *a priori* grounds indeed one might suppose the answer would have to be 'yes' – that Dante must have held that mere unbelief *alone* could not account for the want of grace in anyone; taking 'mere unbelief' strictly as simply an absence of faith that would not *per se* involve any voluntary opposition to the Christian message; and assuming that Dante's thinking as to the moral state of the pagan world was consistent with his own ethical principle, stated in a different context, that where there is no act of free will there is neither merit nor culpability.[45] Which of course was sound theology. For the theologians *infidelitas negativa*, mere not-believing as such, did not of itself entail any act of the will, and so could not be classed as a sin. Aquinas states this with his usual clarity: 'Unbelief (*infidelitas*) can be understood in two ways: first, purely negatively (*secundum puram negationem*), so that a man be called an unbeliever merely because he has not the faith. Secondly . . . by way of opposition to the faith, as when a man refuses to hear about it or despises it. It is this that completes the notion of unbelief, and it is this sense that unbelief is a sin; whereas unbelief *in the purely negative sense*, as in those who have heard nothing about the faith, *does not have the character of sin*, but rather of punishment, such ignorance of divine things being a result of the sin of our first parents'.[46] And the words I have underlined were later officially endorsed in the Church's condemnation, in the sixteenth century, of the proposition of Baius that 'purely negative unbelief, in those to whom Christ has not been preached, is a sin'.[47] I must add however, that to separate, in the abstract, 'negative unbelief' from moral imputability is not to affirm that in the concrete anyone – at least any adult – *has* ever been a purely 'negative unbeliever' with respect to God's offer of grace through faith.

Now it seems hardly credible that on this simple matter Dante would have differed in principle from St Thomas. Yet it is by no means clear that the principle of the non-culpability of merely negative unbelief is applied, in the *Comedy*, to the case of the pagans in Limbo. On the contrary, there is a good deal in the poem to suggest *prima facie* that Virgil and his companions are relegated to Limbo simply and solely because of the bare fact of their want of

45. *Purg.* XVIII, 64-6; cf. XVI, 70-2.
46. *Summa theol.* 2a2ae. 10, 1; cf. 34, 2 ad 2.
47. Denzinger-Schönmetzer, op. cit., no. 1968.

Christian faith, a want that involved no act of will on their part. This may be brought out in the form of an answer to the second question put above, which rephrased becomes: Does Dante in any way show us the good pagans as unbelievers who had rejected an opportunity of believing?

The hypothesis envisages, in the first place, an opportunity only for an *implicit* faith, since the at one time 'possible' belief envisaged would be that of pagans like Virgil to whom Christ in fact was never preached. Now it had always been accepted in the Church that the Old Testament was the record of the first stage in God's self-revelation to mankind; and, by the same token, of a kind of inchoate faith in the Christ to come on the part of the pious Jews. And this reading of the Bible was expressed theologically by speaking of faith in Christ as passing through stages of gradually increasing explicitness. Foreshadowings of Christianity were also looked for in the records of paganism, though less seriously and systematically. Still, since Dante himself looked in that direction for 'prophecies' of Christ – taking the Sibylline oracles, for example, to be such, as so many medieval Christians did – one might expect to find some suggestion in the *Comedy* that pagans too might be saved by an implicit faith in Christ analogous to that of the Hebrew patriarchs and prophets. But it is hard to find even a hint of this. Indeed, apart from the Jewish heroes and heroines whom Virgil saw being led out of Limbo by Christ in person after his Passion, there seems to be no *certain* case of merely implicit faith in Christ in the whole *Comedy*. Let us now test this statement.

The persons in question are all the pagans before Christ and the unbaptized since, leaving out of consideration all who died in childhood before becoming capable of an act of personal faith; our concern being only with moral adults. Now, with three exceptions, all the non-Christian adults – whether they had lived before or after Christ – are located either in Limbo or in Hell. The exceptions are Cato, who has been in Limbo but whom we meet on the shores of Mount Purgatory, and the Emperor Trajan and Ripheus the Trojan. I shall return to these last two presently. As for Cato, the majestic guardian of Purgatory though a pagan and a suicide, it seems almost certain that his eventual destiny is Heaven, but we are told in fact nothing of his faith. Perhaps he represents in the *Comedy* a kind of pagan analogue to the implicit faith of the pious Jews; but if so he is

singular in this, as in most other, respects. All the other adult pagans
who, being in Limbo, escape full damnation, and so may be reckoned as 'good', all these, so far as the question of *faith* is concerned,
seem to be presented as mere non-believers and in terms which convey no suggestion that they were ever potential believers and so
had, at some time, a real chance of salvation — *unless* there is a hint
of this in those allusions to a flawed worship and a rebellion against
God's law, which have already been noted. True, Virgil gives no
such hint in his first explicit confession of unbelief:

> Io son Virgilio; e per null'altro rio
> lo ciel perdei che per non aver fé . . . [48]

but it has been argued that his words a few lines on do allude to a
positive and culpable refusal to believe (in the Saviour who was to
come): [49]

> Non per far, *ma per non fare* ho perduto
> a veder l'alto Sol che tu disiri
> e che fu tardi per me conosciuto. [50]

On this view Virgil's 'non fare' would be some voluntary exclusion,
while he was yet living, of faith, and so of a consequent state of
grace and eventual glory. It is a tempting interpretation; indeed I
am inclined to think it correct, as will appear later on. For after all
we cannot forget or ignore Virgil's open confession, made to Dante
on their first encounter and before their voyage began, that he had
been a 'rebel' and that this was why he could not accompany Dante
into Heaven. With that confession in mind it is hard to know what
else to make of 'per non fare/ho perduto', etc. Yet difficulties are
presented even by the immediate context. For in this context the
direct meaning of 'per non fare' is surely only a repetition of the

48. *Purg.* VII, 7-8, See note 44 above.
49. See G. Busnelli, S.J. in *Studi Danteschi*, XXIII, pp. 79-97. F. Mazzoni, in the art.
cited above at note 37, rejects Busnelli's view, maintaining that D's Limbo-dwellers are excluded from grace simply and solely for *infidelitas negativa*; and this because (a) D's Limbo
theology is more Bonaventuran than Thomist; (b) in *Purg.* VII, 31 Virgil alligns himself
with the 'innocent children' who have died unbaptized; (c) that if D. had thought of Virgil
and his companions as sinners, he would not have honoured them as he does by setting
them apart from the other Limbo-dwellers in the Noble Castle. I am not convinced by
these arguments, not even by (b) which seems to me the strongest one. As will appear in the
course of this essay, I incline to think that on this crucial point Busnelli was right.
50. *Purg.* VII, 25-7. 'Not for doing, but for not doing, have I lost the sight of the high
Sun that you desire and that was known by me too late.'

negation in line 8, 'per non aver fé'; simply a confession of 'negative unbelief' (and note 'e per *null'altro* rio'). Again, the last clause here 'e che fu tardi per me conosciuto' seems almost to exclude the idea that God had in fact given the Roman poet a glimpse of his designs sufficient for 'faith' in them; at the very least that clause enforces the mere *implicitness* of whatever faith Virgil may have been offered the chance of. In any case the general stress of the five lines quoted falls so sharply on Virgil's non-belief and on his innocence in all *other* respects, that the natural impression left, surely, on most readers is that what he is confessing here is a purely 'negative unbelief', in the sense explained by St Thomas. And this impression, even if questionable in the wider context of the poem, seems to be rather strongly supported by several other considerations.

In the first place, to understand Virgil's unbelief as culpable would seem to eliminate any essential moral difference between Virgil and the damned proper – the *Inferno*-dwellers from canto V down to the bottom of Hell. For if he culpably chose not to believe, then Virgil is a sinner, as Francesca, say, or Ulysses is. It is true that, unlike these, Virgil would have sinned only by omission ('per non fare'), but the whole Catholic tradition taught, and Dante elsewhere plainly accepts, the culpability of sins of omission.[51] And if Virgil sinned, then, by the logic of Dante's system, he deserved his exclusion from Heaven – he and the other 'great spirits', his companion in the 'noble castle' in Limbo. But in that case we can hardly be meant to feel any *strangeness* in Virgil's exclusion from grace; whereas I think I speak for most readers if I say that a sense of bewilderment is of the essence of the Dante-personage's attitude to the fate of his companion through Hell and Purgatory; a sense of dismay at the exclusion from divine favour of a man so noble and good; of a dismay which therefore is an implicit protest; the very protest, in fact, that is finally made explicit in the Heaven of Justice, the protest at the exclusion from grace of those who have *innocently* lacked faith (*Paradiso* XIX, 70-8). Because it is perfectly clear that this final, and finally explicit, protest is couched in just these terms: it all hinges on a supposition of innocent unbelief. Here if anywhere, where the Eagle of God's justice replies to Dante's protest, would be the place – if the unbelief of Virgil and the rest were really *not* in-

51. See *Dict. de théologie catholique*, XII, col. 154-6; O. Lottin, *Psychologie et morale au XIIe et XIIIe Siècles*, III, 2[a] partie, pp. 40-51; M. César-Louvain, 1949.

nocent — for the crushing counter-assertion, that they are excluded
from Heaven because, while they *could* have believed, they had
chosen not to. But in fact nothing of the kind is said: the exclusion is
left mysterious — seemingly as much beyond human understanding
as the Godhead itself (*ibid.* 40-69, 82-90). And this is strange; for
has not Virgil, at the beginning of the *Inferno*, already connected his
and the other noble pagans' exclusion from grace with his and the
others' sin of impiety, as we have seen? Why should the Blessed in
the Sixth Heaven (so much more enlightened than the poor poet in
Limbo), when called upon to explain the same thing, have recourse
to mystery?

My point is that there is at least a certain apparent inconsistency
between, on the one hand, Virgil's initial self-confessed guilt before
God and, on the other, the innocence that seems to attach, through
the rest of the Poem, to that fatal unbelief of his. How, in the light
of that 'I was a rebel', can this innocence be genuine? Unless, indeed, we are supposed to separate, morally, the unbelief from the
rebellion: but how is this possible if, as we have seen, the two faults
converge to make one explanation of Virgil's ungraced condition?
Yet the sense of Virgil's innocence remains with us, stirring a sense
of the strangeness of his fate, such as we do not feel, or need not
feel, with respect to the fate of the truly damned (from canto V
onwards). Thus we may feel that the doom of Ulysses is tragically
strange (*Inferno* XXVI). But it isn't at all tragic or strange when
seen from within the moral structure of the *Commedia*. Within this
structure the doom of Ulysses is *deserved*; whereas, even in this
perspective, it is hard to see how Virgil deserves his; and this
because Dante never discloses the connexion between that initially
confessed impiety of Virgil and his unbelief; except so far as it is implied that both factors together account for Virgil's lack of grace.
But this lack is much more closely associated, throughout the Poem,
with unbelief than with impiety; and it is just this that can arouse
our sense of its strangeness. For the unbelief is actually presented *as
though* it were blameless — with reference to Virgil personally in
Purgatorio VII, 7-36, and to the pagans generally in *Paradiso* XIX,
70-8. In other words, it does not appear as the result of a choice
between alternatives. The only alternative to pagan unbelief that we
are allowed actually to see in the *Comedy* is the miraculously induced
explicit faith of Trajan and Ripheus — two highly abnormal cases, as

we shall see. For the 'normal' good pagan unbeliever, represented by Virgil, there would never seem to have been any alternative to unbelief. It is as though the concept of *implicit* faith had no relevance at all to him.

One might object: is this concept not involved in the Dantean Virgil's function as a link, through his poetry, between paganism and Christianity? Had not he, with other ancient poets, 'dreamed on Parnassus' of the state of unfallen Man? [52] Was not *Aeneid* VI, in some Christian sense, inspired? [53] Above all, had not Virgil prophesied the Incarnation? How could the poet of the fourth Eclogue not be regarded, from Dante's standpoint, as an implicit believer? [54] But the answer to these questions is in those very words of Statius which declare the Christian sense of Eclogue IV and are the chief tribute in the *Commedia* to Virgil's religious inspiration:

> 'Facesti come quei che va di notte,
>   che porta il lume dietro *e sé non giova*,
>   ma dopo sé fa le persone dotte,
> quando dicesti: 'Secol si rinova;
>   torna giustizia e primo tempo umano,
>   e progenie scende da ciel nova'.
> Per te poeta fui, per te cristiano . . .' [55]

'E sé non giova': the whole answer is in this phrase: Virgil drew no benefit from his own vision; he showed others the way, not himself. But our question returns – was this his own fault?

The problem thickens if we glance at the two exceptions mentioned above, at the two pagans in Dante's heaven, Trajan and Ripheus, whose salvation is affirmed, with all solemnity, by the Eagle of Justice. There are two points here, one dramatic and one doctrinal. The dramatic point is that the Eagle's assertion that those two pagans are saved comes in answer to Dante's bewilderment at the exclusion of virtuous non-Christians from salvation. And the dramatic tension of the episode is heightened by suspense. In

---

52. *Purg.* XXVIII, 139-48.
53. *Inf.* II, 13-27.
54. *Purg.* XXII, 64-81.
55. *Ibid.*, 64-73: 'You were like a man walking at night, and who carries a light behind him and gets no good from it himself, but enlightens those who are following him, when you said, 'The world is renewed; Justice returns and the first age of mankind, and a new progeny descends from heaven'.'

Paradiso XVIII Dante, having been raised to the heaven of Jupiter,
is confronted by an immense golden Eagle formed of the souls who
on earth loved justice. His bewilderment is voiced in the following
canto, at first indirectly, then directly. First, addressing the Eagle,
the poet speaks of a 'great hunger' that has long tormented him, a
hunger that has found 'no food on earth' to relieve it (XIX, 22-23).
Then the Eagle gives voice to that 'hunger', making explicit the
question in Dante's mind:

> . . . 'Un uom nasce a la riva
> de l'Indo, e quivi non è chi ragioni
> di Cristo né chi legga né chi scriva;
> e tutti suoi voleri e atti buoni
> sono, quanto ragione umana vede,
> sanza peccato in vita o in sermoni.
> Muore non battezzato e sanza fede:
> ov' è questa giustizia che 'l condanna?
> ov' è la colpa sua, se ei non crede?'[56]

The 'case', let us note, is adduced in the present tense, it is contemporary — or of any age: a man far out of reach of the Christian
message, but obedient to the light of reason, just and good; how can
he be blamed for not believing in Christ? The case, in fact, is the
same as Virgil's, and surely we are meant to recall, at this point,
Dante's 'father' and guide and companion now left so far behind;
and it may well seem a little strange that the Eagle's final reply, in
canto XX, to Dante's plea to be shown the justice of excluding such
men as Virgil from salvation — of forever separating moral goodness
from happiness — should bring such peace in the end to Dante's
heart and mind:

> Così da quella imagine divina,
> per farmi chiara la mia corta vista,
> data mi fu *soave medicina*.[57]

56. *Par.* XIX, 70-8: '. . . a man is born on the bank of the Indus, and there is no one there
who speaks of Christ, or who teaches or writes about him; yet all that man's willing and
doing is good, so far as human reason sees. He dies unbaptized and without faith: where is
that justice that condemns him? where is his fault, in not believing?'
57. *Par.* XX, 139-41: 'So from that divine image, to make clear my limited vision, I took
a gift of sweet medécine'.

Relief has come, the intellectual tension is relaxed. But what, in essence, is the answer of the Eagle? Analysed, it falls into three statements. First, since God's mind infinitely transcends ours, or any creature's, his providence *must* be mysterious, seen from our limited point of view (XIX, 40-63, XX, 130-2). Secondly, our human idea of justice itself derives from the uncreated Word, of which every created intelligence is but a partial and limited reflection. Man did not invent the idea of justice[58] and it is only as possessed of this idea, itself a reflection from God, that Dante or any man can call upon God to show himself as just (XIX, 64-6, 86-90). Thirdly, the exclusion from salvation of those who lack faith and baptism is not, in principle, total. God can always, so to say, break his own rules. If, for a man to be saved, he must normally be baptized, this is not an absolute requirement. On the other hand, the requirement of faith is (it is implied) absolute. But God can elicit faith where baptism is impossible, where indeed faith itself seems impossible because of total ignorance of the Christian message; as he has done in fact in the two cases stated here, Trajan and Ripheus. Yes, but how was faith elicited in these two pagans? By means which are — and this is emphasised — quite extraordinary: in the one case, Trajan's, by a miracle (and such a miracle!), in the other, Ripheus', by a special revelation which disclosed to the mind of this Trojan the secrets of the distant future. And clearly, the reason why such strange means were required is that the faith to be elicited had, in both cases, to be *explicit* faith.

Take Trajan first.[59] There was a story that this Emperor, who died in A.D. 117 and as an unbaptized pagan was presumed to be damned, had been brought back to earth, by the prayers of St Gregory the Great, for just as long as was needed for him to make an act of faith in Christ; after which he died a second time and his soul went to heaven. One may regret that this legend found a place in the *Comedy* — or at least this place, where it is used to support a theological thesis, namely that unbaptized adults may after all be saved, for all things are possible to God and he is prepared to work miracles to make the requisite faith a real possibility. But the point

58. Compare Pound's fine lines in the Pisan Cantos: 'Pull down thy vanity, it is not man/made courage or made order, or made grace/pull down thy vanity, I say pull down...'
59. *Par.* XX, 106-117.

to be stressed is the doctrine on faith implied in this use of the Trajan legend. Clearly, Dante is assuming that Trajan could only be saved by a faith that was perfectly explicit; otherwise the need for that astonishing miracle would not have arisen. And exactly the same lesson comes through the Ripheus case; the only difference, doctrinally speaking, is that here the 'miracle' is interior and spiritual.[60] As a poetic invention it has indeed this further difference that Dante's placing Ripheus in heaven is a pure product of his imagination and his love for Virgil. From this point of view it is a stroke of genius. The obscure Trojan companion of Aeneas is named only three times in the *Aeneid*, but the third time in terms that gave Dante the hint he required:

> cadit et Ripheus, *iustissimus* unus
> qui fuit in Teucris et *servantissimus aequi*;
> *dis aliter visum* . . .[61]

Whereas in Virgil the extraordinary moral goodness of Ripheus goes unrewarded by the gods, in Dante the true God rewards it; thus displaying at once his merciful justice and his utter difference from the 'false and lying gods' of paganism.[62] And another and subtler contrast may also be felt: Ripheus fell in battle (*cadit*) but not in spirit (to Hell or even to Limbo) because God — who is what the pagan divinities really *mean* — thought otherwise (*aliter*). Theologically speaking, however, the case of Dante's Ripheus is basically the same as that of his Trajan; to reach heaven he had to make an explicit act of faith in Christ the Redeemer. Only the conditions making this possible differed in the two cases: in Trajan's case a physical miracle, his temporary restoration to bodily life, in Ripheus' a spiritual miracle, his being granted, in the privacy of his own mind, a prophetic vision of the Christ who was to come:

> 'L'altra [the soul of Ripheus], per grazia che da sì profonda
>   fontana stilla, che mai creatura
>   non pinse l'occhio infino a la prima onda,
> tutto suo amor là giù pose a drittura:

---

60. *Par.* XX, 67-72, 118-29.
61. *Aeneid* II, 339, 394, 426-8: 'Ripheus also fell, the most just of the Trojans, the most obedient to reason; but the gods took a different view'.
62. *Inferno* I, 72.

per che, di grazia in grazia, Dio li aperse
l'occhio a la nostra redenzion futura;
ond' ei credette in quella' . . .[63]

And this explicit faith in the future Redeemer, accompanied by hope
and love, took the place, for Ripheus, of sacramental baptism:

'Quelle tre donne li fur per battesmo
che tu vedesti da la destra rota,
dinanzi al battezzar più d'un millesmo'.[64]

The conclusion then seems clear, that while Dante allows in principle for the salvation of pagans, he represents this, in his poem, as
extremely exceptional; not necessarily so, perhaps, in respect of the
number of pagans who may be saved, but certainly in respect of the
way they may be saved.[65] For this way must be by an explicit faith
in Christ; which, in the two cases described by Dante, required the
working of miracles. Thus the episode would seem to show that for
Dante grace and the faith that lays hold of it, was emphatically not
available to all men through the ordinary workings of Providence;
or at least that it had nothing of that 'normality' which we
nowadays tend to attribute to it by extending to the utmost the concept of implicit faith. Medieval theology possessed this concept, but
did little with it; Dante seems hardly aware of it.
B. *The Damnation of the Pagans.* There is a strongly positive side to
Dante's attitude to historical paganism. One aspect of this, touched
on above, was his tracing in Virgil's poetry adumbrations of Christian dogma; of an original 'state of grace' of mankind and of the
restoration of that lost state through the coming of a heavenly
Child. Another, more obvious, and in the *Convivio* and especially the
Monarchia more systematically argued, aspect of the same thing is,
of course, Dante's belief in the providential vocation of Rome and

63. *Par.* XX, 118-24: 'The other [Ripheus], by that grace which wells from so deep a
spring that never has the eye of a creature penetrated down to its first wave, set all his
heart, here below, on justice; for which cause, with grace added to grace, God opened his
eyes to our future redemption.'
64. *Par.* XX, 127-9: 'Those three ladies stood as baptism for him, whom you saw at the
right wheel [*Purg.* XXIX, 121-6], more than a thousand years before baptizing began'.
65. The idea that some pagans attained to faith in Christ through miraculous illumination
of some kind was not uncommon in the middle ages; it emerges, rather strangely, in the
Summa theologiae, 2a2ae. 2, 7 ad 3.

its Empire to prepare the world for Christ and even to collaborate in the Redemption itself.[66] Yet another may be discerned, though less clearly, in the way he handles the pagan myths, the gods and heroes.[67] So rich indeed is all this 'pagan' component in Dante's writings that it is not easy to understand how, at the same time, he could, in other respects, judge the pagan world so harshly. But these contrasts are in the very grain of his work, are different facets of one poetic vision.

For the moment however it is the negative side of his view of paganism that I am concerned with. We have seen that one aspect of this is his stress, in the *Comedy*, on the pagans' lack of saving faith; and that he tends to regard this, without nuance or qualification, as total. Yet he does not seem to present it as a *moral* defect; when he dwells on the pagans' lack of faith *qua* faith, it is always with reference to persons whom in all other ways he seems to admire or even revere. The exclusion of the adult Limbo-dwellers from grace is associated with a want of something in the intellect rather than the will; with the lack of a grace that would be a 'light' (*lumen gratiae*) [68] rather than a restoration of moral health (*gratia sanans*). [69] To be sure, this distinction must not be pushed too far, as the key-example of Ripheus the Trojan shows. For he, we are told in *Paradiso* XX, 118-23, was prepared for the enlightening grace (which 'opened his eyes' to see, prophetically, 'our future redemption') by a prior grace that had kindled his singular love for justice (with obvious allusion to Virgil's 'iustissimus unus/qui fuit in Teucris') and that clearly pertains to morality:

> ' . . . per *grazia* che da sì profonda
>   fontana stilla, che mai creatura
>   non pinse l'occhio infino a la prima onda,
> tutto suo amor là giù pose a drittura:
>   per che, *di grazia in grazia*, Dio li aperse
>   l'occhio a la nostra redenzion futura'.[70]

And perhaps, on this analogy, one might argue that if Dante's Virgil, like Ripheus, had been enabled to believe, he too would first

66. *Conv.* IV, iv-v; *Mon.* II, x-xi.
67. See P. Renucci, *Dante, disciple et juge du monde gréco-latin*, Paris, 1954.
68. See Aquinas, *Summa theol.* 1a2ae. 109, 1 and 8; 110, 3.
69. *Ibid.*, 109, 3 and 9.
70. *Par.* XX, 118-23. See note 63 above for a translation.

have been brought by grace to some higher moral perfection (but still in the natural order) than he actually possesses in the *Comedy*. But we should not make too much, I think, of the Ripheus case. Taking a broad view of Dante's poem two differences, in relation to the present discussion, stand out as more important than any *moral* difference between Ripheus and Virgil. These are, on the one hand an intellectual difference (as relating to knowledge) between Ripheus and the adults in Limbo; and on the other, a moral difference between these last and the rest of the damned. On the one hand the line is drawn between knowledge and ignorance: the eyes of Ripheus were '*opened* to our future redemption', those of the adults in Limbo were not. On the other hand the line is drawn between good and evil: the goodness of Virgil and his companions, the wickedness of the rest of the damned (from *Inferno* V onwards). To put the point in another way, Ripheus was granted a crucial experience denied to Virgil; but morally Virgil is closer to Ripheus than, say, to Achilles or Ulysses.

These last two names bring in another matter relating to my theme, namely Dante's relegating to Hell proper — that is, to one or other of the regions of the *Inferno* below Limbo — a number of persons whom one can presume that he counted as 'pagans', that is as neither Christians nor Jews nor Moslems. In passing, it seems to me that curiously little attention has been given to what may be called the religious distribution of Dante's damned. Apart from the Limbo-dwellers and omitting the Devils and the various Monsters, about 116 damned souls are actually named in the *Inferno*. Of these some 80 are Christians and there are two Jews (Caiaphas and Judas Iscariot) and two Muslims (Mahomet himself and his son-in-law Ali). All the remainder are 'pagans' — thirty two on my reckoning (counting Priscian, in canto XV, as a Christian, but including as pagans the Giants of canto XXXI). This is a high proportion — a quarter of the human population of the *Inferno*. It is of interest to note in passing how these pagans are distributed among the categories of sinners punished. I would group them roughly as follows: sexual sinners (cantos V and XVIII), seven: tyrants and shedders of blood (XII), five: blasphemers and rebels against God (XIV and XXXI), five: diviners and witches (XX), five: frauds and tricksters (XXX), three: false counsellors (XXVI), two: traitors (XXXIV), two: flatterers (XVIII), one: sowers of discord

(XXVIII), one: 'heretics', but in fact materialists (X), one. And among the better-known of these 'pagan' damned are Achilles, Helen of Troy, Dido, Cleopatra (V); Alexander the Great (?) and Attila the Hun (XII); Jason (XVIII); Epicurus (X); Tiresias (XX); Potipha's wife (XXX); Ulysses (XXVI); Nimrod (XXXI); Brutus and Cassius (XXXIV).

Clearly, in one sense all these personages are symbols of moral deformity of one or other kind, while in another sense they are identified with human beings who had had for Dante historical existence (however mythical some may be for us). Considered then in this second way, we can take them as expressing, collectively, a judgement on historical mankind — on man in history as given up to unreason or the misuse of reason; but specifically on pagan and unbaptized mankind as so 'given up'. The question then may be put: Is there any reason to hold that Dante thought of these pagan sinners as persons who had ever been offered grace by God, and so a real chance of deliverance from sin and eventual salvation, in the sense of admission to heaven? Shocking as it may appear, it is hardly plausible to answer other than negatively — such at least seems to be the answer conveyed by the dramatic pressure, so to say, of the scenes unfolded in the *Comedy*. True, it is just possible, as we have seen (and as will be shown in more detail in Section III of this essay), to read Virgil's chief statement of his unbelief — that in *Purgatorio* VII — as alluding, implicitly, to some past fault on his part which had blocked his access to grace. And Virgil is the chief spokesman of paganism in the *Comedy*. On the other hand, we have also seen how the Trajan and Ripheus episode in *Paradiso* XX gives a very different picture of the situation of the pagan world in relation to grace — representing the offer of grace as an exceedingly singular privilege, the successful outcome of which would entail miracles. We can safely rule out the notion that Dante thought of Cleopatra, say, as having been accorded such a privilege. Can we rule out her having been offered grace in a dimmer, less dramatic way? The possibility, in short, for her, of *implicit* faith. Not, I suppose, in theory; for Virgil — granted that possibility in *his* case — may perhaps be taken to represent pagan man in general. Yet in the concrete action of the *Inferno* not the faintest hint is dropped that the poet thought of its pagan inhabitants — from canto V onwards — as having ever been brought by God within reach of saving grace.

Why then are they damned? The answer is given, quite clearly, in *Inferno* XI, 81-3 (combined with 22-66). The pagans, like the rest of Dante's human damned — excepting the Heretics and prescinding from the Devils who are fallen angels — the pagans in this poet's Hell are there as having sinned according to one or other of the three evil 'dispositions' analysed by Aristotle: 'incontenenza, malizia e la matta/bestialitade' (81-3). They have sinned, that is, against the precepts of natural ethics and, so far as this goes, Christian theology throws no light at all on their fate; this, in the text, being simply the effect of this or that action done against the light of reason, the natural law — that law against which the adults in Limbo did *not* sin. From this point of view, then, the damned pagans express the notion that a sin that is simply against the natural law, the law of reason, may yet be what traditional theology calls 'mortal'; that is deserving of the direst conceivable penalty, eternal torment in mind and body. They also *appear* — so far as their actual presentation goes — to exemplify the possibility that such mortal sin may be committed in the absence of any counter-attraction by the Christian God, the God who must be presumed to offer grace to all men. Now what is, or has been, the standing of such a concept of mortal sin in Christian theology? This is a question I must leave to the historians of theology; but those readers who have had the patience to follow me so far will perhaps agree with me that the concept in question is hardly compatible with the doctrine of God's universal will to save; and hence to agree also that if and in so far as the concept of mortal sin occurring in a purely natural context has ever been upheld by theologians, they can only have upheld it, either as idle speculation or because of the relatively slow development, in the Church, of concern with the implications of the doctrine of God's will to save all men; and particularly as regards development of the idea of implicit faith.

11

THE TWO DANTES (II)

The Goodness of Virgil

Let us turn back now to Virgil and his Limbo companions and consider them not precisely as unbelievers – on this aspect perhaps enough has been said for the present – but as figures of goodness, moral virtue; not so much, however, in terms of particular virtues as of their representing a certain general idea of human perfectibility.

A kind of lofty resignation seems to brood over that region of Limbo where Virgil has his dwelling with the other 'spiriti magni', the great spirits of the noble unbelievers, at the sight of whom Dante feels himself 'exalted' as with a glow of pride in human achievement.[1] They have their seven-walled domain, the Noble Castle with its fair river and wide parkland, all luminous, like Virgil's own Elysian Fields, with light from a hidden sun (*Aeneid* VI, 639-40). There they dwell, calmly wise, conversing from time to time in soft musical voices. A large company, of whom thirty five are named or indicated, they fall into three groups: the poets, led by Homer; the soldiers, rulers and noble women; the philosophers, scientists and moralists, led by Aristotle, with his great commentator Averroes ending the list. In essence their spiritual condition is fixed by a contrast between their past as mortal men and their present and future as immortal souls. As to the past, they are content in the knowledge of having lived well as human beings, of having realised the inherent human capacities for courage, patriotism, statecraft, military glory, splendour of verbal utterance, accurate knowledge, profound thought. All this constitutes their present and perpetual 'onore', their special glory. But now, forever conjoined with this glory, is a future entirely without hope: 'sanza speme vivemo in

1. *Inf.* IV, *passim.* See the excellent study of this canto, already referred to, by F. Mazzoni, *Studi Danteschi*, XLII, pp. 29-206. Also G. Padoan, 'Il Limbo dantesco' in *Il pio Enea, l'empio Ulisse*, Ravenna, 1977, pp. 103–23.

disio.'[2] Their comfort is that they lived nobly as mortals on earth; but all that is now irrevocably past and they survive only as spirits, conscious of the essential spiritual need, which is to see God, and knowing that this need and desire will never, in fact, be satisfied. That desire is the same 'natural thirst' of the intellect on which Dante had so insisted in the *Convivio*; while insisting, at the same time, that, since this desire was for something beyond our reach in the present life, since it could be satisfied only in a life after death, we should limit our aims, for the present, to nearer objectives: there is so much else to be desired and done in this world here and now. But, once in Limbo, there is nothing left for the human soul to desire except its final fulfilment, and that is now forever out of reach. In the *Convivio* Dante had seemed to speak of the intellect as self-propelled towards God, its supreme Object. But here in the world of the *Comedy* all is conditioned by grace; and God withholds his grace.

In the *Convivio* Dante is conscious of writing as a philosopher, or as a would-be one.[3] Through most of Books I-II of the *Monarchia* too he is, in a sense, philosophizing. But with Book III of this work he is deep in theology, and it was certainly from theology that he drew the governing ideas of the *Comedy*. Nevertheless, many lines of thought in the poem are obviously intended as philosophical, that is as accessible in themselves to reason, quite apart from faith in the Christian revelation. Such are the doctrinal discourses of Virgil; such, clearly, is even much of the doctrine about God in the *Paradiso*.[4]

But my concern in this essay is mainly with Dante's philosophy of man and human conduct, in so far as this may be discernible in the figures of Virgil and his fellow-adults in the Dantean Limbo. And though inquiry into this topic leads inevitably (as we have seen) to some extent into theology, it can also send us back to the *Convivio*, and particularly to the fourth Book, which in its own way is a small treatise on ethics (and this too has been said above, though hardly yet shown). Now to turn back to the *Convivio* for light on the *Comedy* is to raise, of course, the question whether ideas that Dante put out at an earlier stage, and speaking as a philosopher,

2. *Inf.* IV, 42: 'we live in hopeless desire'.
3. See the very personal — and beautiful — outline of what 'filosofia' means in *Conv.* III, xi.
4. E.g., I, 103ff.; VII, 63-75, 124-44, XIX, 40-51, XXIV, 130-4, etc.

may not have undergone some modification when assumed into the theological context of the poem. But that is a question to be solved *ambulando* — by simply pursuing the inquiry proposed. A further question is as to the philosophical sources of such texts from the *Convivio* (or the *Monarchia*) as I shall cite. But there is no need to hesitate as to the main source of Dante's thinking on human nature and ethics: it is certainly Aristotle, especially his *Nicomachean Ethics*[5] (cited thirty four times in the *Convivio* alone). Let us try to see, then, what help we may derive from Aristotle for an understanding of the theory of man — especially of man as a moral agent — that is implicit in the adult figures of Dante's Limbo. I shall limit my considerations — less or more extensive as the subject may seem to require — to the four following topics: (1) the immortality of the soul; (2) the 'human good'; (3) virtue as a human product; (4) religion as part of virtue.

1. *The Immortality of the Soul*. On this point relatively little need be said in the present context. Dante was firmly persuaded that Aristotle had taught the survival of the human soul after death; and that it survived as personal, that is as numerically individualized, so that there are as many immortal souls as there are human beings. In interpreting Aristotle in this highly disputable way Dante was probably following St Thomas; but he must have been aware that other Aristotelians of his time took a different view of the master's teaching. Some took the line (favoured by Albert the Great for a time) that philosophy was anyhow incompetent to decide on this matter. Others followed Averroes and claimed that since our intellect has no bodily origin — as its immaterial activities show — it is not individualized and numerically multiplied as our bodies are: that there is only one Intellect for the whole human race: and that this was a truth discoverable by philosophical analysis and discovered, in fact, by Aristotle. On this view, of course, the souls of men as individuals would perish with their bodies; only the single supra-personal Intellect would survive. It is indeed a little curious that Dante never mentions Averroes in connection with the immortality of the soul, since he explicitly rejects the Averroistic view of the relation between the intellect and the body.[6] The only philosopher he names

5. See E. Gilson, *D. et la philosophie*, op. cit., pp. 102, n. 1; 144-6 etc.; and my essay 'St Thomas and Dante' in the present volume.
6. *Purg.* XXV, 61-6.

as decidedly against the immortality of the soul is Epicurus.[7] He
ignores the hints of scepticism as to a future life that Aristotle lets
fall in the *Nicomachea Ethics* —[8] to say nothing of the *De Anima*.[9]
He probably understood them, with St Thomas, in the sense that
Aristotle was waiving the question of a life after death as irrelevant
to his present subject; which, so far as it goes, was a correct interpretation. Aquinas's comment on the *Ethics* I, 10 (1100a 10-15)
shows that he understood the secular, this-worldly emphasis of the
work: 'note that the Philosopher is not speaking here of happiness in
a future life, but only of the present life.' [10] But we shall see that this
secular emphasis of the *Ethics* was reflected in Dante's thinking in
ways that are hardly reducible to a distinction between 'points of
view', such as it no doubt was for St Thomas. This point should
become clearer as we proceed.

2. *The Human Good*. Broadly speaking, what Aristotle does in the
Nicomachean Ethics is, first, to give an outline definition of the good
life for man — or, as he puts it, what 'the human good' is (I, 1-12);
and then to fill in this outline with a fairly detailed account of the
various 'virtues' which the achievement of this human good involves
(II-X). Two points should be noted here; first, Aristotle's concrete
and *practical* approach, and then his making the whole discussion
hinge on the idea that what is distinctively human about man is
mind or reason.

The practical slant appears almost at once in the sharp criticism of
Plato's Idea of the Good as a guide to human ethics (I, 6). Aristotle
is not, as a moralist, interested in the universal idea of Good; his exclusive concern is with the good-for-man, with such goodness as
man can achieve here and now, in this world, as a result of his own
activities.[11] And this turns out to be the happiness attainable by a
small minority of men (for decidedly favourable circumstances are
presupposed) through performing the proper task or function (*ergon*)
of man, which is to live according to the 'rational principle' (*kata
logon*).[12] Aristotelian ethics all hinges on this notion of man *qua*

7. *Inf*. X. 14; cf. *Conv*. II, viii, 7-8. See also A. Pézard, 'Un Dante éicurien?', in *Mélanges
offerts à E. Gilson*, Paris, 1959, pp. 499-536.
8. E.g. at III, 2, 1111 b 22; I, 10, 1100 a 10-1101 b 6. See A. Mansion, *Revue philos.
de Louvain*, 51 (1953) pp. 444-72.
9. III, 5, 430 a 20-5; see R.-A. Gauthier, *La morale d'Aristote*, Paris, 1973, pp. 21-2.
10. *Sententia libri Ethicorum*, Rome, 1969, I, p. 54.
11. *N.E.* I, 6, 1096 b 7-34; 7, 1098a 15.
12. *N.E.* I, 7, 1097 b 21-98a 17; 1102 a 13-18.

man, of a style of life and conduct, inward and outward, befitting a
being endowed with reason; and on the identification of this with
happiness. And Dante made this insight his own, drawing from it
his ideal of a happiness attainable before death and consisting in the
realisation of what man as such is capable of. Moreover – and this
can hardly be overstressed – in the *Monarchia* he presents this ideal
as entirely a matter for philosophy to define, independently of the
Christian message and theology. The ideal includes both the end to
be aimed at and the means to its achievement. The former is temporal happiness, 'beatitudo huius vite'. The latter are the 'moral and
intellectual virtues' which result from man's bringing into activity
his specifically human 'capacity', his *'propria* virtus', where the adjective marks off the virtues of which man *qua* man is capable from the
Christian 'theological' virtues (faith, hope and charity) which
presuppose divine grace – or, as Dante calls it here, a 'divine light'
superadded to that of reason. But this rational light, as displayed in
the writings of philosophers ('per phylosophica documenta') is quite
sufficient to show us how to live in this world, aiming at that time-
bound end ('beatitudo huius vite') which God has pre-fixed for his
rational creatures *in so far as they are also mortal.*[13]

From this humanist ideal it is a short step to the Dantean Limbo;
to Virgil, there, and Cicero and Saladin and the Master-Philosopher
himself enthroned amid his 'filosofica famiglia'. For by what other
ideal had these human paragons lived? Everything about them
reflects one or other aspect of the famous portrait of 'the highmind-
ed man' in *Nic. Ethics*, IV, 3; their dignity, the 'honour' that sur-
rounds them, their composure and gravity, their rare and gentle
speech; everything except the one thing which in fact makes all the
difference, that Dante's 'great spirits' are, precisely, *spirits*. They
have passed through that death which Aristotle could, virtually, ignore, but which the Christian Dante cannot. For the pagan moralist
all that mattered was to define the good-for-man, *t'anthrōpinon ag-
athon*, and his whole argument assumed that this is to be achieved, if
at all, before death. Aristotle is simply not concerned with the
hereafter. Nor, again, indeed is he directly concerned with any end
beyond man himself, beyond a self-achieved perfection of human
nature in and through the best activities of which it is capable.[14]

13. *Mon.* III, xv, 7-9.
14. *N.E.* I, 7 passim.

This is the guiding idea in the *Nicomachean Ethics*: even in Book X, which treats in part of the contemplative life of the philosopher, the point of view is still anthropocentric; the 'divine things' the philosopher contemplates are regarded in function of the philosopher who aspires to know them and, so aspiring, finds his own human perfection – discovers indeed his own true self. [15]

Now I would say that outside the *Comedy* Dante as a moral philosopher goes a long way with Aristotle, following the path which led to the deliberate paradox at the conclusion of the *Monarchia*; where man's happiness in this life is declared to be his 'ultimate end', notwithstanding that *another* 'ultimate end' awaits him in eternity (and the difference, as already indicated, is not only between the temporal and the eternal but between the end that we can reach to by our own 'virtue' and that which we cannot reach to except 'as aided by a divine light', i.e. by grace). [16]. That, in fine, is Dante's position outside the *Comedy*. But within it? Here matters are less simple. For if we ask where, in the poem is the 'place' and, as it were, the embodiment of man's temporal happiness and perfection, we have to answer with a distinction according to whether divine grace does or does not come into the picture. There are, in fact, two answers, each pointing to a distinct region of Dante's after-world. If we prescind from grace there is only one symbol standing for this-worldly perfection in the poem, and that is Limbo, the great Dantean image of the 'so far and no further' of human nature – of man fixed in a condition of serenity without hope; in a condition which in a sense is thoroughly 'natural' – natural indeed *by definition* – and yet can hardly strike us as other than radically *unnatural* (though perfectly 'logical'); where a state of perfection that is in essence *temporal* is transferred into a condition of eternity and there becomes entirely pointless, a suspension *in vacuo* (as Virgil himself puts it, 'Io era tra coloro che son *sospesi*'); [17] in short, a dead end. But, far removed from Limbo, at the summit of Mount Purgatory, we meet another great image of human perfection in time, of the 'happiness of this life'; only now envisaged as a state of grace: the 'divine forest' of Eden, the Earthly Paradise. For I fully agree with Charles Singleton that the sacred wood which Dante

15. *N.E.* X, 7, 1177 a 12-17; 1177 b 26 – 1178 a 3.
16. *Mon.* III, xv, 7.
17. *Inf.* II, 52 (cf. IV, 45): 'I was among those who are suspended'.

enters in *Purgatorio* XXVIII images a state of grace (though on earth, not in heaven) and not one of mere 'nature' on the hither side of grace.[18] . This is surely implied by the wood's position on the summit of the mount of purification – which is a work of grace – and again by Virgil's disappearance from the scene at this point, and Beatrice's entrance. The whole place, clearly, is an image of man's condition before the Fall – which in the theological tradition, on this point wellnigh unanimous, was precisely a fall from grace. And the radiant nymph Matelda, who comes to meet the voyager as he enters the wood, is part of the same figurative expression, indeed she brings it to a focus. But, granted all this, two interesting consequences seem to follow.

The first is that Dante has changed the meaning of the Earthly Paradise (considered as a symbol) in passing from the *Monarchia* to the *Comedy*. The difference is very remarkable. In the last chapter of the prose treatise we are distinctly told that 'terrestris paradisus' figures 'the happiness of this life' as this is understood by 'the philosophers' and is attainable by the practice of natural virtue; whilst the happiness of which Holy Scripture speaks and is attainable through the supernatural virtues of faith, hope and charity is identified exclusively with the *eternal* life of heaven whose appropriate image is the 'paradisus *celestis*'.[19] In other words, in the *Monarchia* the whole meaning of 'earthly paradise' is humanistic – is coterminous with something attainable by human power alone – whereas in the *Comedy*, if my interpretation (and that of most critics) is correct, this image retains its traditional Christian sense. And this contrast comes out only more clearly if we compare what is said, on the one hand in the treatise, on the other in the poem, of the 'happiness of this life' – figured in both works by the Earthly Paradise – from the point of view of its status as an 'end' of human desire. In the *Monarchia* the stress falls on its self-contained *sufficiency*; it is an 'ultimate' end (with respect, to be sure, to man's nature precisely as a mortal being); whereas in the poem all the emphasis is on the transitional and provisional nature of the temporal bliss that is signified by the sacred wood and by the joy of Matelda. This bliss, Matelda tells Dante, was that of the unfallen Adam and Eve, and it was

18. *Journey to Beatrice*, Harvard U.P., 1958, Part I.
19. *Mon.* III, xv, 7.

granted to them simply as a 'pledge' — let us say, in function — of the ulterior eternal bliss:

> 'Lo sommo Ben, che solo esso a sé piace,
> fé l'uomo buono e a bene, e questo loco
> diede *per arr*' a lui d'etterna pace'.[20]

And the second consequence also involves Matelda. For surely one important 'sense' conveyed in and through this radiant figure is a contrast by opposition with Virgil and the other adult Limbo-dwellers; especially in the contrast between her merriment and their gravity.[21] Virgil has usually been correlated with Beatrice, and this is certainly right, but it involves Virgil chiefly as regards his function in the poem as Dante's guide, not as regards his permanent situation as a dweller in Limbo. In this respect Matelda is Virgil's clearest correlative; in this respect he and she stand in contrast exactly as the good-for-man *minus* grace is in contrast with the good-for-man *plus* grace. And finally — to repeat a point already made — all this entails, from the point of view of the action of the poem, a wider constrast which must set the *Comedy* at a certain distance spiritually, not only from the Aristotelian ethic but specifically (so it would seem) from the *Monarchia*. This work, as we have noted, makes earthly, temporal happiness an 'ultimate end'; but there is nothing ultimate, as also has been noted, about the Earthly Paradise in the *Comedy*. As Jacques Goudet succinctly says: 'le Paradis Terrestre n'est plus un but, mais un relai avant le Paradis céleste; l'on y passe pour aller plus loin'.[22] The humanist ideal has become a phase through which Dante passes on to his true goal, the 'trasumanar' of *Paradiso*.[23]

3. *Virtue as a Human Product.* Aristotle characteristically sees the good life as *activity*; though the highest activity, in the end, is thought itself, whose work (*ergon*) is to know truth.[24] Happiness

---

20. *Purg.* XXVIII, 91-3:

> 'The highest Good, who alone finds joy in himself, made man good and for a good, and gave him this place as a pledge of eternal peace'.

'Arra' (1.93) echoes St Paul, 2 *Corinthians*, 5, 5; cf. St Augustine *De spiritu et littera*, 3, 5.
21. Compare *Purg.* XXVIII, 40-81 with *Inf.* IV, 112-4. Merriment, for D., is one of the signs of grace, see *Purg.* X, 64-9.
22. *Dante et la politique*, Paris, 1969, p. 163.
23. *Par.* I, 70.
24. *N.E.* VI, c. 2, 1139 a 17-39 b 12.

involves activity of both soul and body, but the principal agent is the soul; and so we come to the clinching phrase: 'the human good turns out to be activity of the soul in accordance with excellence (*aretē*)'.[25] What Aristotle means by *aretē*, in its narrower sense of 'moral virtue', is then set out in Books II to V of the *Ethics*; and Dante faithfully follows this exposition in *Convivio* IV, xvii, 4-8, and presupposes it throughout much of the *Inferno* and the *Purgatorio*. But running through all Aristotle's teaching on moral virtue is a cheerful confidence in man's power to discern and to perform his proper *ergon*, which was bound to arouse mistrust in his Christian readers, once the *Nicomachean Ethics*[26] began to be widely studied (in Grosseteste's translation) after about 1250. In theological circles such confidence smacked of Pelagianism, of the heresy that man, even in his 'fallen' condition, could obey the law of God (the morality revealed in the Scriptures, in particular the law of love declared by Christ), and so achieve salvation, by exercising his power of free choice, without any special divine assistance (traditionally called 'grace'). Grace might be required indeed in the form of instruction to the human mind; but the will, once instructed, could fend for itself in the choice between good and evil. Of course, the Church's condemnations of Pelagianism had been couched in specifically Christian terms – had been aimed, in the first place, at ruling out any suggestion that man can cooperate in his *supernatural* salvation (union with God through Christ) without his will being healed and restored by grace. And it might be argued that this left open the question as to man's need of grace on the *natural* level; whether, that is, a perfect practice of virtues consonant with his nature might not, in principle, be within man's power without special assistance from God – assistance in the form of power superadded to the specifically human powers of reason and free will. Nevertheless, the general sense or bias of Christianity has always been against allowing the possibility, for fallen man, of such unflawed human excellence. In common with most theologians, St Thomas rejected it.[27]. But there is a strong case for holding that Dante allows

---

25. *N.E.* I, c. 13, 1102 a 13-18; c. 7, 1098 a 16-17.
26. On Christian reactions to the *N. Ethics*, see R.-A. Gauthier, art. cit. in *Archives d'histoire doctrinale* etc., XVI, 1946-7; and his essay 'S. Thomas et l'Ethique à Nicomaque' in the Leonine ed. of Aquinas's *Sententia libri Politicorum*, 1971, Appendix, pp. v-xviii.
27. See the previous essay 'Limbo and Implicit Faith', note 41.

it, by implication, in his fiction of Virgil and the other adults in Limbo.

Returning to Aristotle, the point to be stressed is that for him, as A. H. Armstrong puts it, 'virtue and vice are within our own power'.[28] The virtue of a good man is his own product; he is morally self-made. It is true that he will need, as a rule, a good start in life and the benefit of a good education.[29] The good life, as Aristotle understood it, was normally possible only for an upper-class male elite. But the gifts of fortune were a mere prerequisite to virtue; for a young man of good education and able to dispose of his own time the task of achieving human goodness had scarcely begun. All would depend on the use he made of his time, and this on his own exercise of choice, *prohairesis*. It is in analysing this term that Aristotle comes nearest to formulating a theory of free will, though he does hardly more than clear the ground for deeper investigations.[30] However, and this is the point, he does seize strongly on the idea of human self-direction, human autonomy. This comes out with special clarity in two passages of the *Ethics*. The first is where he insists that *prohairesis*, that deliberate choosing through which happiness is in fact achieved, must be of things that are within our power to do or not to do; unlike mere 'desire', which is not moral at all, and unlike mere 'wish' which can be for things which, on reflection, we know to be impossible. Properly speaking, we cannot *choose* the impossible; for choice in this sense entails our understanding, after reflection, that a given action is within our power.[31] The Aristotelian idea of choice implies full capacity and self-direction in the chooser. This was a point, as we shall see, which very strongly impressed Dante. The other place I allude to is where Aristotle raises the question whether happiness (= virtue) is a 'gift of the gods'. In his reply, he first seems to side-step the question as not properly ethical (but rather theological); but then proceeds to answer it, brilliantly, in a thoroughly humanistic way. There are, he says, three kinds of 'goods' involved in virtuous living: (a) pre-existing 'conditions of happiness' (e.g. not to be born a slave); (b) accompaniments useful

28. *Introduction to Ancient Philosophy*, London, 4th ed., 1965, p. 105.
29. N.E. VI, 13, 1144 b 4-6 (cf. 1103 a 24-5); X, 9, 1179 b 21-1180 a 17; 1177 a 6-10. See R.-A. Gauthier, *La morale d'Aristote*, Paris, 1973, pp. 54-7.
30. N.E. III, cc., 1-6; see R.-A. Gauthier, op. cit., pp. 35-8.
31. N.E. III, c. 3, 1112 a – 12 b 28.

as 'instruments' (e.g. good health or riches); (c) the thing itself, virtuous activity of the soul; and this is at one and the same time exclusively the result of our own efforts *and* a thing 'godlike and blessed'.[32] Clearly, Aristotle is not scoffing at the notion of the 'godlike' or divine; he is merely identifying one form of it with *human* virtue. And R.-A. Gauthier's comment shows the relevance of this to our present subject: 'Ces lignes éclairent d'un jour cru l'abîme qui sépare l'humanisme aristotélicien de la doctrine chrétienne de la grâce: celle-ci enseigne la défiance de l'homme, la confiance en Dieu, celui-là la défiance des dieux, la confiance en l'homme'.[33]

Christian confidence is in God, not in man. If Dante in his two prose works followed (as it seems to me he did) the contrary emphasis of the pagan moralist, this was presumably because that emphasis seemed to him true to experience, so far as it went; and also because of the passionate intensity of his conviction – displayed in everything he wrote after his exile from Florence – that human affairs, private and public, could be managed a very great deal better than they were. And in Aristotle's *Ethics* he found, he thought, this conviction authoritatively upheld. The philosopher had clearly marked out that area of human activity where alone moral – and political – virtue is created, and where everything depends on volition guided by reason, that is on deliberate choice. For us it is clear, of course, that Aristotle, not being a Christian, could ignore the typically Christian problem as to the ultimate sufficiency of such man-directed, man-created goodness. He did not have to take account of the idea of a divine-human drama working itself out in the souls of men by the issue of which – a Yes or No to God's offer of love, and a love that goes on into eternity – all merely human goodness or badness must be measured in the last resort. This idea Dante did, in his own way, eventually take account of in the *Comedy*. Meanwhile however, in *Convivio* IV and in the *Monarchia* he could and did respond enthusiastically to the lucid humanist commonsense of Aristotle; that men, individually and socially, are virtuous or vicious according to the use they make, freely and of

32. *N.E.* I, c. 9, 1099 b 9-31.
33. *L'Ethique à Nicomaque*; transl. and commented by R.-A. Gauthier and J. Y. Jolif, II, part 1, Louvain-Paris, 1970, p. 74.

themselves, of the nature and powers they find themselves endowed with.

This is the chief theme of Book IV of the *Convivio*. But in order to see our way through the rather bewildering richness of this part of the treatise — Dante's greatest achievement in Italian prose — it will be as well to distinguish between three main concepts that recur in it: human nature, human nobility, human virtue. Of these three concepts, that of human nature is the most basic, since the other two presuppose it. But it belongs more closely with nobility than with virtue: a human being may be entirely devoid of virtue, but never entirely devoid of as much nobility, at least, as comes from sharing simply in human nature; for this, in the last resort, is a created image of God. Nobility, for Dante, is a concept that extends as widely as 'nature'; only it more directly involves the notion of 'degree' — of less and more, of higher or lower. Every nature in Dante's universe, taken as a given *species*, stands at a greater or less remove from God: and again, every *individual* of each nature, so taken, exists at a greater or less remove from an ideal 'perfection' proper to its species as such; and the nearer it approaches this ideal, the more natural 'nobility' it has. Thus we may predicate nobility of a stone, a tree, a horse, a hawk, a man; [34] . meaning in each case that the individual thing shows a high degree of excellence in its kind or species.

In *Convivio* IV of course Dante is concerned above all with nobility in its human form; and by this he means broadly two things. First, something inherent in an individual from the start, as a natural gift, prior to any excellence he may acquire through effort or training; essentially, it is a certain equilibrium of soul and body favourable to subsequent human development. [35] . Secondly, human nobility means precisely this development, in the form of virtues, both moral and intellectual, actually possessed. Thus the concept of human nobility overlaps nature on the one side and virtue on the other: on the one hand it is an excellence merely received, a 'divine gift'; [36] on the other, an excellence personally achieved, the fruit of individual reason and choice applied to the changing circumstances of life through time. In *Convivio* IV, where Dante's interest is chiefly ethical, he leaves aside the intellectual virtues — by which he

34. *Conv.* IV, xvi, 4-5.
35. *Conv.* IV, xx, 9-10.
36. *Ibid.*, 6-10.

means scientific abilities of various kinds – to concentrate on the 'fruits of nobility' which are the moral virtues and in the exercise of which consists 'the happiness of the *active* [as distinct from the contemplative] life'.[37] . But it is worth noting that all the ethical reasoning in the *Convivio* presupposes an idea of nobility which transcends the ethical sphere, transcends indeed the entire human world; being the idea of a graded participation, at every level in the universe, of a 'perfection' that has its source and exemplar in God.[38]. This metaphysical vision makes Dante's point of view, even in the *Convivio*, rather different from that of Aristotle's in the *Nicomachean Ethics*. Where Aristotle starts from the function, *ergon*, proper to man, and then works out his system of the appropriate human virtues, Dante begins from the abstract idea of nobility as a participation in 'the divine', and then tries to show how this idea may be realised through human life on earth and in time.[39] There is a Platonic strain in the *Convivio* that is largely absent from the *Ethics*.

However, what I wish to stress in the work is its strong Aristotelian component, as this comes out particularly in the treatment of moral virtue in Book IV; which in general is about virtue and nobility and how they are interrelated. It takes the form of a commentary on a didactic poem which Dante had written a decade earlier to refute a prevalent 'error' concerning 'that human goodness which is sown in us by nature and whose right name is "nobility".' The error was to identify nobility with such things as rank and wealth and lineage.[40]. In his poem (*Le dolci rime d'amor*) Dante did three things:[41] first, for that worldly concept of nobility he substituted an unworldly one, based on metaphysics and religion; next, he showed how nobility, as he understood it, could flower into the moral virtues; finally, he related these virtues to the different stages of life, so that his last two stanzas sketch the course of a truly noble human life from birth to death. But there is another, very significant thing to note: the poem opens with a kind of farewell (or *au revoir* at least) to speculative metaphysics, expressing – by an implication which the commentary will bring out into the open –

37. *Conv.* IV, ix, xvi-xx, xxiv-xxviii.
38. *Conv.* III, ii, 2-16; vii, 1-5.
39. Cf. *Conv.* III, vii, 8-13; IV, xvii-xviii.
40. *Conv.* IV, v-xv.
41. See *Dante's Lyric Poetry*, ed. K. Foster and P. Boyde, Oxford, 2 vols., 1967 (where this poem is no. 69, but in the standard Italian editions it is no. LXXXII).

Dante's conversion to a kind of philosophy more directly relevant to human affairs in this temporal life. It is not irrelevant to note that the poem was written at about the time when Dante first began to participate actively in Florentine politics (1295-'6); nor that it is the first of his works to allude expressly to Aristotle's *Ethics* (line 85); indeed it may well have stemmed from his first serious reading of that work. In short, the branch of philosophy he was now making particularly his own was ethics, conceived of in close relation to social life and politics.

Ten or twelve years later, when *Convivio* IV was written, Dante was in exile from Florence, but no less concerned with politics. In a sense he was more concerned than ever, for he now knew more clearly where he stood; he had discovered his concept of the Empire, and in *Convivio* IV, iv-ix he sets it out in what reads like a kind of rough draft of *Monarchia* I-II. What is more to our purpose, Dante's whole philosophy of man has now entered a new stage. This appears in the transition from Books III to IV of the *Convivio*, which corresponds, at a more mature level, to the switch from speculative to practical philosophy implied in the opening stanza of *Le dolci rime d'amor*. The theme of most of Book III had been the beauty and nobility of philosophy as a participation, through love, of created minds, human and angelic, in the divine Wisdom itself. But the final chapter (xv) brings us suddenly back to earth; the argument abruptly takes a *restrictive* turn. Man, we are told, being a composite of soul and body and deriving all his knowledge from sense-data, can have, in this life, only a very remote and inadequate idea of God; he knows *that* God is, he does not and cannot know *what* God is. This is how things are in the order of nature; this is how the human intellect, used correctly, can see that they are. Let the human will, then, come into line and renounce, for the time being, all vain desires for that perfect fulfilment of the intellect which, for the present, is impossible. With this argument in III, xv, 6-10 (recalled in IV, xiii, 7-9) Dante sets the scene for his concentrating all through Book IV on the human world, on man's doings here on earth and in time; in short, on ethics and politics, the proper field of human volition.

This last phrase makes the essential point, but to understand it we have to seize the underlying concept of 'human activity', 'l'umana operazione'. It is in his handling of this concept that Dante shows his Aristotelianism most clearly in the *Convivio*. In the course of the first half of Book IV, through all the polemic against vulgar notions of nobility, Dante's very personal insight into 'human activity' gradually comes to the surface. We see it first in the long c. vi where, to define more closely the supreme political authority (that of the Emperor, already sketched in cc. iv-v), he introduces the complementary supreme philosophical authority; which naturally turns out to be that of Aristotle. It is not irrelevant, at this point, to note that the political theory of the *Convivio*, unlike that of the *Monarchia*, omits all consideration of the Church. This is in line with the spirit of the work as a whole. The writer is a believer, but he discusses moral and political issues as though Christianity had nothing specific to say on them. In this sense at least the *Convivio* is 'pure' philosophy. It is indeed rather remarkable that a Christian should write so wide-ranging a treatise on human nature as *Convivio* IV, and only once introduce, marginally and with dubious orthodoxy, a notion from moral theology.[42] True, the Bible is quite often cited; but the chief authority all through is 'the glorious philosopher' Aristotle. And he is regarded chiefly as a moral philosopher, indeed as *the* master of ethical wisdom. It is important to understand why this is so.

The clue, I think, is in the concept of the sort of activity that would be specifically human – 'l'umana operazione'. When, in *Convivio* IV, vi, Aristotle is brought decisively into the argument he is closely associated with this concept. Dante is arguing that Aristotle has a unique and supreme 'authority' in moral philosophy, and the gist of his reasoning is as follows. Everything in the universe exists, in the last resort, in order to 'act', and to act in the manner most consonant with its own specific nature, to perform its 'propria operazione'. Now the nature of man is to be an intellect and a will conjoined with a mortal body. Hence he has a twofold 'proper activity'. Considered simply as intellectual, he can find his natural fulfilment only in knowing the 'supreme Intelligible', namely God (cf. IV, xxii, 13). But such knowledge as this is beyond man's reach (as already noted) while he lives in the body, in this mortal life: it belongs only to the future life where the intellectual soul, released from the body, will come at last fully into its own. What then is

---

42. *Conv.* IV, xxi, 11-12. I return briefly to this text later on.

man's 'proper work' here and now, what is his natural 'end' in the present life? Philosophers have given various answers, but Dante finds only three worth considering. The Stoics identified this 'end' with disinterested truthfulness and justice. The Epicureans, considering that all sentient beings naturally seek pleasure and avoid pain, and that man is no exception to this rule, concluded that the natural end of man was pleasure or, what to them seemed the same, freedom from pain. However, both of these answers are inadequate in that both overlook an essential fact — that human life is a sequence of activities which are all motivated by some desire but are all performed in different circumstances; and which therefore should be reckoned as 'right' or 'wrong' inasmuch as they hit or miss a mid-point, between excess and defect in desiring, in relation to the particular circumstances in which the agent happens to find himself. Hence the 'more subtle' and the truer answer is to say that the 'proper work' of mortal man *qua* mortal is constantly to achieve this mid-point, this mean between extremes; which is precisely what is meant by moral virtue, 'operazione con virtú'. And this correct answer, adumbrated by Socrates and Plato, was at last worked out to perfection by Aristotle; who is therefore the supreme moral philosopher, the 'master and guide of human reason as aiming at its end-activity' ('inquanto intende a la sua finale operazione').[43]

The proper function of man on earth, then, is to practice moral virtue conceived as a habitual right choice between extremes (of desire or non-desire); and since this implies discernment and deliberation, to live virtuously is to live according to reason, i.e. *humanly*.[44] This will sound platitudinous until we grasp the peculiar sense in which Dante understands 'living humanly'. In its most exact and proper sense this means action which, to the highest possible degree, *is our own*; as depending, to the fullest possible extent, on our human power of volition. Dante's reasoning here is fairly subtle and calls for close attention. Its gist is as follows. If *human* activity is that which brings into play our specifically human powers of reason and will, our actions will be *more* human in the degree that they bring *both* of these faculties into play together. Now there are four ways in which our reason can be related to 'activities': (a) as considering the activities (the 'works') of Nature — as in the natural

43. *Conf.* IV, vi, 6-16.
44. Cf. *Conv.* IV, vii, 11-15.

sciences; (b) as considering our own *rational* activities – as in logic
or in 'the arts of speech'; (c) as considering activities which we bring
about as effects in the external material world – as in the
'mechanical arts'; (d) as considering our acts of choice as such, that
is our activity precisely as proceeding from our *will*. Now in none of
the first three cases is the thing itself that is considered under our
power, under human control. True, it is within our power, in each
case, to consider or not to consider, to direct or not to direct our
attention to the works of Nature, or to the way our intellect works,
or to external matter as worked on by the various 'arts'; but the *object* of our attention is in each case governed by factors – the structure of the non-human universe, or the laws of logic, or the 'laws' inherent in matter – which are not of our choosing and are not, ultimately, under our control; for they do not originate from us; 'we
do not *make* them, we *find* them', as Dante tersely puts it. Only in
the last case (d), where the action considered is that of the will itself,
do we find an activity that depends entirely on ourselves and may
therefore be properly called our own. Consequently, it is only as exercising free and deliberate choice – in other words, as moral agents
– that we are autonomous; and conversely, we are autonomous in
the degree that we are moral agents. But to act rightly as moral
agents is to be morally virtuous. Hence Dante can conclude, in
words which Gilson justly described as 'un trait de lumière': 'it is
the moral virtues above all else that are *our* products, because *they are
within our power in every respect*'.[45]

It seems to me clear that this insight into man's autonomy as a
moral agent derives from the *Nicomachean Ethics*. The last sentence
quoted fuses, as it were, into one formula two interrelated theses of
that work: that man has his proper specific function (*ergon*) which is
to live by reason (*kata logon*), and that it depends on man alone to
realise this function and so to achieve the 'human good'.[46] And of
course it was the latter thesis that suggested the phrase I put at the
head of this section, 'virtue as a human product'.

But the reader will have noted that Dante has added something
to the Aristotelian thesis, namely a further stress on the autonomy –
I had almost said the creativity – of the will, the effect of which is
to present moral virtue as not only man's product but as, in a sense,

45. *Conv.* IV, ix, 4-7; xvii, 2: Gilson, *D. et la philosophie*, op. cit., p. 112.
46. See above, pp. 193-99.

his *only* product; in the sense that a man who becomes just or temperate is achieving something that depends 'in every respect' on himself. The argument is open to several objections but one may, I suppose, concede to Dante that 'products' like a particular man's justice or temperance do depend more exclusively on his own freedom of choice than his acquisition of any science or of any technique in the manipulation of external matter. The point, in any case, is that on this view human life not only connotes moral virtue (as it connotes the sciences and arts), it properly *consists* in moral virtue. And this formula may be Aristotelian but it is still more Dantean. However, it is enough for our immediate purpose to note that this formula includes the other and milder one, that virtue is a 'human product'. If it is through a man's acts of free choice that he is most creatively and originally 'himself', and if he displays this autonomy most in acquiring moral virtue, then surely Aristotle's thesis is conceded that the 'human good' consists in the virtues, moral and intellectual, and that these depend principally on man himself. From this point of view Dante's stress on the humanness of the moral virtues — as being 'the fruits that are most properly *ours*'[47] — merely underlines the Aristotelian confidence in man's ability to perform his proper *ergon* in this world and so attain to the 'human good' which is his natural end *qua* man (though Dante would say '*qua mortal* man').

At this point in the argument I must, in fairness to the reader, recall an idea I threw out at the start of this essay but which I have not developed since and which I do not, in fact, intend to develop. It was the idea, or rather the question as to how far Dante's philosophy of man may be called 'dualistic'; whether, that is, Dante did not draw the distinction between man as mortal (the rational soul as embodied) and immortal (the rational soul in itself) in such a way as, implicitly, as to locate human nature proper only on *this* side of death, while regarding the rational soul *per se* as being intrinsically of a higher nature — a nature which, so regarded, may be called 'angelic' and is only 'human' by the circumstance of its being temporarily joined to a body. Some such dualism is, as we have seen, suggested here and there in the *Convivio* and in the final chapter of the *Monarchia*. But so far as the present essay is concerned the

47. *Conv.* IV, xvii, 2.

hypothesis of this dualism has served only as a starting point for the line of thought I wish to pursue now to the end, making it alone my chief concern; the line which has led me to connect the adults in Dante's Limbo with the *Nicomachean Ethics*, inasmuch as both those fictions and that text raise, for the Christian reader, the issue of 'pelagianism', as suggesting a view of man's perfectibility which virtually leaves grace out of account. To this matter I now return and the next three or four pages will offer a closer analysis of those Limbo adults than I have so far given. I leave it, in passing, to the reader to ponder the plausibility of linking the texts we have just been considering from the *Convivio*, which stress the peculiar *humanness* of moral virtue, with the hypothesis of Dante's dualism, in the sense suggested. For if after all moral virtue represents, on the one hand, a perfection proper to *this* life, and, on the other, the 'product' of man that is most properly and distinctively *his*, then it is hard to see what *human* perfection is left for the life after death. Does not Dante speak, as we have seen, of the soul after death as surviving 'in a more than human nature'?[48]. And does he not also say that the knowledge of God, such as only a release from the body makes possible, 'is not possible for our nature'? [49] . There is a problem here, but I cannot discuss it adequately within the limits of this essay. In any case it is raised much more sharply by the *Convivio* than by the *Comedy*. And I am now concerned principally with the poem.

*   *   *

The moral qualities and limitations of the adults in Limbo are described by Virgil in *Inferno* IV, 33-42 and in *Purgatorio* VII, 25-36; and in the latter passage more positively than in the former. Let us paraphrase each in turn. The lines in *Inferno* IV give, first, a general moral description of all the souls in Limbo (33-34a) and then rapidly distributes them into three groups (34b-42).[50] Of all the Limbo-dwellers Virgil says, 'they have not sinned' ('ei non peccaro'), where 'sin' obviously means what theologians call actual or personal sin, not the state of 'original sin' which all human beings in-

48. *Conv.* II, viii, 6.
49. *Conv.* III, xv, 10.
50. The best general study of *Inf.* IV is the work, already cited, of F. Mazzoni, *Studi Danteschi*, XLII, pp. 29-206; cf. the study by G. Padoan, *op. cit.* in note 1.

herit from the Fall, and in which all remain until released by faith in
the Saviour and baptism (whether sacramental or somehow
'desired'). Then, within the sum of these non-sinners, Virgil begins
to differentiate. First (34), he distinguishes between those who died
in childhood (the 'infanti' of line 30) and those who reached the age
of moral choice and so were able to merit by good deeds, to acquire
'mercedi'. But the latter are in no better case than the former ('non
basta', 35) so far as salvation goes, because they are equally unbaptized (34-36). Then, within this latter *adult* division, Virgil distinguishes between those who died when Christian baptism was
already possible but did not in fact receive it (like Saladin, line 129)
and those who lived before Christianity but who are not thereby excused, and consequently saved, because they did not give due
honour to God (37-8). To this third group belongs, of course, Virgil
himself (39). Finally lines 40-2 summarise the fate of *all* these Limbo-dwellers: they are all 'lost' (41), but only for the defects
enumerated (40: 'Per tai difetti, non per altro rio'); namely, in the
children, want of baptism, and in the adults, either the same want,
or, in the case of those who lived B.C., that their religion was at
fault, 'they did not adore God as he should be adored'. This last
phrase, of course, brings us back to the knotty problem already in
part discussed – the question, in brief, whether this phrase is intended as a mere paraphrase for unbelief or as pointing to some sin over
and above that merely negative condition. But without pursuing this
point for the moment, let us have Virgil's distinctions set out thus:

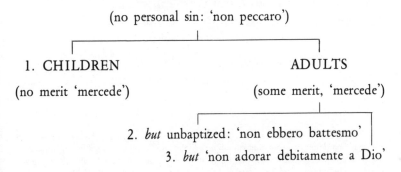

LIMBO-DWELLERS

(no personal sin: 'non peccaro')

1. CHILDREN   ADULTS

(no merit 'mercede')   (some merit, 'mercede')

2. *but* unbaptized: 'non ebbero battesmo'

3. *but* 'non adorar debitamente a Dio'

For 'such defects' (40) all three categories are 'lost' (41) and doomed to 'hopeless desire' (42). The defect of group 3 in particular remains to be considered. But immediately our concern is rather with the merits ('mercedi', 34) of the adults; or rather with that noble quality of their lives on earth which is now, in fact, rewarded by a kind of 'grace' from heaven, manifested in the 'honour' so emphatically paid to them and the zone of light in which they dwell (67-78).

Speaking with Sordello at the end of the first day on Mount Purgatory, Virgil returns to the subject. His tone now is more personal than in *Inferno* IV; but more interesting is the fact that he now ignores the difference between the B.C. and the A.D. adults. This difference in *Inferno* IV had turned, implicitly, on the availability or not of baptism (lines 35-7); whereas now in *Purgatorio* VII baptism is alluded to – periphrastically – only in connection with the Limbo children (32-3). This means that, as regards the Limbo adults, the whole stress here is on the *inward* factor, on their lack of the 'three holy virtues', i.e. faith, hope and charity; a lack which is *not* made up by their full possession of 'all the other', i.e. all the natural virtues (35-6):

25 'Non per far, ma per non fare ho perduto
    a veder l'alto Sol che tu disiri
    e che fu tardi per me conosciuto.

28 Luogo è là giù non tristo di martiri,
    ma di tenebre solo, ove i lamenti
    non suonan come guai, ma son sospiri.

31 Quivi sto io coi pargoli innocenti
    dai denti morsi de la morte avante
    che fosser da l'umana colpa essenti;

34 quivi sto io con quei che le tre sante
    virtù non si vestiro, *e sanza vizio
    conobber l'altre e seguir tutte quante.*' [51]

---

51. *Purg.* VII, 25-36: 'Not for doing, but for not doing, have I lost the sight of the high Sun that you desire and that was known by me too late. There is a place down below, not sad with torments but with darkness only, where the lamenting sounds not as wailing but as sighs. There I abide with the innocent children seized by death's fangs before they were exempted from the guilt of the human race; there I abide with those who were not clothed with the three holy virtues, but without sin knew the others and followed them all'.

The last three lines define, one might say, the Limbo adults spiritually. And with respect to *Inferno* IV, 34-9 the definition is new; but not necessarily so new as to supplant the previous one. Indeed our presumption must be that the two definitions substantially concur, that the difference is only that now certain aspects of the situation are left in the shade and others, hitherto passed over, are brought more into the light. Two aspects anyhow (as regards the adults) now drop out of sight: sacramental baptism and (as regards those who, like Virgil, lived B.C.) their failure to adore God 'debitamente'. And what now comes clearly into the light is that all these adults have lacked the specifically Christian, the so-called 'theological' virtues, but have not lacked, indeed have fully possessed, all the natural virtues, those traditionally classified as 'cardinal': prudence, justice, fortitude, temperance. This stress on the adults' natural virtues is very strong: they have had these *to perfection*, for this surely is the sense of 'sanza vizio', and they have had them *all*, 'tutte quante'. And the point becomes unquestionably clear if we recall the obviously parallel case of the good pagan evoked in Dante's 'protest' in *Paradiso* XIX, 70-8: [52] that Indian who, living far out of reach of the Gospel, had nevertheless conformed himself *entirely* — not in deeds only but even in interior acts of the will ('voleri e atti', 73) — to the law of reason (74), and so had been 'without sin in life and words'. It would seem then that Virgil and his companions are morally perfect up to the limit of their nature as rational beings; that in them humanity, as defined by this limit, has reached its optimum. The only alternative would be to say that Virgil's account of himself and his adult companions, and Dante's of the good Indian, are too favourable; that they are one-sided and incomplete as glossing over something to the discredit of the good pagans. Virgil's account — here in *Purgatorio* VII — in particular would seem to be suspect since it contains no allusion to that flaw in the B.C. pagans' religion and his own 'rebellion' against God's law which he had mentioned earlier (*Inferno* IV, 38-9 and I, 125).

Waiving this point for the present, and taking Virgil's *Purgatorio* self-portrait at its face value, let us reflect a little on how this picture of an achieved human perfection tallies with the idea of the human condition put out by traditional Christianity. It is clear that the two

52. See above, pp. 182-87.

things are not easy to reconcile. Every reader of the New Testament
knows that the original Christian message took the form of a
promise of God's forgiveness for human sin — both the inherited sin
of the race, that of its common father Adam, and the sins of individuals. There is no place in New Testament teaching for
blameless men (excepting Jesus himself) whether born within or outside the Judaic Law. 'Are we Jews any better off?', cries St Paul,
'No, not at all; for we have already formulated the charge that Jews
and Greeks alike are all under the power of sin, as it is written:
"There is no just man, not one; no one who understands, no one
who seeks God" . . . . But now, quite apart from law, the justice of
God has been manifested (though both the Law and the Prophets
bear witness to it); the justice according to God through faith in
Christ for all who believe: for all without distinction. For all have
sinned and fall short of the glory of God, and all are justified by
God's free grace alone, through the redemption which is in Christ
Jesus'.[53] To be sure, this Pauline teaching on sin and grace has a personal emphasis; still, it is obviously authentically Christian. But to
get the whole matter into clearer perspective, theological and
historical, let me attempt a quick sketch of the development of the
idea of grace in the Western Church, the medium through which
Dante received that idea.

Common alike in secular Greek and in the Septuagint, the word
charis, 'grace' was an apt term for Christian uses. In the Septuagint
it renders the Hebrew *hen*, — meaning favour or good will and
presupposing the idea of active and generous love, especially on the
part of God. Again, as derived from *charein*, 'to be glad', *charis* connoted joy and goodwill in both parties to a gift or favour, in the
giver and the receiver. Thus it could carry a sense of being in com-
munion or fellowship and in the New Testament, especially in St
Paul (but cf. John 1, 14-17, Luke 1, 28-30; 2, 40, 52) it became
the chief term signifying the Christian experience of being loved by
God, in Christ, and of returning this love, in Christ — or simply of
being 'in Christ'. Thus around *charis* gathered the other Christian
words, faith, love, peace etc., as well as, in Paul especially, the con-
trast-term 'law' and the term for grace's antagonist, 'sin'. In time
these words came to be defined more precisely, and as each became

53. *Romans*, 3, 9-24.

more precise all the rest were affected too. The Church could not understand 'love' or 'faith' except in the context of grace, and in particular, and more quickly, she found that her understanding of grace was bound up with its Pauline correlative 'sin'. Here Augustine led the way, exploring St Paul's division of all mankind into two states only, that of sin and that of the grace given in Jesus (Romans 3, 23-4); and this exploration naturally opened up questions about the nature of man and free will.

Underlying all Christian discourse on grace is, of course, the idea, common to the whole Bible, of the absolute 'otherness' of God, and hence the presupposition that no communication from God to man is *owed*, any more than creation itself was owed, but must always be God's free initiative. Human nature as such has no 'divinity', in the sense of a share in the life proper to God. Moreover, this 'apartness' of God from man has nothing in principle to do with man's being in fact in a state of sin. It is part of the God-creature relationship, which is prior to the God-sinner relationship. This idea is partly obscured in the New Testament by the great Pauline stress on man's apartness as *sinful* and on grace as the remedy for sin. But even in the New Testament there are texts that indicate grace as a raising of man's *nature* towards God, apart from direct reference to salvation from sin. Thus St John says that the result of faith in the Incarnation is a new divine birth which does not arise from human nature (1, 13, cf. 1 Peter 1, 23); and in John 1, 18 (cf. 1 Cor. 2, 10-11; Gal. 1, 11-12) we learn of a new knowledge of God, made possible through Christ, where the contrast seems to be with the knowledge accessible to human nature as such, quite apart from man's 'fallen' condition.

It is not surprising then that Christian thinking about grace went on to develop in a twofold way according as the stress was put on one or other of the two chief terms that contrast with grace: nature and sin. The Greek Fathers tended to see grace as a share in 'divinity', received by human nature as a result of the Incarnation. They used the Greek ideas of participation (*methexis*) and divinization (*theopoiēsis*) and looked into human nature to find some pre-existing capacity for this divinization. Thinking of grace in the Johannine terms of light and life even more than in the Pauline terms of justification, they show a tendency to take the cause of grace back to the Incarnation itself rather than to concentrate on the redemptive

Passion. This was only a difference of emphasis, but it suffices to distinguish a 'Greek' approach to grace-theology that was more on-tological than ethical. As a motto, so to say, for this line of develop-ment we 'Latins' might take the phrase *gratia elevans*, although this only appears, so far as I know, rather late in the Church's official teaching, at the Council of Vienne in 1311-12.[54]. More directly relevant to our present subject is the other line that runs from St Paul through Augustine to the first official definitions of grace, at the Councils of Carthage (418) and Orange (529). Here grace is understood chiefly as the healing and rectification of the sinful human will, as *gratia sanans*.[55]. Historically its starting point was St Paul's break with Judaism and so with the Law, as the way by which man may come into harmony, effectively, with God. Paul re-jected the Law in this sense. For him, as we have seen, there was no difference, in point of sinfulness, between Jew and Pagan; and there was no remedy except in faith in the atoning sacrifice of the Cross. Chiefly owing to St Paul, this aspect of grace is the more con-spicuous one in the New Testament; and it led, far sooner than the other, to ecclesiastical definitions. That it did so was due above all to St. Augustine. Augustine's refutation of Pelagianism is Paul's refutation of Judaism over again, but aimed at the self-directing Stoic free will instead of against the Jews' legal righteousness. It has had an absolutely decisive effect on Catholic Christianity. It settled once and for all two basic points: that man without grace (God's help) is necessarily a sinner, and that man can never take the in-itiative in his liberation from sin, the first move being always with God. Clearly, this is a predominantly *moral* conception of grace, focussing directly on the human will's relation to God and touching only in a secondary way on the status of human nature as such in relation to grace.

And so, broadly speaking, it remained, in the West, until the Aristotelians of the thirteenth century drew out a clear and distinct idea of *nature* from the newly translated works of the Philosopher, the so-called *libri naturales* (in which term were comprised the *Metaphysics* and the *De Anima* as well as the *Physics* and the astronomical and zoological treatises). And, along with this new conception of nature as a relatively autonomous system with its own

54. Denzinger-Schönmetzer, *op. cit.*, no. 895.
55. *Ibid.* nos. 222-30, 371-97.

intrinsic structures and finalities, there arose also, quite naturally, the idea of a specifically human kind of knowledge bounded by sense experience and the range of reason. Thus for the first time in the Christian West philosophy clearly appeared as a discipline distinct from theology.[56] But how did these two new factors, the Aristotelian idea of nature and the idea of a strictly human science and philosophy independent of faith and theology, affect Christian thinking about grace?

They would seem to have affected it in broadly two contrasting ways: as contributing to the progress of theology and at the same time as posing difficulties and favouring the growth of a non-Christian mentality in Europe. In one way the Greek idea of nature as an intrinsically intelligible structure of being and activity was a positive boon to theology of the sort practised by St Thomas; even as regards the theme of grace conceived as a 'super-natural' gift that transcends all natural capacities. There is perhaps no more striking instance in the *Summa* of St Thomas's genius for transforming, while appropriating, the Aristotelian concept of nature than the use he makes of it (in 1a2ae. 110, 3-4) to render intelligible the New Testament teaching on the New Birth and the New Creation – a use which, at the same time and precisely through this recourse to the pagan philosopher, is a refutation of views propounded in the standard theological text-book, the *Sentences* of Peter Lombard. The thing is done so easily and quietly that its audacity may pass unnoticed.[57]

To this kind of bridge-building between Greek thought and the Gospel St Thomas devoted his talents and energies; and with considerable effect on his contemporaries and in the decades immediately following his untimely death in 1274. Gilson has said 'ce solitaire n'a pas écrit pour son siècle',[58] and one sees what he meant, but the fact is that Thomas's reputation stood very high by the turn of the century; and no less as a philosopher than as theologian, indeed

56. There are, of course, many good studies on or around this theme; two may be mentioned here: E. Gilson's *History of Christian Philosophy in the Middle Ages*, London, 1954; F. Van Steenberghen's *The Philosophical Movement in the Thirteenth Century*, London, 1955.

57. This aspect of Aquinas' teaching on grace gets special attention from C. Ernst, O.P., in his edition of vol. 30 of the new English translation of the *Summa theologiae* (gen. editor, T. Gilby, O.P.): *The Gospel of Grace* (1a2ae. 106-114), London, 1972.

58. *La philosophie au moyen-age*, Paris, 2nd ed. 1952, p. 590.

perhaps especially as a philosopher, owing to his great series of commentaries on Aristotle (c. 1268-73) which were quickly and widely
appreciated as the best available instruments (along with those of
Averroes) for the study of the common Master. Nevertheless it is
also true that in the years when Dante was growing to manhood,
and on into the fourteenth century, philosophical activity in the
West — always carried on by men whose training was wholly
Aristotelian — was very far from being dominated by St Thomas. In
moral philosophy, the field I am concerned with, the solutions
offered by him to the problems raised for the Christian mind by
what R.-A. Gauthier calls 'l'humanisme exclusif' of the *Nicomachean
Ethics*, these solutions were read and discussed and criticized; [59]
they did not form the tenets of a widely influential 'school', outside
the Dominican Order. As for those problems, in any case, two in
particular were felt, and both (but the first more directly) are relevant to the present inquiry: (1) the nature and degree of that happiness which, according to Aristotle, man can achieve in this world
by his own efforts (especially *Nic. Ethics* I, 7-10); (2) the compatibility of Aristotelian 'magnanimity' (*megalopsychia* — which Ross
renders by 'pride') with Christian humility (especially, *N.E.* IV, 3).

Now as regards the first of these questions — the one that more
directly concerns us — we have good evidence of the existence,
before the end of the thirteenth century, of a critical reaction against
St Thomas's benign interpretation of the *Nicomachean Ethics*, his effort, as it were, to defuse the pagan 'charge' in that work; a reaction
which in fact represented, on this point, a more exact assessment of
the spirit of the *Ethics*. The crucial point was how best to understand the phrase at the end of I, c. 10: *makarious d'ōs
anthrōpous*, which Ross renders '... but happy *men*', and the version used by St Thomas, 'beatos autem ut homines'. Aristotle's drift
here seems to be that, whatever may be the case with souls after
death, and granted that various misfortunes are unavoidable in this
present life, still we ought to aim, in this life, at the highest happiness of which our nature is capable. Now Aquinas understood that
qualifying phrase 'ut homines' in the sense of *faute de mieux*; Aristotle, with his hazy notions of a future life and fully aware of the im-
perfections of this life, would be saying, 'Well, let's make the best

59. art. cit. in *Archives d'histoire doctrinale et littéraire du Moyen-age*, XVI, 1946-7, pp.
187-335.

we can of an unsatisfactory situation'.[60] And elsewhere St Thomas
— with a precision and subtlety that betrays his intense interest in the
matter — draws out the implications of this text, as he understood it,
in terms of a key-distinction between *beatitudo imperfecta* and
beatitudo perfecta; between that provisional and extremely incomplete happiness which is the best we can hope for in this mortal
life, and the total and eternal bliss of heaven. In this way he made
even Aristotle come into line with the Christian sense of the radical
inadequacy of our life before death.[61]

But another, more 'philosophical' interpretation of 'beat(i) ut
homines' was possible and it soon found discreet expression. It con-
sisted in taking this qualifying phrase, not in the sense of a resignation to a *faute de mieux*, but as pointing to the limits within which
man's specific nature as such has to operate and seek the perfection
proper to it. It shifts the stress away from the factual conditions of
human life in this world — which is what Aquinas had chiefly in
mind — towards an abstract conception of the 'end' of man *qua* man.
And this was to circumvent Aquinas's distinction; for this was not
primarily a distinction between man *qua* man and man as
'divinized', or between the natural order and the supernatural order,
but between the state of man as on the way towards God and his
state at the end of the journey; between man *in via* (*homo viator*) and
man *in patria*. The brilliant analysis in *Summa theologiae* 1a2ae. 1-5
is all based on this alignment, so to say, of the imperfect towards the
perfect; so that the best that can be said (but how much it is!) of the
'beatitudo imperfecta' of this life is to call it a 'beginning', or a
'hope', or a 'kind of participation' in the 'beatitudo perfecta' of
heaven (the vision of God's essence) which is the *only* 'ultimate end'.
As compared, then, with this eternal life in 'beatitudo perfecta', life
in time, however 'blessed' (imperfectly) is not fit to be called an *end*
at all. But now, suppose we change the perspective and take
Aristotle's phrase in the sense of St Thomas's critics: then to be 'happy as men (*ut homines*)' becomes the *aim* we should pursue in order
to fulfil the nature that is proper to us precisely as human beings —
neither brute animals, nor angels, nor God, but animals endowed

60. *Sententia libri Ethicorum*, Rome, 1969, I, p. 59-60 (ed. Pirotta, § 202; and cf. §
2136).
61. *Summa theol.* 1a2ae; 3, 2 ad 4; 3, 6; 5, 3 and 5; cf. *Contra Gent.* III, 25-48.

with reason. And this aim becomes man's ultimate end — at least so far as this life is concerned.

Here we are evidently in sight of the passage at the end of the *Monarchia*, declaring that man has 'two ultimate ends', one as a compound of body and soul, the other as an immortal spirit. For man is the 'horizon-line' where two 'natures' meet, each with its own distinctive end or perfection; so that each of these ends is 'ultimate' with respect to the nature whose perfection it is. And these abstractions arose naturally out of thirteenth century Aristotelianism. St Thomas had resisted, in advance, the dualism they represented, but it had been prepared for by the critical reaction to his Christian interpretation of the Philosopher in the decades following his death. To illustrate this let us glance at two texts: first, an anonymous commentary on the *Nic. Ethics* which R.-A. Gauthier has dated c. 1290; second, the better known little treatise *De summo bono* by Boethius of Dacia, probably written at Paris before 1280.

The chief interest, here, of the anonymous commentary is that its author takes issue with St Thomas's interpretation of that phrase of Aristotle about being happy 'as men' (*N.E.* I, end of c. 10).[62] To our commentator it seemed that Thomas was reasoning too much as a theologian — not *philosophically* enough. To a philosopher it should be clear that there *is* a sense in which 'beatitudo perfecta' must be possible for man in this life. True, such happiness will not be perfect 'absolutely' (*simpliciter*): *that* degree of perfection can only be found in the life after death — which is the theologian's business. But every philosopher knows that 'of all the animals man is the most perfect', and therefore that man 'must have it in his power to reach his ultimate end [in this life on earth] ... which is human happiness .... Otherwise man would never reach the perfection proper to his nature'. And this is what the Philosopher meant where he said he was speaking of happiness for *men* and 'in so far as it is possible for happiness to be realised in human nature in this life'. The evil and misfortunes of our present life — with which the theologian tries to support his notion of 'beatitudo imperfecta' — these do not affect the philosophical principle that 'the most perfect animal' must, as such, have an attainable 'ultimate end' — the happiness possible, here and now, to him precisely as possessed of this nature.

62. See R.-A. Gaùthier, art. cit. in *Archives* etc., pp. 278-81.

So the philosopher puts the theologian right on the concept of man *qua* man. What we then find on turning to Boethius of Dacia's little work [63] is an exaltation of the philosopher to the status of the *model man*. Boethius is the purest of intellectualists and at the same time the serenest of 'pelagians' (though naturally he never alludes to so theological an issue as that term implies). His subject is the *summum bonum*, the 'supreme good' – not 'absolutely speaking but as possible for man'. And this must be the good that man can acquire by the use of the 'divine thing' in him, the intellect; and this both in the way of pure 'knowledge of the truth' and of the direction of the will to the practice of moral virtue. And this double use of the intellect is supremely delightful, and in it 'human happiness' is achieved, 'the supreme good of man'. Only a few, a happy few, live in this way, but only they truly live 'according to the order of Nature' (*secundum ordinem naturalem*). And 'these are the philosophers' (*et isti sunt philosophi*). Moreover the way of philosophy is a way leading to perfect moral rectitude; and those who follow it consistently 'never sin' (*nunquam peccant*).

Now, probably neither of these texts I have glanced at – almost certainly not the *De Summo Bono* – would have met with Dante's entire approval; not even when writing the *Convivio*. But they are, I think, extremely indicative of a temper, an approach, a way of thinking about and formulating the situation of man on earth without which neither *Convivio* IV, nor *Monarchia* III, xv, nor the Dantean Limbo would in fact have been possible. What had emerged here and there in the West was the conception of a humanist ethic based more or less exclusively on the 'natural order' – of an area of human activity that would be self-contained and autonomous; virtually independent of grace whether *elevans* or *sanans*. It was against just such a conception that the Augustinian Petrarch was later fiercely to react; but in the meantime it had deeply affected the Aristotelian Dante.

---

63. Boethius of Dacia, *De summo bono* (text in M. Grabman *Mittelalterliches Geistesleben*, Munich, 1936, II, pp. 200-24). Boethius taught philosophy at Paris and was involved with Siger of Brabant (see *Par.* X, 133-8) in the condemnation of 'Averroism' in 1277. The naturalism he represented spread to Bologna, as appears from the *Quaestio de felicitate* of James of Pistoia, dedicated to Dante's friend Guido Cavalcanti; see *Medioevo e Rinascimente, Studi in onore di B. Nardi*, Florence, 1954, II, pp. 427-63.

12

THE TWO DANTES (III)

The Pagans and Grace

I n the foregoing section of this essay I began to sketch an
approach to Dante's Limbo as a product of late thirteenth century Aristotelianism, of the type that has come to be called
'integral' or 'radical' (in preference to the older term 'Latin Averroism'). Viewed in this light the Dantean Limbo would be one
effect — a very personal, even peculiar one — of the emergence
in the European mind at that time of an idea of human perfectibility
to be realised before death and within the limits of human nature;
this being now distinguished, with a quite new precision, from the
'new man' of Christian teaching, from our nature as transformed by
divine grace.[1] This new idea of the properly human sphere and
capacity drew its inspiration, so far as morals were concerned, mainly from the Nicomachean Ethics; and, as everyone may see, it was
tendentially non-Christian.

I want now to pursue this topic with special regard to the Christian doctrine of grace, and to begin by asking (at the risk of
repeating things already said): What presuppositions, in the mind of
its inventor, are discernible in the Dantean Limbo? To this question
the obvious general answer is that the poet was a Christian, but with
a mind formed by the culture of his time. As an heir of the Christian
tradition Dante, like Aquinas before him, took for granted an
irreducible difference between the natural order and the order of
grace, between what man could do of himself and what, over and
above this, God in his sovereign independence might choose to do.
As a believer Dante inherited the conviction, derived from the
Bible, that there was an upper limit beyond which mere human
endeavour could never rise. But he belonged, in addition, to the
historical form of western culture that we call scholastic. Now the

1. *Ephesians* 2, 15; 4, 24; *Galatians* 6, 15 etc.

great germinal insight of thirteenth century scholasticism was the discernment of an 'order of nature' as something to be explored and defined *per se*, in clear distinction from the 'supernatural order' (the correlating of the two 'orders' being the special task of theology). It was a discernment and an appreciation, unprecedented in Christendom, of the intrinsic structures and specific finalities of Nature, and so of man as a part of Nature. Nor, presumably, would this have been possible but for the impact of the new versions of Aristotle and of his Arab commentators, an impact that aroused consternation and endless controversy but nevertheless was borne victoriously along by the chief agents of intellectual renewal in that age, the Orders of the Friars and the new Universities. And with all this came the discovery of philosophy as *distinct* from theology, of science as *distinct* from faith, of rational ethics as *distinct* from the following of Christ – a certain intensification, at many points, of the natural tendency of the rational faculty to conceptualize and distinguish and draw boundary lines.

For what, after all, are the figures in Dante's Limbo but images of Man as distinct from Christian Man? But if that is what they are, is the idea of manhood which they express compatible with any theory of man that can plausibly be called Christian? The Christian question to any theory of man is, how does Christ fit into it? Now in orthodox (Catholic) Christianity Christ stands in essential relation both to man as evil and to man as capable of goodness: he is both Crucified and Resurgent; both the peace-offering for our sins and the bearer of a new life-relationship with God; which in technical theology is expressed, in part, by saying that Christ brings to man both *gratia sanans* and *gratia elevans*; both the healing and correcting of our corrupt wills and the lifting of our nature into a love-union with God that will terminate eventually in the Beatific Vision. How does all this tally with the idea embodied in Dante's Limbo-dwellers? It is hard to see what it has to do with them at all. For, on the one hand they seem quite uncorrupt so far as natural goodness of theirs seems to entail no reference to God as the source of any *further* perfection.

Grace under both of its aspects – *sanans* and *elevans* – would seem to be ruled out in advance. As regards the first of these apparent exclusions of grace, something has already been said, in Sections I and II of this essay. The second has hardly been touched on yet. But it may help to bring the matter of *gratia sanans* into sharper focus if we compare what I take to be the theological oddness of Dante's fiction here with the views of St Thomas Aquinas where he touches on the same underlying question – that is, the question whether man needs grace as a moral remedy against himself. This will occupy the rest of the present part 3 (that dealing with the third of the four 'topics' to be examined which I distinguished early in Section II). Then in part 4 I shall try to deal – perforce briefly – with the difficult matter of that precluding of *gratia elevans* which Dante's fiction appears to entail, inasmuch as it would seem, at least, to represent human nature as wholly self-contained and self-enclosed, as not open to any perfection that is not merely *human*; and this not because of any moral obstacle in the human will, but simply because this nature is what it is – no less *and* no more.

St Thomas was the leading Christian Aristotelian of his time and yet his views on the point I am now concerned with – a point, as we have seen, very closely related to Dante's debt to Aristotle – differ sharply from those of the poet. In the *Summa theologiae*, discussing man's need of grace, 'de necessitate gratiae', St Thomas asks (1a2ae. 109, art. 2) whether man 'can will and do what is good without grace'.[2] In his reply (speaking here very much as a theologian and for the moment forgetting Aristotle) he first distinguishes the two traditionally accepted 'states' (*status*) of human nature, the one as intact (*in sua sua integritate*) in Adam before the Fall, the other as 'spoiled in us' (*corrupta*) since. In either state nothing at all is willed or done except, ultimately, through the power of God, but this general dependence as such does not involve 'grace'. Grace only comes in when we consider what is peculiar to each 'state'. 'In the state of intact nature . . . man could by his natural endowments will and achieve the goodness proportionate to his nature, the goodness of the virtues he can make his own. . . . But in the state of corrupted nature man *falls short even of the goodness which is in line with his nature*, so that of his own power he cannot perfectly bring into act even this kind of goodness. It is true that, since human nature is not entirely ruined . . . man can achieve some goodness even in this

---

2. In what follows I am indebted to the work, already cited in Section II, of C. Ernst, *The Gospel of Grace*, London, 1972 (vol. 30 of the annotated transl. of St Thomas's *Summa theologiae*, General Editor, T. Gilby).

state . . . . *But he cannot, in this state, realise completely the goodness that is conatural to him, so as to fall short in nothing* . . . . Thus, in the state of intact nature it is only in one respect that man needs to receive a power given as a 'grace' (*virtus gratuita*) over and above the powers he has by nature – namely, in respect of achieving and willing the good that is *supernatural*. But in the state of corrupted nature he is in need of such a superadded capacity in *two* respects; first, in order to be healed (*ut sanetur*) and then in order to achieve the goodness that belongs to virtues that transcend his nature (*ut bonum supernaturalis virtutis operetur*)'.

This conclusion is then further analysed in the course of the same Question 109. Article 8 is particularly relevant to our subject since it raises the question as to whether a certain *attitude to God* is part of morality, which is the topic I shall come to presently (under 'Religion as part of Virtue'). But it will be useful to examine this article forthwith. It puts the question whether man 'can avoid mortal sin without the help of grace', and St Thomas's 'reply' will be found, I think, to hinge on two points: (1) that sin is something *unnatural* – 'sinning is simply a failure to act according to [human] nature'; (2) that both the failure to follow the true bent of nature, which is sin, and the healing or rectifying of corrupted human nature, which is the work of grace, begin in that 'part' of man which is most specifically human, the mind or reason – with a proviso as to the starting point of sin which will appear in due course.

Having noted then that sin is out of line with 'nature', and that once our nature had turned sinful it can only be 'healed' by God's grace (implying that it could not heal itself), Aquinas goes on to remark that this healing is a gradual process, for 'in our present [temporal] life this healing begins in the mind (*secundum mentem*), with carnal desire not yet fully reintegrated; as the Apostle says (Romans 7, 25): "I serve the law of God with my mind, but with my flesh the law of sin". In this state a man can entirely refrain from mortal sin, which of its essence involves the rational part of us, as has been shown. But he cannot wholly refrain from venial sin, owing to the disorder existing in the lower sensual impulses'. The situation Aquinas is speaking of – as the Pauline reference makes clear – is that of Christians beset by temptations but presumed to be 'in grace'; so let us skip a few lines and come to where he considers the case of people like Dante's good pagans, morally responsible but *ex hypothesi* not 'in grace'. 'Similarly, even before a man's reason, which is the essential factor in mortal sin, be restored ... by grace, he is able indeed to refrain from particular mortal sins, ... he does not have to be always actually sinning; but he cannot remain for long without sinning mortally. ... This is because, just as the lower impulses ought to be subject to reason, *so reason itself should be subject to God, directing the will towards him (in ipso constituere finem suae voluntatis)*. All human activities should be ruled by their proper end, as the lower impulses by the judgement of reason. Therefore, just as there must be disorder in our lower impulses so long as they are not subject to reason, so too many disorders are sure to arise in the rational part if it is not wholly subjected to God; for when a man's heart is not so firmly grounded in God that he would not choose to be separated from him for the obtaining of any good whatsoever, or the avoiding of any evil, then many things are sure to present themselves, to obtain or to avoid which a man will withdraw from God, setting at nought his precepts, and thus will commit grave sin'.

Let us pause here to make two comments. First, it is clear that the pith of Thomas's argument is that the moral state of a man, for good or evil, depends on how his mind — or 'heart' — is related to God. The right relation is one of filial submission, the wrong the absence of this, entailing actual or potential rebellion. The biblical word 'heart' here obviously signifies interior thoughts and intentions, and more particularly the will, as the root of responsible activity. Everything then depends on the state of a man's will. If it be disengaged from God, this must sooner or later have its consequences in practice, for as Thomas concludes, 'a man cannot for long remain without acting in accordance with a will not rightly disposed towards God' — unless, to be sure, God himself intervenes to right the situation. Secondly, it is clear that Thomas here assumes a strict correlation between having one's heart properly disposed towards God and being in a state of grace. He implicitly excludes the hypothesis that a man might have his heart duly subject to God and yet *not* be in a state of grace.

If this be the sense of Thomas's teaching, how does it help us with Dante's good pagans? We can take it that Dante accepted the traditional division, repeated here by Thomas, of the 'states' of human nature on earth; an original 'intact' state followed by a state of 'corruption', which in turn is now in process of being 'healed' by the grace that comes from Christ. But besides this, I think the three following points can be safely presupposed. (a) Dante would have accepted the distinction St Thomas has drawn between two moments in moral behaviour: the first in the mind, as submissive or not to God; the second in consequent action, good or bad. (b) Precisely as regards the *second* of these moments, Dante's good pagans are *always* represented as blameless (see the texts commented on in Section II above, especially *Purgatorio* VII, 34-6 and *Paradiso* XIX, 73-5) – except, and only except, in Virgil's allusions, early in the *Inferno* (I, 125 and IV, 38), to a fault in the religion of the old pagans and to his own 'rebellion' against God's law. (c) But these good pagans are represented as *never* having been actually in a state of grace.

Now, these being my assumptions, I find that four alternatives present themselves with regard to the moral condition of adult un-graced humanity, as Dante saw this. The first would represent the Thomist position. The other three are alternative suggestions as to what may be implied, doctrinally, by the adults in Dante's Limbo. The four may be set out, rather baldly, thus:

(i) The heart is *not* subject to God. Consequent behaviour is (sooner or later) bad.

(ii) The heart *is* subject to God, but *not* because of grace. Consequent behaviour good.

(iii) The heart is *not* subject to God, but has never actually *rejected* an offer of grace. Consequent behaviour good.

(iv) The heart is *not* subject to God and it *has* rejected an offer of grace. Consequent behaviour good.

It is essential to note that in none of the last three alternatives is grace regarded as necessary for integral goodness in the natural order, i.e. for the full round of natural virtue; and this even though the doctrine of the Fall ('Original Sin') is presupposed – as of course it is in every part of Dante's poem. This is the point which would most sharply differentiate Dante from St Thomas, and it is the one I have been especially concerned to stress in this part 3 under the heading 'Virtue as a Human Product'. But our analysis can also serve to introduce my next sub-section, namely part 4, 'Religion as a Part of Virtue'. For it is clear that our alternative (ii) differs from (iii) and (iv) in that it would represent the good pagans as good in a sense *not* included in the two latter alternatives; in that their hearts would be subject to God in the first of the two moral 'moments' which St Thomas has distinguished. Hence if it is alternative (ii) that applies to Dante's good pagans, then the latter are to be thought of as not only virtuous in word and deed but also as radically pious and religious. On the other hand it seems absurd to say that this piety of theirs, supposing it to have existed, was an effect precisely of divine grace, if this by definition is 'super-natural' and if one accepts (as one must, I think) that Dante always represents the virtues of his good pagans as merely 'natural'. What sort of spiritual unity would Virgil represent if his 'heart' were in a state of grace while all the good actions that sprang from it and expressed its goodness were simply of and in the 'natural order'? But if that interpretation of (ii) is ruled out, and if we still wish to understand these pagans in terms of (ii), then we have to say that the whole goodness envisaged under this alternative is composed of *natural* virtues rooted in *natural* piety; both the piety and the virtues being simply dispositions of human nature as such, of man *qua* man. Is this, then, how Dante presents his Virgil? One is very much tempted to answer 'yes' in view of the general character of Dante's Guide. But how can we forget that admission of a flaw in his piety, let fall at his first meeting with Dante and before they start on their voyage together: 'I was a rebel against his [God's] law' (*Inferno* I, 125)?

These words − coupled with *Inferno* IV, 37-9 − certainly put Virgil's piety in question; but the matter needs to be further examined. For in considering Dante's Virgil as, in some sense, a symbol of the natural virtues, one cannot ignore the fact that among these virtues the thirteenth century theologians tended to include piety towards God (*religio*). So we have to ask whether Dante follows the same line of thought, in what he shows us of 'natural' virtue in the *Comedy* or says about it elsewhere, and particularly in *Convivio* IV. But before I pursue this point I want to raise once more, and rather sharply, the nagging question that has underlain so much of the discussion hitherto: how far, if at all, does Dante's presentation of his Limbo-dwellers allow us to say that he thought of them as ever having had access (as a possibility, of course, not as a realised fact) to divine grace? Plainly, they are not *actually* in the 'state of grace' in the usual and orthodox sense of the phrase − the condition of those who are their way to heavenly glory, to the Beatific Vision. But was such a condition ever a real *possibility* for them? Now I want to suggest here and now (anticipating one of the conclusions of this essay) that the right answer to that question may well be that Dante conceived of his good pagans as having in some mysterious way been offered access to grace in the sense of *gratia elevans*, without having been offered – *because they did not need it* – access to grace in the sense of *gratia sanans*. Theologically this may seem an absurd hypothesis – for of course these potential receivers of *gratia elevans* would be descendants, presumably, of sinful Adam; but where Dante's theology is concerned the strangeness of a concept is no reason for excluding it in advance.

4. *Religion as a Part of Virtue.* Aristotle was aware of modes of being intrinsically superior to the human ('man is not the best thing in the world' [3]); to this extent his thought is not quite irreligious. But religion as a worship that is strictly owed to God (or the gods) by man finds no place in his ethics [4] ; so that when philosophical theology revived in the West after the Dark Ages, the theologians could get little help from Aristotle in the matter of defining 'religio'. In this respect the philosopher they turned to was Cicero who, in a passage already recommended to his fellow-Christians by Augustine, had linked *religio* with *iustitia*.[5] Adopting this idea theologians began to make 'religion' part of the cardinal virtue of justice; it was a giving to God of what was due to him. The matter however remained for a time rather confused; for what, after all, is due to God, according to Christ's teaching, but total love? How then is religion, properly understood, anything else but charity, *caritas?* But in that case how can it be merely a subdivision of natural justice? Here, as elsewhere, it was St Thomas who drew the required distinctions most clearly. I need not repeat his analysis in detail; enough to draw out the points more relevant to our theme. First then, for Thomas both religion, considered in its essence, and charity are virtues in the will, that is, the soul's appetitive capacity. Secondly, whereas charity names the will as bearing on God *directly*, religion names it as bearing on God *at a remove*, as the Creator and Governor of the universe, and so as owed submission and reverence from all rational creatures. Thirdly, whereas man is both able and

---

3. *Nic. Ethics* VI, 7, 1141a 22.
4. See R.-A. Gauthier, *La morale d'Aristote*, Paris, 1973, pp. 107-110.
5. *De inventione rhetorica* II, 53; see O. Lottin, *Psychologie et morale aux XIIe et XIIIe siècles*, III, 2, pp. 313-26.

morally obliged to be, in this sense, religious, he is by nature
altogether incapable of charity, as defined; and this because the
human mind, being created and therefore finite, can only apprehend
God in a finite way, that is, indirectly and through created *media*;
and by the same token can only indirectly and mediately love him.
Therefore, fourthly, whereas religion (so defined) does *not* presuppose divine grace, charity absolutely does; it is essentially *supernatural*, being in essence a sharing in the love-life of God himself.[6]

This distinction springs straight from the Christian tradition, yet
it may seem odd that religion has been defined, to start with, in
terms of the natural virtue of justice; one might have expected it to
get a higher or more central place in a theological ethic that sees the
whole of life in terms of an approach to, or estrangement from God.
But, in the first place, that definition of 'religio' as a part of justice,
was not Christian in origin; it came, as we have seen, from Cicero.
Moreover, what, for Aquinas, links religion with justice is the notion of obligation; but what distinguishes it from every other form
of justice is the unique Object which, in this case, governs the
obligation. Again – and this is more directly to our purpose – it is
clear that St Thomas regards this virtue of *religio* as the nearest approach, from the human end, to the life of grace 'in Christ', although
it cannot, by definition, be called intrinsically Christian. For, having
distinguished religion from charity and placed it far lower in the
moral scale, he goes on to say that among all the (natural) moral virtues *religio* is preeminent, as the one that most directly bears on the
final point and purpose of all virtue, which is to bring man into contact with God. This proposition is so important in the present context that I give the saint's own words; 'Ea quae sunt ad finem sor-
tiuntur bonitatem ex ordine in finem; et ideo quanto sunt fini
propinquiora, tanto sunt meliora. Virtutes autem morales ... sunt
circa ea quae ordinantur in Deum sicut in finem. Religio autem magis
de propinquo accedit ad Deum quam aliae virtutes morales, inquantum operatur ea quae directe et immediate ordinantur in honorem
divinum. *Et ideo religio praeeminet inter alias virtutes morales*'.[7] Thus
for St Thomas religion represents the apex of human conduct in the
natural order. We are a long way indeed from the Nicomachean

6. This analysis is based chiefly on *Summa theol.* 2a2ae. 23 *passim*, for charity, and on
2a2ae. 81, for religion.
7. *Summa theol.* 2a2ae. 81, 6.

Ethics! If for Aquinas, as for Aristotle, there is a goodness befitting man *qua* man to which we should strive, this for the Christian thinker is only fully achieved in the worship of God; on which Aristotle had nothing to say.[8]

But it is equally important to realise that for Aquinas and the Catholic tradition generally, this 'apex morality' of religiousness is of strict obligation. No one is excused! It is binding on all men to acknowledge, as best they can, and even – in some way or other – to worship the divine Presence in the world.[9] And the relevance of this point to Dantean ethics is crucial, as we shall see. But before we turn back to the poet I want to press this same point a little further in its Thomist context. It might be objected against my stress on the obligatoriness of 'religion', as Aquinas presents it, that I am taking a tone that is not characteristic of Aquinas himself, whose ethical discourse and vocabulary seldom remind one of Kant; so that one of his ablest interpreters has said, 'it may be doubted whether "obligation" represents a specific interest for St Thomas' (T. Gilby).[10] And certainly, in the *Summa* the moral imperative is never presented as an 'absolute' prescinding from the pursuit of happiness. Every argument about right and wrong depends on non-ethical premises about the nature of man and his inbuilt dynamic relationship to God. It is by a compulsion of his nature that man desires God.[11] Morality proper only begins at the point where this desire is required to take effect in a free choice, a self-directing towards God, the 'due end', *finis debitus*, of the human will.[12] Nevertheless the adjective 'debitus' has the strongest possible sense here, so that deliberately to exclude the End in question is 'mortal sin'.[13] And if men commonly seek happiness in things more directly known than God, and more immediately attractive, this does not cancel the prior obligation to seek God in and through all things. But of course there can be no obligation to seek an object of whose existence one is wholly unaware. And just what knowledge of God – of the God in whom *he* believed – did St Thomas think was

8. This is perhaps too sweeping: see *Nic. Ethics* I, 12, 1101b 20-27 and St Thomas's *Expositio*, I, lect. 18.
9. *Summa theol.* 2a2ae. 81, 3 ad 2; 4. *Contra Gentiles* III, 115-6.
10. English transl. of *Summa theol.* cit., vol. 18 (1966) p. 124.
11. *Summa theol.* 1a2ae. 2 *passim*; 3, 8. *Contra Gentiles* III, 25-63
12. *Summa theol.* 1a2ae. 89, 6.
13. See Note 12; also *Summa theol.* 1a2ae. 87, 3.

available to the pagan part of mankind (in the sense of those to whom the Christian message has never in fact been announced)? Anything like a detailed answer to this question would be out of place in this essay; let it suffice for the present to note that Aquinas certainly thought, following St Paul, that *some* awareness of God must, as a general rule, be within the reach of pagan man; an awareness sufficient, at least, to serve as the psychological ground for an implicit 'turning to God' which would amount, in fact, to an implicit plea for grace.[14] In *Romans* 1, 18-23 St Paul had refused to countenance the idolatry of the pagan world precisely because the true God had not left that world in total darkness: 'So they are without excuse; for, knowing God, they have not honoured him as God or given thanks to him, but instead have become futile in their thinking and their foolish minds were darkened ... and they exchanged the glory of the immortal God for images resembling mortal man or birds or beasts or reptiles'. And both the main points in this indictment are subscribed to by Aquinas in his commentary on the epistle – that God never left the pagans without some incipient knowledge of himself, and that that is why idolatry was sinful. The great general sin of the pagans was false religion, 'peccatum impietatis', an implicit refusal to render to the true God the honour due to him, 'Dei debitus cultus'. But the premiss behind this hard judgement on the pagans is that no man begins the moral life in total ignorance of the Creator; some light is given, initially, to all men.[15]

Returning to Dante with this Pauline and Thomist teaching in mind, we might expect that when he writes as an ethical philosopher – that is, chiefly in Book IV of the *Convivio* – he would consider seriously the place of religion in the moral life. But it is not so – not, at least, when he descends from metaphysical generalities to consider the particular forms of moral goodness (the virtues) that should characterize a good human life. Certainly the *Convivio* is in some sense a religious work, but one can hardly doubt that St Paul and St Thomas would have found it in this respect inadequate. It implies a generally orthodox idea of God, but its central concern is man, and man is viewed in it, for the most part, not in relation to God but in relation to the cosmos, so far as this is intelligible (Books II-III), and to his own nature, so far as this includes a latent 'nobility' which

14. *Summa theol.* 1a2ae. 5, 5 ad 1; 109 4 ad 2. *Contra Gentiles* III, 159.
15. *In Epist. ad Romanos* I, lect. 7. See ch. 9 above, 'The Son's Eagle', note 25.

can be developed into moral virtue (Book IV). Certainly this inborn human nobility derives from God, it is a participation – at a level only 'a little lower than the angels' – in a divine 'likeness' deriving from the archetypal Light which is also transcendent Unity and infinite Goodness. This is the 'religion' expressed in the *Convivio* (particularly in Book III): the affirmation of a 'divinity' in things, especially in intellectual being. There is nothing, of course, specifically Christian about this.[16]

Throughout the work Dante writes as one who takes all the Christian things for granted – prayer, the sacraments, the Church, the Incarnation – but whose principal concern is to express the insights of reason. Not that these insights are very coherently organised. We have already noted the sudden shift of perspective between the mainly Neoplatonist Book III and the mainly Aristotelian Book IV; a shift the author excuses, with disarming candour, by his being baffled by a metaphysical problem.[17] If, as Jacques Goudet remarks, Dante in the *Convivio* was 'un penseur novice, mal assuré de toutes ses conclusions',[18] he sometimes shows himself aware of his limitations. But occasionally he speaks with breath-taking assurance, and one instance of this is worth noting. It comes not far from the end of Book IV where Dante, after distinguishing 'nobility' (roughly, the complex of natural endowments, at their ideal 'best', with which a human life begins) from virtue (the due effects of that nobility drawn out by moral endeavour) is so delighted by his vision of human nature that he expressly identifies the natural endowments of man with the traditional seven 'Gifts of the Holy Spirit'.[19] The orders of nature and grace, the distinction of which is elementary Catholicism, have seldom been so innocently confused. But I mention this confusion chiefly because of its function in the text as fixing, so to say, one of the two 'sacred boundary points' between which the course of human life is depicted as proceeding in what may be called a *secular* manner. To put this more clearly, if rather crudely; in the tableau of human life presented by *Convivio* IV, God is all-important at the beginning and at the end, but not in between. At the beginning, because natural 'nobility' is his gift; at the end

16. *Conv.* III, ii, 2-19; vii, 2-7; viii, 1-8; xii, 6-14, etc.
17. *Conv.* IV, i, 8.
18. *Dante et la politique*, op. cit., p. 17.
19. *Conv.* IV, xxi, 11-12.

because it is when the good man draws near to death that he should turn to God, says Dante, 'with all his mind and heart'. Such religious 'conversion' is one of the two appropriate 'acts' of the noble soul in the last of the four stages ('etadi') of human life, the stage of 'senio' which begins at the age of seventy. The soul should *then* 'turn to God', looking forwards to life after death, and 'bless the time past', looking backwards, gratefully, over the three previous stages through which it has passed ('adolescenza', 'gioventute', 'senettute').[20]

This matter is so important that I give Dante's own words (and it is a beautiful passage). He is glossing lines 136-9 of his poem *Le dolci rime d'amor*.[21] '*Poi ne la quarta parte de la vita*; per la quale lo testo intende mostrare quello che fa la nobile anima ne l'ultima etade, cioè nel senio. E dice ch'ella fa due cose: l'una che ella ritorna a Dio, sí come a quello porto onde ella si partio quando venne ad intrare nel mare di questa vita; l'altra si è, che ella benedice lo cammino che ha fatto, però che è stato diritto e buono, e sanza amaritudine di tempesta. E qui è da sapere, che . . . la naturale morte è quasi a noi porto di lunga navigazione e riposo. Ed è cosí come lo buono marinaio, come esso appropinqua al porto, cala le sue vele, e soavemente . . . entra in quello; *cosí noi dovemo calare le vele de le nostre mondane operazioni e tornare a Dio con tutto nostro intendimento e cuore*, sí che a quello porto si vegna con tutta soavitade e con tutta pace'.[22] Let us pause here to note two things: that the good man's *direct* concern with God is reserved for extreme old age; and then the sweet serenity of this picture of life's ending. This becomes still clearer as we read on: 'E in ciò avemo *da la nostra propria natura* grande ammaestramento di soavitade, che in essa cotale morte *non è*

20. *Conv.* IV, xxviii, 1-10. Dante probably took his fourfold division of human life from Albert the Great. The 'ages' are: puberty to 24; 25 to 44; 45 to 69; 70 onwards. The differences between the ages are due to variations in the proportion of the 'contrary qualities' in the body: heat, cold, moisture, dryness. Each age has its appropriate moral dispositions. All this is explained in cc. xxiii-xxviii.

21. See K. Foster and P. Boyde, *Dante's Lyric Poetry*, Oxford, 1967, vol. 2, pp. 210-28.

22. *Conv.* IV, xxviii, 1-3: '*Then in the fourth part of life*: here it is intended to show what the noble soul does in the last age, that is in extreme old age. And the text says that the soul does two things: first, that it returns to God as to the port which it had left on first entering the sea of this life; then that it blesses the journey it has made, as having kept to a straight course, and been untroubled by storms. And here you should know that natural death for us is like a harbour and a resting place after a long sea voyage. And just as a good sailor, when nearing a harbour, lowers the sails and, steering gently, comes smoothly into port; so we ought to lower the sails of our worldly activities and turn to God with all our mind and heart, so that we enter the harbour softly and smoothly in perfect peace'.

dolore né alcuna acerbitate, ma sí come uno pomo maturo leggiermente e sanza violenza si dispicca dal suo ramo, cosí la nostra anima sanza doglia si parte dal corpo ov'ella è stata. Onde Aristotile . . . dice che 'sanza tristizia è la morte ch'è ne la vecchiezza'. E si come a colui che viene di lungo cammino, anzi ch'entri ne la porta de la sua cittade, li si fanno incontro li cittadini di quella, cosí a la nobile anima si fanno incontro . . . quelli cittadini de la etterna vita; e cosí fanno per le sue buone operazioni e contemplazioni: chè, già essendo a Dio renduta e astrattasi da le mondane cose e cogitazioni, vedere le pare coloro che appresso di Dio crede che siano'.[23] In the serenity of such a death — so sweetly natural, like the falling of a ripe fruit — there seems little place for any fear of God.[24] Death is only the gentle release of the soul into an 'eternal life' which is made to seem as natural, and as naturally happy, as the temporal life through which the noble soul has passed.

What are the factors which make for this happiness, temporal and eternal? Bare human nature, of course, does not suffice. Temporal happiness, that of the 'active life', is the fruit of virtue, involving the strenuous life-long exercise of reason and will. As for the happiness after death — conceived of as pure joyous contemplation — this too seems to depend on right choices made during life in time.[25] But this prerequisite is only very lightly touched on in the *Convivio*. Dante is much more concerned here with errors and wrong choices that would prevent or impede temporal happiness. With the possibility of a failure going on to eternity he shows little interest. Compare, for example, the welcome that he here imagines given to the noble soul after death, by the 'citizens of the eternal life', with the welcome given to Virgil on his return (with Dante) to Limbo in *Inferno* IV, 79-96. This latter passage surely echoes the same text of Cicero (*De Senectute* 23, 83) which appears, translated by Dante,

---

23. Ibid. 4-5: 'And here we can take a great lesson in sweet gentleness from our own nature; for according to nature a death of this sort has no pain or bitterness, but just as a ripe fruit is easily and effortlessly plucked from the bough, so our soul painlessly leaves the body wherein it has dwelt. Hence Aristotle says, 'death in old age is not sad' [*De respiratione*, c. 23, 479a 20]. And as when a man returns from a long voyage, even before he enters the gate of his city, the citizens go out to meet him, so do the citizens of eternal life go to welcome the noble soul, because of its good deeds and thoughts; for that soul, having already given itself to God, and being now purified from worldly things and concerns, seems already to enjoy the sight of those whom it believes to be with God'.
24. Compare 2 *Corinthians* 5, 10; *Hebrews* 10, 30-31.
25. *Conv.* IV, xxviii, 11-12.

immediately after the words from the *Convivio* last cited: 'Odi che dice Tullio, in persona di Catone vecchio: "A me pare già vedere e levomi in grandissimo studio di vedere i vostri padri, che io amai...." '[26] But the tone is very different in the two cases: serene in the *Convivio*, touched with deep melancholy in the *Inferno*:

> Intanto voce fu per me udita:
> 'Onorate l'altissimo poeta;
> l'ombra sua torna, ch'era dipartita'.
> Poi che la voce fu restata e queta,
> vidi quattro grand' ombre a noi venire:
> *sembianz' avevan né trista né lieta*.[27]

The happiness of old age, then, as the *Convivio* presents it (we are far indeed from Leopardi's 'di vecchiezza/la detestata soglia'!) comes from happy expectations and happy grateful memories; Cicero being cited with regard to the former, Lucan with regard to the latter. It is wholly in keeping with the treatise as a whole, and indeed with its period, that both 'authorities' are pagans. But Dante writes as a Christian, and with patent sincerity, though we may find the examples he adduces of conversion to God in old age rather curious: Lancelot and Guido da Montefeltro (both, incidentally, are soldiers): 'Rendesi dunque a Dio la nobile anima in questa etade, e attende lo fine di questa vita con molto desiderio e uscir le pare de l'albergo e ritornare ne la propria mansione, ... uscir le pare di mare e tornare a porto. O miseri e vili che con le vele alte correte a questo porto, ... e perdete voi medesimi là dove tanto camminato avete! Certo lo cavaliere Lancelotto non volse entrare con le vele alte, né lo nobilissimo nostro latino Guido montefeltrano. Bene questi nobili calaro le vele de le mondane operazioni, che ne la loro lunga etade a religione si rendero, ogni mondano diletto e opera disponendo'.[28]

---

26. Ibid. 6: 'Listen to what Tully says, in the person of the elder Cato: "Already I seem to see, and with intense desire I rise to gaze upon, those fathers of ours whom I have loved" '. A rough version of *De senectute*, c. 23, 83.

27. *Inf*. IV, 79-84: 'Meanwhile I heard a voice that said: 'Honour the great poet, whose shade, which had departed, now returns'. When the voice had ceased and was still, I saw four great shades come towards us, in appearance neither sad nor joyful'.

28. *Conv*. IV, xxviii, 7-8: 'So in this age the noble soul gives itself back to God, waiting for the end of this life with eager desire, feeling as though it were leaving an inn on the roadside and returning home ... leaving the sea and returning to port. Oh how wretched and base are you who speed to this harbour with all sails spread ... and perish at the end of so long a voyage! Certainly Sir Lancelot did not choose to enter harbour under sail, nor

And here Dante reminds the reader that 'religione' bears a deeper meaning than its common one of 'religious order' of 'community'. He gives it in fact more or less the sense we have seen the theologians give to 'religio': 'E non si puote alcuno escusare per legame di matrimonio . . . chè non torna a religione pur quelli che a santo Benedetto, a s. Agostino, a s. Francesco e a s. Domenico si fa d'abito . . . ma eziandio a buona e vera religione si può tornare in matrimonio stando, chè Dio non volse religioso di noi se non lo cuore'.[29]

It would be rash to read into this last sentence an anticipation of later Humanist criticism of religious vows.[30] But isn't there something a little odd, from the Christian point of view, about the chief idea expressed in this beautiful passage on 'senio'? I mean the very close association it establishes between religion and *old age* – religion, that is, in the sense of piety and filial attention to God. But to appreciate the force of this association we have to set the poet's account of the attitudes appropriate to old age ('senio') in the whole context of the treatment of the moral virtues which occupies the second half of *Convivio* IV (cc. xvii to xxix). It is clear that Dante has carefully considered the whole subject; his exposition is lucid, logical, coherent. First, in c. xvii, he gives a general definition of moral virtue and enumerates eleven principal forms of it as distinguished by Aristotle. In the three following chapters he discusses the relation of moral virtue to inborn 'nobility'; which then leads off into a digression, in two chapters of extraordinary brilliance (xxi-xxii), on the deeper nature and divine origin of this 'human nobility'. Then, having thus prepared the ground for a correlation of the moral virtues with the actual course and process of human life, Dante sets out, in c. xxiii, his division of man's life into the four periods already noted, the four 'etadi': 'adolescenza' from puberty to twenty four; 'gioventute' from twenty five to forty four; 'senet-

---

our noble Italian Guido of Montefeltro. Well did these heroes lower the sails of worldly activities, who in old age gave themselves to a life of religion, setting aside every worldly pleasure and activity'.
29. Ibid. 9-10: 'And no one is excused on the ground of the marriage tie . . . for those who don a religious habit – that of St Benedict or St Augustine or St Francis or St Dominic – are not the only converts to religion, for in the married state too one can well and truly turn to religion, since the only thing in us that God has willed should be religious is the heart'.
30. For example in Valla's *De professione religiosorum*, as to which I may refer to my essay 'Christ and Letters', *Blackfriars*, April 1963, pp. 155-6.

tute', forty five to seventy; 'senio' from seventy on. The next five chapters then run through these stages in succession, distinguishing the good dispositions appropriate to each. In all, Dante enumerates thirteen such good qualities and virtues, but we need not consider them in detail; the point is that not one of those he regards as appropriate to the first three 'etadi', covering the whole active life of a man from puberty to the age of seventy, has anything directly to do with religion. They all involve only an individual's relations to himself or to other human beings. Only as regards men over seventy – a great age in the medieval world – is there any allusion to God; only when physical vitality is ebbing away and there is nothing left to be done in this world, does it become, explicitly, part of a good man's goodness to remember God and to pray.[31]

To put the matter thus is to point to a certain unreality in this picture of human life. For after all there is a fair amount of Catholic piety in the *Convivio* itself, some fervent allusions to Christ and to Mary, some warm professions of faith in the Church; [32] and yet when Dante wrote the work, between 1304 and 1308, he was still only in his second 'etade', that of 'gioventute'. The author's Christianity does not seem quite to tally with his more or less pagan ethical system; and this begins to seem something of an abstract construction, a system contemplated in the mind and not very closely related to life in the concrete. In this respect the *Monarchia*, for all the academic rigour of its style, is more *practical* than the *Convivio*. Its theme of course is the authority of the supreme – in theory – civil power in the medieval world, that of the Emperor; a topic on which Dante had already written at some length in *Convivio* IV (cc. iv-ix). And it was a topic which inevitably, in the first decades of the fourteenth century, raised the very practical problem of the relations between the Empire and the Church, the problem thrashed out, at a high theoretical level indeed but with intense earnestness, in *Monarchia* III. By comparison, the treatment of the Emperor's authority in the *Convivio* is remote from practical considerations, for here the correlative and contrasted authority is the purely intellectual one of Philosophy, represented by Aristotle. Of course, when Dante, in 1304-'08, was balancing these two authorities, his hero

31. I am glad to find myself in agreement on this point with J. Goudet; see *D. et la politique*, Paris 1969, p. 26.
32. *Conv.* II, v, 2-3; viii, 14; III, vii, 16; IV, v, 4-9; xv, 5, etc.

Henry of Luxembourg had not yet entered the scene to bring the old Church-Empire issue to a new point of crisis. Even so, the choice of the Philosopher rather than the massively present institutional Church, to represent the idea of non-political, purely doctrinal authority, is surely symptomatic of a certain withdrawal into a world of abstractions of Dante at this time; of a preoccupation above all with abstract ideas, that of political authority as such, of 'reason' as such, of 'man' as such. These are philosophical rather than theological ideas, and therefore all the more easily detachable, in the Christian society of the time, from immediately practical issues. Moreover, by 1304 when the *Convivio* was begun, Dante had probably had enough, for the time being, of immediately practical issues. He was enjoying a period of rest and retirement after the political upheaval in Florence at the turn of the century, and the personal disaster of his basnishment from the city. The opening chapters of the *Convivio* reflect the joy and relief he felt on returning to his books and to study. And his studies had not hitherto included theology. Nor does the *Convivio* itself reflect any special theological interest (in contrast with the third Book of the *Monarchia*).

The deeper problems raised by *Convivio* IV are, as I view the matter, inseparable from the general subject of the present essay. The particular problem I am raising at the moment (and perhaps exaggerating a little) is that of explaining a lack or omission: the virtual absence from the ethical system propounded in this work of specifically Christian ideas and problems. It is as though the author, without consciously prescinding from Christian ideas (in the field of morality) were in fact largely supplanting them with a different system. Clearly, there is no intended opposition to Christianity. But neither will it do, I think, merely to assimilate *Convivio* IV to the type of those various 'opuscula' *De vita philosophi* or *De felicitate* by medieval academics whose methodological prescinding from the data of faith and theology was an accepted literary procedure. There may be something of this stance in the *Convivio*, but the work as a whole is too unacademic, too personal and — despite the detachment from practical issues noted above — too earnestly engaged with life to fit the type. Dante's aims and general procedure were irreducibly personal and his own.

How then shall we describe this procedure? I would distinguish three 'moments' in it (inseparable in time). First, he conceived an idea of human nature and life, drawn from Neoplatonism and Aristotelian sources. Then he worked this idea out in some detail, drawing on his own rich experience of life, and, as regards literary sources, chiefly on Neoplatonism for the metaphysical background and on the Nicomachean Ethics for his vision of life on earth as a strenuous acquisition of moral excellence which would also be an achievement, constantly, of happiness; working in *en route* suggestions and examples from Cicero, Seneca and the Latin poets, especially Virgil. Finally, he made some effort to relate the result obtained, his achieved 'model' human life, to his Christian faith. Now it was always a characteristic of Dante's religious outlook to view the Christian faith precisely in function of, in relation to, life after death. This is the aspect of it that he always most emphasises. In terms then of his philosophical 'model', he found no difficulty in relating the faith to the idea of the intellect as a power transcending the body, a thing essentially immortal. And because intellect *qua* intellect lives by increase of knowledge, and because its bodily existence seemed in many ways to impede such increase, he thought of immortality as consisting above all in a maximum satisfaction of the mind's desire for knowledge; and of the Christian faith as, above all, a certainty, guaranteed by Revelation, about the real existence of such a satisfaction — in the eternal vision of God — and about its availability to man. The Christian message then is 'news' about the Beatific Vision and its availability; and he represents it (in the context of a division of the 'sciences') as formulated in what he calls 'theology'. But theology, 'la divina scienza', is for Dante (in the *Convivio* at least) hardly distinguishable from Revelation itself. As such it is possessed by faith alone and is out of reach of — quite undisturbed by — the disputatious and questioning reason.[33]

So much, very summarily, for the way in which Dante as a Christian was able to confirm and complete his philosophy with respect to life after death and its availability to mortal man. It was much less easy to find Christianity a place, *consonant with the philosophical model*, within the course of human life on earth; for here philosophy seemed already to provide all the required concepts. True, the Church is there, teaching and dispensing the sacraments; but neither

33. I have treated this subject in more detail in an art. 'Teologia', to be published in vol. 5 of the *Enciclopedia Dantesca*, Rome; and cf. E. Gilson, *De. et la philosophie*, op. cit., pp. 114-22. See also *The Mind of Dante,* ed. U. Limentani, Cambridge, 1965, pp. 55-8.

Church nor sacraments are represented as having any relevance to man's moral life in this world, the subject of *Convivio* IV. The reader is left wondering (if this matter interests him) whether Dante regarded them as important *only* in view of the afterlife. The influence of divine grace in the human soul and body in the present life – a central issue for Christian ethics – is entirely ignored. The word 'grazia' appears at *Conv.* IV, xx, 3, because it occurs in the poem which Dante is glossing (line 115), where it signifies the nobility of human nature as a gift of God to the individual before birth: in the commentary it is called 'this divine thing' but the meaning is the same, a *natural* endowment. As for grace as 'healing', *gratia sanans*, this naturally finds no place in an ethic which, as we have seen, makes virtue an entirely human product. On the other hand, grace as 'divinizing', *gratia elevans*, may be implied in the occasional allusions to the future life in 'glory' (the most striking instance of this is the reference to Beatrice in heaven, at II, viii, 16).

It is of some importance to note that the *Convivio* is not a young man's work; Dante was in his early forties when he composed Book IV. Now the latest possible date for the composition of the first cantos of the *Inferno* would be around 1310; and they were probably written earlier. It is exceedingly unlikely that more than three years passed between Dante's finishing *Convivio* IV and writing *Inferno* IV, the canto of Limbo. During this interval he may well have undergone a religious conversion of some kind; but even so the relative nearness in time of these two compositions makes it plausible to expect that the philosophy of man that fills *Convivio* IV should leave its traces in *Inferno* IV; and in my opinion – as the reader, I hope, will have gathered by now – this is indeed the case. But my immediate concern is with the *Monarchia*, in relation to *Convivio* IV.

The *Monarchia* – which can hardly have taken less than a full year to prepare and compose – cannot be dated firmly (as *Inferno* IV can) to within three or four years after the *Convivio*; it may have been written as much as ten years later. Yet on all essential points relevant to my argument, I find that it stands very close to *Convivio* IV. However there are some interesting differences which I would summarise as follows:

(1) The reader of the *Convivio* can forget the Church most of the time. The allusions to it, though always respectful, are few; it never enters into the argument. In the *Monarchia* the Church is massively

and formidably present: Book III is all a sustained dialogue between Dante and the Church of his time.

(2) The Church, thus brought right to the foreground through one third of the *Monarchia*, is clearly presented, in this work, as the carrier of the Christian message directing man to his supernatural end in the life to come. Now the interior contact between man's soul and that message – and, consequently, that supernatural end – is only touched on vaguely and intermittently in the *Convivio*, whereas at the end of *Monarchia* III it appears as an integral part of the argument, with the mention of the theological virtues, faith, hope and charity (III, xv, 8).

(3) The Fall of man and Original Sin, virtually ignored in the *Convivio*, are brought into the argument of the *Monarchia*, and in two connections: with the Atonement effected by Christ (II, xi *passim*) and with the need – given man's 'fallen' condition – for some external authority to make and enforce laws, as a curb on disorderly passions (III, iv, 14; xv, 9-11). And in both of these connections the Empire is necessary: in the former, because it was not enough that Christ in his innocent humanity should bear the punishment of Adam's sin, but this punishment had to be inflicted by corporate Humanity acting in the person of its supreme representative, the Roman Emperor, himself acting through his deputies, Pilate and the executioners of Jesus; and in the latter connection because, just as fallen man cannot be trusted to observe the supernatural virtues without the guidance of the Church and the sanctions of Canon Law, so too as regards the natural virtues, he needs to be guided and governed by laws enforced by the Emperor.

(4) In the *Convivio*, whenever the afterlife is alluded to (in the sense of 'glory' or 'heaven' or 'vision of God'; e.g. at II, viii, 6-16; III, xiv, 14-xv, 10; IV, xxii, 10-18) there is no distinct mention of any need of special divine help to bring the soul to that state; whereas in the *Monarchia* this need is explicitly recognised: ' . . . the happiness of life eternal . . . to which man cannot rise of his own power, unless this power be aided by a divine light (*nisi lumine divino adiuta*)' (III, xv, 7). The stress here on light, 'lumen divinum', is characteristic, though it may be an echo of the theologians' 'lumen gloriae'.[34]

(5) The distinction between man as mortal (soul and body) and as

34. Cf. St Thomas, *Summa theol.* 1a. 12, 5-6.

immortal (the soul *per se*) the chief function of which in the *Convivio*
was to support an ethic hinging on the difference between the active
life and the contemplative life, is now in the *Monarchia* drawn out
very sharply indeed, to the point of dividing the 'essence' of man
into two 'natures', each with its own 'ultimate end' (III, xv, 3-6). In
its context this distinction is politically motivated, but its effect is to
reinforce (with dubious metaphysics) the tendency to dualism
already noted in the *Convivio*.[35]

These are the chief points relevant to my theme in which the
Monarchia differs from the *Convivio*. As they show, Dante was
much more concerned with the Church and with the data of Christian theology than he was in the vernacular work. The reason lies in
his purpose in writing the *Monarchia*. If *Convivio* IV is a string of
reflections on human nature by an Aristotelian poet-moralist of
genius, the *Monarchia* is the same man's heroically strenuous effort
to see deeply into the actual situation of mankind as he found it; and
not just to see that situation, but to change it. Hence at the outset
the author's explicit statement that his present aim in writing is not
primarily speculative but practical; which is as much as to say,
political. And the political interest envisaged is not, of course, that
of any city or nation, but that of all mankind conceived of as united
in a common 'civilitas', a single society, with one single aim in common, the fullest possible achievement and enjoyment of 'the happiness that belongs to this world' ('beatitudo huius vitae'); which
would consist in man's bringing into act the latent capacities of
human nature precisely as such ('que in operatione proprie virtutis
consistit'). The society envisaged is universally human, as embracing
all men, and the good envisaged as its aim is strictly – indeed exclusively – human; as, with exquisite precision, the phrase last
quoted shows: 'in operatione *proprie* virtutis'. Similarly, the appropriate means to this end are human: the light of philosophical
reason and the practice of the natural virtues. And these purely
human factors would suffice to bring about peace and happiness on
earth, were it not for Original Sin and the consequent 'bestial' disorder in man's impulses. And it is just to remedy this disorder
that God has set up the office and authority of the Emperor. Thus
the origin of the Empire is divine and supernatural, but its function

35. I may refer to what I have said on this point in *The Mind of Dante*, ed. U. Limentani,
Cambridge, 1965, pp. 71-3.

is limited by the purely natural – humanly natural – 'end' for which
it was instituted, the temporal wellbeing of man *qua* man. Thus on
its own level Dante's Empire is a kind of 'analogue' of the Church.
For of course the Church is of divine origin and the Church also
presupposes Original Sin, being the Servant of Christ who came
precisely to remedy that disaster, though on the supernatural level.
And so we have, with the similarity, the difference: *here* the
'natural', *there* the 'supernatural'. As the Church, teaching by the
light of Scriptures inspired by the Holy Spirit, guides man to an end
beyond time (and to which, finally, only a 'lumen divinum' will
raise the human spirit), so the Empire, using the light of reason,
guides man (but it is the *same* man, and there's the rub!) to an end
within time, an end bounded by death.

Two institutions, two distinct spheres of influence, two distinct
ends aimed at – of which one is *not* a means to the other, for *both* are
'ultimate' ('duo ultima'). And yet, alas, one common subject, mortal
man: no wonder Dante has to fight the Canonists, hammer and
tongs, through his passionately argued Book III! But I am not concerned with the explicit point at issue in this Book, namely whether
the Emperor's jurisdiction comes to him directly from God and not
through the Pope. What I want to stress is the premiss, or set of
premisses, from which, rather than towards which, Dante's
arguments proceed; though he brings it out clearly enough in the
splendidly terse summary of his general position in the final chapter
(III, xv, 4-10). And the premiss is this, that the whole business of
man's achieving 'perfection' in this world, as a being endowed with
reason and nevertheless mortal (whose optimum state would be at
once physical moral and intellectual, in short a full flowering of
natural 'virtue') is presented as something to be carried out by means
entirely intrinsic to human nature itself. The only factors directly involved are all contained in man's 'propria virtus' (sustained, of
course, by God as Creator). Nor does the bringing of Original Sin
into the argument represent any significant alteration, in the
Monarchia, of the man-centred outlook which has been noted in the
Convivio. 'Gratia sanans' is as absent from the one treatise as from
the other, at least so far as man's achievement of natural 'virtue' is
concerned, the aim of his life as terminated by death, 'prout corrup-
tibilis est'. And if, after all, fallen man is plagued by bestial impulses,
the remedy, so far as the argument of the *Monarchia* goes, is not

divine grace but the 'bit and bridle' of the laws of the secular Empire. So far as man *qua* mortal is concerned, the Fall is left unconnected with any grace coming from Christ: its ill effects must find their remedy in the State.[36]

The question whether Dante's ethical ideal (for man as mortal) includes what the theologians meant by 'religio' seems less relevant to the *Monarchia* than to *Convivio* IV; but we may safely say that the absence of it, noted above, from the latter work is not made good in the Latin treatise. Nor does it seem to be made good even in the *Comedy*. Here of course we are in the afterlife, in the world of disembodied souls. The relevant distinction now is not between man as mortal and as immortal, but rather between man as left in the state of fallen nature, whether in Limbo or in Hell proper, and man as transferred to the state of grace, in Purgatory or Paradise. We are concerned with the former category. Does 'religion', then, find a place in the ungraced souls of the *Comedy?* The obvious soul to consider is Virgil, in whom ungraced humanity is shown as its best. Now Dante's Virgil is certainly religious, even zealously so. Not only is he aware of the true God — whom Roman-wise he calls the heavenly 'Emperor' (*Inferno* I, 124) — but in his very first speech to Dante he dismisses with contempt the *ersatz* pagan divinities as 'dei falsi e bugiardi' (ibid., 72). Strangely, however, this piety towards the true God leads him later to rebuke very severely the pagan Capaneo for irreverence to one of those false gods [37] — or so it seems at first sight. Capaneo had scoffed at Jupiter and is now punished for this among the damned blasphemers. On seeing Dante and Virgil approaching he begins to mock Jupiter once more. Evidently Jupiter now stands in some way for the true God, and his mocker is a blasphemer. I agree with André Pézard that Dante's meaning here is that there was a true, if confused, idea of God latent

---

36. This analysis is based on *Mon.* III, xv, 7-12 (ed. Ricci, 1965). Note especially §§ 9-10: 'Has igitur conclusiones et media, licet ostensa sint nobis hec *ab humana ratione que per phylosophos tota nobis innotuit*, hec a Spirito Sancto qui ... supernaturalem veritatem ac nobis necessariam revelavit, humana cupiditas postergaret nisi homines, tanquam equi, sua bestialitate vagantes 'in camo et freno' compescerentur in via. Propter quod opus fuit homini *duplici directivo secundum duplicem finem*: scilicet summo Pontefice, qui secundum revelata humanum genus perduceret ad vitam ecternam, et Imperatore, *qui secundum phylosophica documenta genus humanum ad temporalem felicitatem dirigeret'*. Earlier Dante had declared that both Church and Empire were remedies against the effects of Original Sin, and that otherwise neither institution would have been needed; see III, iv, 14.
37. *Inf.* XIV, 43-72.

in pagan religion.[38] The same insight appears elsewhere in the *Comedy*, especially in connection with the war of the Giants against Olympus. Capaneo is a kind of advance-image of the Giants in *Inferno* XXXI, who themselves foreshadow Satan in canto XXXIV. This kind of oblique justification of pagan religion raises a problem with regard to the Limbo pagans to which I shall return, briefly, before the end of this essay.

Virgil's own kind of piety is a fact entwined in the narrative of the *Inferno* and *Purgatorio*, more or less visible as the occasion requires. It is always in character; never Christian; always at a certain remove, like his discernment of those points of doctrine which he has to leave to Beatrice to instruct Dante in. Is it a purely personal piety, not shared by his Limbo companions? A 'charism' given him for the duration of the voyage which he has undertaken, at the behest of Beatrice, as Dante's guide?[39] These questions seem rather farfetched, and this is to the credit of Dante the artist; so plausibly non-Christian is his image of a pagan traveller in the Christian Other World (yet how different is the paganism of Dante's Virgil from that of Virgil's Aeneas!).

There is no need then to regard the Limbo adults as irreligious. Limbo is not a Humanist Society. We are not shown its inhabitants praying, but neither are we shown Virgil praying — except indeed at the opening of *Purgatorio* XIII, where he addresses God through the sun-symbol (lines 16-21). And the Limbo adults are all in reception of a kind of divine blessing, the wide zone of light in which they dwell and for which, presumably, they are grateful (Virgil even calls it a 'grazia', *Inferno* IV, 78). Even Farinata, after all, who is much lower down, seems grateful for the very much dimmer light which he and his companions still receive: 'cotanto ancor ne splende il sommo duce'.[40] As to whether and how far these Limbo dwellers represent an idea of human nature similar to that which we have gathered from *Convivio* IV and the last chapter of the *Monarchia*, my opinion is that this idea is, in essentials, implied in the Dantean Limbo, so far as the *post mortem* situation of Limbo allows. For, since the Limbo dwellers have passed through death, they can obviously not represent the idea of Man in the context of the 'active

38. *Dante. Oeuvres complètes*, Paris, 'Bibl. de la Pléiade', 1965, p. 965.
39. *Inf.* II, 121-5.
40. *Inf.* X, 102: 'so much light still comes to us from the supreme Lord'.

life' on earth, which was the main theme of *Convivio* IV, or in that of man's pursuit of a temporal 'ultimate end' which was the underlying theme of the *Monarchia*. An ethic of the active life or of life in time no longer, of course, applies in Limbo; except in so far as the adults there are still 'honoured' by the afterglow of the virtues they acquired on earth (*Inferno* IV, 67-78). But, surviving bodiless in this 'honour', there is nothing left for them to *do*. One is tempted to say that the only 'life' left for them is that of the hopeless desire of which Virgil pathetically speaks (ibid., 42). Yet this desire itself must presuppose some knowledge, and appreciation, of God; *at least* as much as — according to *Convivio* III, xv, 6 — is attainable by unaided reason on earth. And on this kind of God-knowledge would be based the 'piety' of Virgil and his companions. There is no hint, of course, of any rebellion on their part, since their arrival in Limbo.

CONCLUDING REMARKS. This essay has stemmed from a perplexity that I have long felt regarding what may loosely be called Dante's humanism and how this relates to his Christianity. Humanism cannot be incompatible with the belief that God has become a man. Nevertheless a certain humanism is or can be anti-Christian; and it is in an anti-Christian sense that the term is more commonly used nowadays in the English-speaking world. And certainly, this sense represents one way of conceiving, and formulating as a practical motive, the basic humanist belief that man should aim at and can achieve a certain excellence, in thought and action, consonant with his nature. Now from the Christian point of view this belief or ideal at once involves man in relations with something greater than himself; it being elementary Christianity that our highest excellence is found in knowing and loving God, and that our achieving this excellence depends principally on God. And the divine initiative implied in the latter point is called 'creation' as regards the existence of our nature, and 'grace' as regards its attaining to that love-knowledge of God. And while creation is something God brings about through the union of a man with a woman, the gift of grace is something he brings about by uniting himself with human nature, directly. Thus the new 'excellence', the 'new life' as the New Testament calls it, which is the effect of grace, is rooted in the manhood of the New Man, Jesus. Nevertheless this new life, this grace-life, both in Jesus and in those who get it from him, is a God-centred life. Such, briefly, seems to be the basis of Christian humanism. At the opposite extreme would be a wholly man-centred humanism. And while, as a widespread social phenomenon, such man-centred humanism is a relatively recent growth, there have been theories of man in the past sufficiently cen-tred on purely human aims and capacities to be given that name without serious risk of confusion. And we have seen evidence for counting Aristotelianism (in the *Nicomachean Ethics*) as such a theory.

Viewed against this background of ideas, Dante can hardly fail to pose a problem. It is easy to say, what is obviously true in some sense, that his whole *oeuvre* is in the tradition of Christian humanism; far less easy to say what, on the evidence, one can exact-ly mean by this. The main difficulty comes from the very strong Aristotelian component in his work; and we have seen some reasons for questioning the full assimilation of that component into the Christianity which Dante nonetheless fervently professed. And this in respect even of the *Comedy*. The question is clearly still less avoidable in respect of the *Convivio* and the *Monarchia*. Analysing *Convivio* IV in particular, we have found it to contain the rough out-lines of a man-centred ethic of pagan derivation, co-existing with ex-pressions of Christian belief of whose sincerity there is no reason to doubt, but which remain, in this work, assertions of belief unsup-ported by any serious reasoning from Christian premises, by any theology. In effect, the two components, the philosophical and the Christian are merely juxtaposed, and the theological problems which this raises are never faced, nor even, apparently, noticed. Theologically speaking, this brilliant work is immature. And if it is a sign of growing maturity that a man takes stock of tensions and con-tradictions latent in himself, then certainly the *Comedy* marks a great advance, in this respect, on the *Convivio*. For the latent tension in *Convivio* IV, between a fullblooded Aristotelian ethic and the Chris-tian outlook on life, now comes to the surface in the tragic figure of Virgil — Virgil who represents human goodness (the Philosopher's 'great-souled man') *outside* Christianity. He is virtue left ungraced.

In adding no qualification here to Virgil's virtue, I know that I have still left unanswered a very pertinent question raised earlier; but to that I shall return before I end. The point I wish to make here

– at the cost of repeating myself – is that, whatever blame one might eventually have to attach to Virgil on theological grounds, in view of *Inferno* I, 125, what he constantly and actively represents in the Poem is goodness at an optimum on the *human* level; that is, on the hither side of Christian holiness (this is a difference in *principle*; it does not mean that we have to find the souls in Purgatory or Paradise more amiable than Virgil). The only sin that we as readers are permitted to ascribe to Virgil is the 'rebellion' which he himself confesses on his first meeting with Dante in the Dark Wood. But this sin, *so far as the reader can see*, entails no flaw in his humanity; that is, no moral flaw, for it certainly and painfully has entailed his losing 'the good of the intellect', the vision of God.[41] In short, the moral nobility of Virgil as a visible *persona* in the Poem is intact. Therefore through him Dante has expressed a certain humanism. Now, does it make any sense to call *this* humanism 'Christian'? To this the only answer I can make is through a distinction – a distinction between Virgil in his temporary function in the Poem as Dante's guide to Beatrice, and Virgil in, so to say, his 'background' condition in the Poem as a soul in Limbo. Under the former aspect Virgil prepares Dante, his 'son', for grace; as in a different way, he had prepared another 'son' of his, Statius, for grace, leading him to look for the fulfilment of the prophecy in the Fourth Eclogue (*Purgatorio* XXII). Now the idea that there is a human 'preparatio ad gratiam', that human powers and desires may play their part in bringing a man to grace, even though the first move is always from God, this idea was accepted, in principle by theology; [42] and one can hardly *not* call it a kind of Christian humanism, whatever else the term may be taken to cover. In this respect then, let us say that Dante's Virgil expresses a Christian humanism. But Virgil considered simply as a soul in Limbo? And his companions there, who are not even granted *his* transient contact with Christian things, 'spiriti magni' though they are? What has Christian humanism to do with them? One is tempted to answer, 'nothing'. And yet they are

41. D. had found this phrase – which he has immortalised – in Aquinas's commentary on the *Nic. Ethics* (I, lect. 12; VI, lect. 3). Before repeating it in *Inf.* III, 18, he had used it in *Conv.* II, xiii, 6, citing it as Aristotle's. Note that as used in *Inf.* III, it occurs before D. and Virgil enter Limbo: thus it applies to the Limbo-dwellers as much as to the damned proper.
42. See Denzinger-Schönmetzer, *Enchiridion Symbol.*, ed. cit., nos. 1525-7; St Thomas *Summa theol.* 1a. 62, 2 ad 3; 1a2ae. 109, 6; 112, 2-3; 113, 8. Cf. C. S. Singleton, *Journey to Beatrice*, Harvard Univ. Press, 1958, pp. 39-56.

an integral part of the *Comedy*. Without them — that is, without the
Limbo state which they embody — the Poem as we have it would
not exist; and we have granted that it is a Christian humanist work
in some sense.

So it seems we have to fall back on the old distinction between
form and content in a poem, between the *Comedy* as a formed work
of art and the ideas that it 'contains' and that could be set out in
prose. The achieved poem shows us the human spirit being drawn
towards union with God: gradually penetrated by divine grace until
a maximum contact is achieved: and this through the image of a
Christian man's voyage into the afterlife. Now in order to reach that
divine union the voyager has to pass beyond human nature, be
'transhumanized' (*Paradiso*, I, 70); and this transition is the work of
grace, operating especially through the successive Guides: Virgil at
the level of a human 'preparatio ad gratiam' (God's initiative
presupposed) and Beatrice and St Bernard at their respective levels
of grace. Yet Virgil's function in the whole action is not only the
positive one of guiding Dante towards grace; less conspicuously but
quite distinctly he stands for just that human nature which has to be
transcended — representing it precisely in its specific humanness;
not, that is to say, as spoiled by sin, and so in need of *gratia sanans*
(which is what the personage Dante may be taken to stand for), but
simply as the finite nature which it is, and so needing — if it is ever
to unite with God — *gratia elevans*. And from this point of view
Virgil, and with him the other adults in Limbo — the whole Lim-
bo-image, in short — stand for human nature as a thing good in its
kind and degree but *incomplete*; and incomplete whether it be regarded in the abstract, in the idea of the human as such, or as considered
historically as pagan mankind (or, with special reference to Virgil, as
the Empire minus its fulfilment in the Church, as 'that Rome' of
which Christ was not yet 'a Roman' — *Purgatorio*, XXXII, 102, and
cf. *Inferno* II, 16-27).

And all this represents, I suggest, the viewpoint of *one* of the 'two
Dantes' in my title. But matters take on a different aspect if, ignor-
ing the way in which all this conceptual material is actually organised by the poet, we consider separately that idea of *mere* human
nature which we have seen that Virgil embodies. Doing this, we
now find ourselves contemplating a 'nature' whose contact with
God (through grace) is minimal, but whose intrinsic excellence, on

its own level and for the duration of life on earth, can, in principle, be complete. And this completeness in human excellence, if achieved, would be *self*-achieved. Grace as *sanans*, as healing the wound of sin, would not, in principle, be needed. Not so grace as *elevans*, as 'divinizing': the necessity, in the *Comedy*, of *this* sort of grace is manifest, for the soul after death. For the soul that lacks it there remains, at best, only an eternity in Limbo, the place of hopeless yearning. And the soul can only lay hold of this grace, which would raise it to God after death, during its life on earth and before death. But we have seen, especially in considering *Paradiso* XIX-XX that Dante represents the obtaining of this grace — for those out of reach of the Christian message — as extremely exceptional, indeed as abnormal, in the sense that it involves miracles (*Paradiso* XX, 100-123).

A strange isolation from God seems then to be the lot of pagan man, as Dante represents him. In order to live perfectly as a human being *tout court* he does not appear to need divine grace; yet if he does not have grace he can only expect, after death, an eternity of unsatisfied longing. And the grace that would save him from this unhappy destiny is not *normally* available to him. The gap between nature and grace has been enlarged to the widest extent consistent with Christian belief.

Such, at any rate, may well be the conclusion drawn by the reader who has had the patience to follow me so far. But there is something else to be said which must qualify, or at least put a query against, that 'isolation' of Dante's pagans from grace, as I have described it. The text which tells most in the contrary sense is *Inferno* I, 121-6. From my point of view in this essay, these are the most puzzling lines in the *Comedy*. I have considered them, in passing, above; let us now take a final look at them. Virgil, it will be recalled, is explaining to Dante that, while he can guide the latter through Hell and Purgatory, God will not allow him to enter Heaven with his pupil; and this, says Virgil, is because he has been a rebel against God's law: 'perch' i' fu' ribellante a la sua legge'. Now, does this mean that Virgil is confessing that he has been guilty of rejecting some offer of grace from God? There is a fairly good case for holding that this is indeed what Virgil means. To make this clear I must ask the reader to recall a paragraph early in this chapter (Section III) of the present essay, in which I set out four alternative interpretations of Dante's view of 'the moral condition of adult un-graced humanity'. The first alternative (i) was a summary of St Thomas's teaching on this matter, and I have given my reasons for ruling it out as a plausible interpretation of Dante's view. The remaining three (ii-iv) were alternative possible interpretations of the doctrine which (we must suppose) underlies Dante's description of the adult Limbo-dwellers. And I now ask: How far does Virgil's statement in *Inferno* I, 121-6 help us to determine which, if any, of this three alternatives is correct?

Well, Virgil's plain declaration that he had rebelled against God's law clearly rules out alternative (ii) according to which the Limbo adults would be blameless in *every* respect (assuming, as we surely may, that Virgil's case is typical of the Limbo adults generally). So we are left with alternatives (iii) and (iv), both of which would represent these souls as having been guilty of some (initial?) sin against God 'in the heart',[43] although their practice of the natural virtues was perfect – 'sanza vizio' as Virgil elsewhere says (*Purgatorio* VII, 35). But whereas, according to alternative (iii) that sin in the heart did *not* imply a refusal of grace, according to (iv) it did entail just this. Now it is surely not possible to interpret Virgil's 'rebellion' in terms of (iii), for the plain implication of his words is, 'had I *not* been a rebel I *would* have received grace' – this being precisely the means for getting to that Heaven from which his rebellion has shut him out. Again, his sin could hardly have been only against the 'natural law', the law of reason, conceived of as not involving a choice for or against grace, for on that score Virgil seems to be as blameless as the good Indian referred to in *Paradiso* XIX, 70-78, all of whose willings and doings were good, 'quanto ragione umana vede'. Was then Virgil's rebellion a 'not honouring God as God', as St Paul puts it in Romans 1, 21? But this, at the least, would be a refusal to 'prepare' for grace, and hence indirectly a rejection of it.

In the light then of Virgil's confession in *Inferno* I, it would seem that we can best understand the situation of the adults in Limbo in terms of alternative (iv). These would all have been guilty of some personal sin 'in the heart', over and above the 'Original Sin' they in-

43. St Thomas, *Summa theol.* 1a2ae. 109, 8. If the reader will turn back to the pages in Section II of this essay where I set out the four 'alternatives7 I am here recalling, he will find a translation of the relevant parts of this important article in the *Summa*

herited as children of Adam; and that personal sin would have entailed a rejection of grace. It need not have been a direct rejection.
We know that the ancient pagans in Limbo did not adore God
'debitamente', and this is given as sufficient reason for their exclusion from Heaven, and also for Virgil's: 'e s'e' furon dinanzi al
cristianesmo,/non adorar debitamente a Dio:/e di questi cotai son io
medesmo' (*Inferno* IV, 37-9). This last line seems implicitly to identify Virgil's 'rebellion' (I, 125) with this false pagan worship; it
would be one instance of the latter — and incidentally, of the cult of
the 'false and lying gods' mentioned at I, 72. Presumably, this
false-worship-rebellion must have involved some culpable omission
of an act of faith, tantamount to a refusal of grace; since grace and
faith go hand in hand, and faith is the primary condition of access to
the Christian God (*Hebrews* 11, 6).[44] Hence, on this view the
unbelief of Dante's good pagans would not, after all, be purely
negative; it would entail some act on their part impeding faith.
Hence too, in interpreting Dante's thought on this delicate point,
we should have to allow that for him the availability of grace to the
non-Christian world was *not* limited to such abnormal situations as
those exemplified by Trajan and Ripheus in *Paradiso* XX. These
conclusions, it will be agreed, particularly the last one, raise
difficulties: yet they can hardly be avoided, it seems to me, except
by taking Virgil's words in *Inferno* I, 121-6 and IV, 38 in a very
loose sense indeed; and Dante is usually a precise writer.

And this interpretation would bring Dante into line, on this one
point at least, with Aquinas. In *Contra Gentiles* III, 159, Aquinas
comes very close to our theme when he puts and answers an objection to the Catholic teaching on grace (let me say in passing,
however, that the *implications* of St Thomas's answer here do not include a Limbo for adults, nor even the requirement of *explicit* faith as
a condition for salvation). That teaching, observes St Thomas, says
that a man commits sin if he fails to 'turn to God', while it also
asserts that no such 'turning' — 'conversio' — is possible except as a
result of God's gift of grace, a gift entirely depending on the Giver.
So the objection follows: How can a man be held responsible for
doing or not doing something the doing of which entirely depends
on someone else? St Thomas's answer is very much to our purpose:

44. 'Prima ... conversio in Deum fit per fidem', says Aquinas, citing this text from
Hebrews: *Summa theol.* 1a2ae. 113, 4.

'While it is true that no one can do anything to merit grace [before receiving it] or to acquire it by an act of his own free will, still a man may hinder himself from receiving grace; thus it has been said of some, *They said to God, Away with you! We do not choose to learn your ways* (*Job* 21, 14) and then again, *Others of them hate the light* (*Job* 24, 13). And since it is in the power of free will to hinder or not the reception of grace, a man may justly be blamed if he does hinder it. For God is ready, for his part, to give grace to all men . . . . But they, and they alone, are deprived of grace who themselves put an obstacle to it'. It is interesting that in the Vulgate the second text from *Job* cited here reads, 'ipsi fuerunt *rebelles* lumini', which is fairly close to the Dantean Virgil's, 'perch' i' fu' *ribellante*' etc. But, whether or not Dante had this passage from Thomas in mind, it does seem to meet the case of the Limbo adults; always provided that the *Inferno* texts which I have been citing do in fact refer to some personal sin on their part.

Nevertheless I find this solution puzzling, and for three reasons. First, if it is the correct one, why should Virgil declare, to Sordello in *Purgatorio* VII, 31-3, that his place in Limbo is with 'the innocent children' who have died unbaptized? This does not sound like the words of a man conscious of personal sin in addition to Original Sin.[45] Secondly, and more seriously perhaps, if the adult pagans in Limbo were all, at some moment of their life on earth, somehow offered grace, why should such a labour of miracles be needed for conveying grace to Trajan and Ripheus (*Paradiso* XX, 100-29)? Thirdly, if we grant that Virgil and his companions were offered grace and refused it, then a nice problem arises with regard to the flawless moral virtue they displayed in the ordinary course of their lives (*Inferno* IV, 33-4; *Purg.* VII, 25, 34-6; cf. *Paradiso* XIX, 70-5). For this seems to imply that the grace they refused cannot have been 'healing grace', *gratia sanans*; for their moral nature, as things turned out, needed no healing. So it could only have been grace as 'divinizing', *gratia elevans*. I am no expert in the byways of the history of Christian doctrine, but I should be surprised to be told by one who is, that such a position as this was not very unusual.

From all the above, in any event, we may conclude, I think, that Dante shows a marked tendency, through the *Convivio* and the

---

45. F. Mazzoni stresses this point (a little too much, perhaps) in his study of *Inf.* IV cited above: *Studi Danteschi*, XLII, p. 79.

Monarchia and even in the *Comedy*, to reduce to a minimum the conceivable contacts between human nature and divine grace; even if
we are persuaded, by the evidence adduced in the last few pages, or
on other grounds, that he did allow a bare possibility of such contact
for *all* adult human beings. And that tendency, with its consequences, is what I have taken as characteristic of the 'other', the *second* Dante implied in the title of this essay. And perhaps it reveals
an important defect, from the Christian point of view, in this great
Christian's thinking about man: an over-readiness to conceive of
moral virtue in isolation from Charity, 'the first and greatest
commandment'.[46]. After all, a certain practice and cult of moral virtue is quite compatible with the radical perversity of indifference to
God.[47] But Christianity requires that the moral virtues themselves
be offered to God as a way – as *the* way – of cooperating with his
grace. In this perspective the natural virtues themselves, ordered under Charity ('the mother of the virtues'), become as it were organs
of grace, are no longer just humanly 'acquired' but divinely
'infused'.[48] Guided by this insight St Thomas could take over the
whole achievement of Aristotle, as a philosophical moralist, while
giving it an entirely new setting and direction. In Dantean terms
this means the difference between Limbo and the *Purgatorio*; in
which we see repentant man recovering, under grace, the lost or
diminished natural virtues, but only in preparation for something
that is utterly beyond their own range, a love-union with the
Infinite. In the *Purgatorio* Aristotelianism is integrated into
Christianity; in the Dantean Limbo it is not.

---

46. *Matthew* 22, 38.
47. St Thomas, *Summa theol*. 2a2ae. 23, 7. Petrarch was perhaps more sensitive than D.
on this essential point; see his anti-aristotelian polemic, *De sui ipsius et multorum ignorantia*
(1367), the best part of which is available in *Fr. P. Prose*, ed. G. Martellotti et al.,
Milan-Naples, 1955, pp. 710ss.
48. *Summa theol*. 2a2ae. 23, 8 ad 3; 1a2ae. 63, 3-4.

INDEX OF THEMES AND TOPICS

INDEX OF AUTHORS

(For Aristotle, Virgil and Aquinas, see Index of Themes and Topics)